The Miegunyah Press

The general series of the
Miegunyah Volumes
was made possible by the
Miegunyah Fund
established by bequests
under the wills of
Sir Russell and Lady Grimwade.

'Miegunyah' was the home of
Mab and Russell Grimwade
from 1911 to 1955.

Donald Thomson in Arnhem Land

Donald Thomson in Arnhem Land

By Donald Thomson
Compiled and introduced by Nicolas Peterson

THE
MIEGUNYAH
PRESS

THE MIEGUNYAH PRESS
An imprint of Melbourne University Publishing Ltd
187 Grattan Street, Carlton, Victoria 3053, Australia
mup-info@unimelb.edu.au
www.mup.com.au

First published by Currey O'Neil 1983
Revised edition published 2003
Paperback edition published 2005
Reprinted 2006, 2010

Designed by Melissa Graham
Typeset by Melissa Graham
Printed in Australia by Openbook Print

National Library of Australia Cataloguing-in-Publication entry

Thomson, Donald F. (Donald Fergusson), 1901–1970.
Donald Thomson in Arnhem Land.

Bibliography.
Includes index.
9780522852059 (pbk.).

1. Thomson, Donald F. (Donald Fergusson), 1901–1970. 2.
Aboriginal Australians – Northern Territory – Arnhem Land.
3. Ethnology – Northern Territory – Arnhem Land. I.
Peterson, Nicolas, 1941– . II. Title.

305.89915

Foreword

This book is about the life of Yolngu people as it was in 1935–1943 when Dr Thomson, an anthropologist, was in our country. He came to Arnhem Land following the killing of five Japanese and three Europeans in the Caledon Bay area. Wonggu was my mother's father and he and the other people mentioned in this book are the parents, grandparents and great grandparents of myself and many people living in the area from Milingimbi to Yirrkala today.

Although this book is written from Dr Thomson's point of view, it is of special interest to us because of the photographs. Dr Thomson was a very good photographer who took over two thousand photographs of our old people's way of life before they settled down at Yirrkala and Milingimbi Missions. It is the best pictorial record of our culture and old people that can now be produced. It is linked to the story of Dr Thomson's travels in Arnhem Land, his reports to the government and his return in the war time to form a coast-watching unit of Yolngu people who helped protect Australia from invasion.

The photographs cover all aspects of our way of life, from house types, fishing methods, material culture and food sources to ceremonial life. Many of the photographs include the names of the people depicted, which makes them of special interest to all of us in north-east Arnhem Land. But this book is for everybody interested in the history and culture of Yolngu people.

Gatjil Djerrkura OAM (1950–2004)

Contents

Preface to the First Edition

When Donald Thomson died in May 1970 he left several drafts and outlines of papers and books. One project he had had in mind for many years was a book on Arnhem Land but it had taken second place to several others and little work was done on it. However, Thomson's wife Dorita and secretary Judith Wiseman, knowing how keen he was that the public should learn something of the events in Arnhem Land during the late 1930s from a point of view sympathetic to Aboriginal people, started to put together an account of his time in Arnhem Land from his published and unpublished writings, with a particular concern to include many of his unsurpassed photographs.

The immense task of preparing Donald Thomson's superb ethnographic collection for use by scholars resulted in a first draft of this compilation being set aside while more urgent tasks were undertaken. In the meantime Dorita Thomson generously gave me free access to the collection, which had a particular significance for me since Thomson had been the first anthropologist to visit the area where I began my own field research thirty years later. Learning of the plans for the book, I offered to take on the task of preparing it. In doing so I have slightly altered the focus to create a narrative akin, in some respects, to the journals of the early explorers rather than an academic account of Aboriginal life in the 1930s or of the history of north-east Arnhem Land in this period. Since Donald Thomson played a crucial role at the turning point of Arnhem Land's history, which although partly published is quite unknown to the general public, I decided to construct a narrative, in Thomson's own words, for the whole period of his involvement. This was not difficult. His style of writing was highly personal, even in government reports, and his passionate commitment to the Aboriginal people kept him constantly in the limelight as advocate, defender and critic, so there was more-than-adequate material. His style suited his view of himself as one of the last of the explorers, which in some ways he was.

This approach seemed all the more important because the accounts of the prewar period gain added significance in the light of Thomson's little-known involvement with the Arnhem Landers during the early days of the Second World War, when he trained and led a scouting and reconnaissance force of Aboriginal people in the area in preparation for the feared Japanese invasion. The report on this guerilla force remained classified until recently but now the fascinating sidelight it throws on defence activity in the Northern Territory can be placed in its proper perspective. Thomson's writing is unique in that it names Aboriginal people, presenting them as individuals and active agents in local history in a way few other writings do.

No attempt has been made, therefore, to turn this book into an exhaustive academic or depersonalised account of this period in Arnhem Land history. Thomson was an important part of that history and his own account and perspective are of interest and significance for that reason alone.

Chapters 2 to 6 are edited composite versions of his reports to the Commonwealth Government, parts of which have been reprinted in modified form in the *Geographical Journal*, expanded by his own journalistic accounts, private correspondence and diaries. Chapter 7 is based on the unpublished army reports. The brief biographical sketch in Chapter 1 is drawn from diverse sources, including discussion with Dorita Thomson, the Australian Archives, the National Library and Thomson's own published and unpublished writings.

The most difficult problem facing me as editor has been deciding on the extent to which I should alter certain phrasings to protect Thomson from anachronistic criticism. The original writing was done in the late 1930s and early 1940s when Aboriginal people were commonly called 'natives' or 'boys'. He used these terms, as well as 'Aborigines'/'Aboriginals', throughout his writings. Today they have a jarring and unpleasant connotation, which would not accurately reflect the relatively progressive nature of many of Thomson's views. Although at times his expression and attitudes were more overtly paternalistic than is acceptable today, there can be no doubt that Thomson was in the forefront of champions of Aboriginal rights, including land rights, recognition of customary law, and the need to respect Aboriginal people as fully responsible Australian citizens with their own views and rights. His sympathy for them, his forceful advocacy to the government on their behalf and his public championing of their cause all serve to underline this. Therefore at the risk of de-

Thomsonising the account I have changed terms such as 'natives' and 'boys' to 'Aborigines', etcetera, throughout the narrative. I have also eliminated repetition, introduced names, dates and as much specific detail as possible and standardised the spelling of all but personal names in accordance with the orthography currently in use in north-east Arnhem Land. Save for a few linking paragraphs indicated in the notes, the account is in his own words. For those who wish to consult the materials from which this book has been compiled I include a note on sources at the end.

From the quickest glance through the book, it will be clear that the photographs are an integral part of it. All but two (those on pages 124 and 162, top) were taken by Thomson. He was a superb and enthusiastic photographer. Using a Thornton Pickard half-plate camera and a Graflex he built dark-rooms in the field at each location where he spent any length of time and he developed the glass negatives on the spot. Often he worked late at night or in the early hours of the morning to develop the negatives because in the summer months these were the only times when water temperatures fell back to suitable levels. The plates published have been chosen from the total of some 2,200 that he took in Arnhem Land because they are directly linked to the text, and the captions have been based on his notes.

This book would not have been compiled without Judith Wiseman's unstinting enthusiasm, energy and attention to detail or the original vision and generous help and friendship of Dorita Thomson. My thanks are also due to Professor G. Dening and the University of Melbourne for providing the funds for me to work on the collection; to the staff of the Department of Anthropology of Museum Victoria for their friendly assistance at all times; and to Hank Nelson, John Mulvaney, Howard Morphy, Frances Morphy and Rosalind Peterson for their help and interest.

Nicolas Peterson
Canberra

Preface to the Revised Edition

The principal change made for this edition is the inclusion of over eighty additional photographs and sixteen new drawings. My intention is to provide a visual ethnography of Aboriginal life in eastern Arnhem Land as it was between 1935 and 1943 and to go some way towards suggesting the vision Thomson had of the Anthropological Bulletin he outlined to the government but never wrote. Thomson's photographic and ethnographic coverage was very broad and as a result this is the best view of a fully functioning, independent Aboriginal existence, at one moment in time, that we will ever have. His coverage includes domestic life, material culture, subsistence, shelter and religious life. In respect of the latter, the only images included are of those parts of ceremonies at which both men and women are present (that is, public sequences). Great care has been taken in checking the selection of photographs with people across eastern Arnhem Land. I have provided detailed captions to the photographs, drawing on my own knowledge of the area where necessary. Readers interested in exploring the ethnography further should consult L. Warner, *A Black Civilization* (Harper Brothers, New York, 1937), which is based on field work done at Milingimbi between 1927 and 1929; other sources are listed at the end of the book. Most of the photographs are placed in the text so that they relate directly to the chronology of their taking and the narrative.

A large number of alterations have been made to the previously published text, mainly involving the addition of further details of people and dates, other material from Thomson's diaries and a few corrections. New ethnographic information includes the addition of a table correlating the seasons with economic activity, food supplies and house types, and extended captions to the photographs. Some additional matter has been included at the end of the biographical sketch (Chapter 1). With the assistance of Frances Morphy, spelling, including that of personal names, has been updated to the current orthography (with the exception of omitting the glottal stop), because many Yolngu now regard its use as standard.

This book could not have been published without the very generous support of the Grimwade Miegunyah Fund on the basis of a submission made by Dr Ray Marginson, Chairperson of the Donald Thomson Collection Administrative Committee – a joint committee of Museum Victoria and the University of Melbourne. Lindy Allen, Melanie Raberts and Rosemary Wrench, at Museum Victoria, are now responsible for the care of the collection. Lindy has been unstinting in her help, support and enthusiasm for the preparation of this edition. She has also been mainly responsible for documenting, with the help of many Yolngu from Milingimbi to Yirrkala, the identities of any unknown people in the images. Thanks are also due to Rosemary Wrench for overseeing the gathering together of the images, to John Broomfield and Jon Augier for printing them (for further details on the illustrations see page 236) and Clive Hilliker for the maps. Last but of course not least, I would like to emphasise my indebtedness to Dorita Thomson and her family for their generous friendship and support throughout.

N.P.
Canberra, May 2003

Amendments to the Paperback Edition

For this paperback edition, a number of the captions have been added to with further identifications of people made possible by recent field research by Louise Hamby and Lindy Allen, supported by an ARC Linkage Project (LP 0347221) between the Australian National University and Museum Victoria titled, 'Anthropological and Aboriginal perspectives on the Donald Thomson Collection: material culture, collecting and identity'.

A Biographical Sketch
of Donald Thomson

by Nicolas Peterson

On leaving school in 1920 Donald Thomson turned down a scholarship to study veterinary science at the University of Melbourne, despite his keen desire to go to university and his need for funds to do so. He wanted to study natural science but as no assistance was offering in this field he determined to find a way of following his choice under his own steam. With the help of a lifelong friend he bought a robust horse, Barney, and a cart and went to work for the Lilydale shire carting materials for the road gangs and breaking stones. At the weekends he would cut firewood, deliver it to Croydon Station, then walk Barney and the cart the twelve miles or so to Camberwell Station, where he would pick up the wood and deliver it to his customers.

With the money from his savings, supplemented by work each vacation, and the sale of Barney and the cart, he raised enough to see him through his chosen course at Melbourne University. Such rugged individualism and determination were typical of Thomson throughout his life. They were combined with a sensitivity to criticism, a keen sense of justice, a somewhat austere nature, a biting wit and a tendency for passionate commitment, all making for an unconventional career as an anthropologist and an often difficult and demanding colleague to whom few people were indifferent.

Thomson's parents were both musicians who came to Melbourne from London. His father set up the Board of Examinations at the Melbourne Conservatorium and spent a great deal of time travelling in connection with his work. Thomson never manifested any musical talent himself, but from an early age he developed a strong interest in natural history, making a collection of birds' eggs and keeping a natural history diary at the age of ten. This interest appears to have developed during a period when he was frequently absent from school because of ill health: he caught diphtheria and suffered from curvature of the spine. Schooling was further broken by a trip to England with his parents and sister Agnes when he was twelve, with the result that he left school altogether at fourteen to attend the School of Horticulture at Burnley, Melbourne. A year's experience there re-interested him in secondary schooling so his father sent him to Scotch College. There his penchant for natural history was reflected in his winning a prize in this field and, more tellingly, by being nicknamed Kanga after one of his pets.

At Melbourne University he took parts one, two and three of both zoology and botany with the aim of working in the field making collections. Inspired by Captain Robert Falcon Scott's antarctic expedition, he wanted to work in the polar regions but realised that he would need to be able to turn his hand to other things besides biology if he were to join any similar expeditions. He thus began systematically to develop a proficiency in photography, particularly of scientific and natural history subjects, embarking on a life-long love.

The desire to join a scientific expedition to a remote region seems to have been an important driving force for Thomson at this time. Early in 1923, during his second year at university, he arranged to see the recently retired Professor of Biology, Sir Baldwin Spencer, who was best known to many people for his anthropological work and writings on the Aranda and other peoples of the Northern Territory. Thomson hoped Spencer might be able to give advice on how to secure a place on the Hubert Wilkins Collecting Expedition, sponsored by the natural history section of the British Museum, which was then advertising for expedition members. Spencer dissuaded Thomson from applying to the expedition and urged him to finish his degree first, promising to help him join an expedition after his graduation.[1]

Thomson graduated in 1925 and in December of that year he married Gladys Coleman, a fellow student from the year behind him. He was offered a full-time post on the staff of the Department of Botany at £200 a year but chose instead to take a better paying cadetship at the Melbourne *Herald*, while his wife finished her degree. While working on the *Herald* it seems he was still concerned to find a way to mount or join an expedition to a remote area. Perhaps mindful of the way in which Spencer had combined both biology and anthropology, and with the support of Professor Wood Jones, who was to play an important part in Thomson's prewar career, he applied for field work funds to the newly established Australian National Research Council's committee on anthropological research. He received a reply from Professor Radcliffe-Brown, the first incumbent of the recently established Chair of Anthropology at Sydney University, indicating that there was money available for field work but that Thomson must first get some training. This he decided to do by taking up Radcliffe-Brown's suggestion that he enrol in the new one-year diploma course in anthropology being started at Sydney. Because Thomson was hard up, Radcliffe-Brown applied for a fee-free year for him and also arranged a part-time demonstratorship in the Zoology Department.

Thomson did well in the course and was awarded the first diploma in March 1928. However, he upset Radcliffe-Brown by not telling him of his marriage until the very end of his course because he was afraid it would be seen as an impediment to doing field work. This, combined with Thomson's admission of a preference for natural history and a keenness to explore the bush, made Radcliffe-Brown an equivocal supporter in the following years and led him to declare that Thomson was not 'wholeheartedly a scientist'. Nevertheless, he supported Thomson's application to the Anthropological Committee of the Australian National Research Council for a grant to work among the peoples of Cape York. Thomson obtained the grant,[2] which was for £600 to £500 for expenses and £100 as a personal allowance, later raised by £50.[3] Without wasting any time he set out the following month, on 28 April, leaving his wife behind.

The expedition itself went well. In the eight months he was away he travelled over a thousand miles with packhorses, crossing Cape York twice in the process. He took more than two hundred superb plate photographs on glass negatives and made a small zoological collection as well as collecting a great deal of anthropological information. He returned to Melbourne in January 1929 and in a letter to Radcliffe-Brown shortly afterwards said: 'I should have given almost anything to have been able to make a cinematograph record of the life of … [the Edward River people] and I shall do in future if I return and can obtain a good machine'.[4]

The doubt about his return to Cape York was occasioned by two factors — one positive, the other negative. The positive doubt was raised by the continued pursuit of his ambition to become involved in polar exploration. To this end he had written on 25 March 1929 to Sir Douglas Mawson who was then organising the Australian Antarctic Expedition, asking to join as the biologist.[5] Although initially accepted, he had to be turned down when the New Zealand Government complained that there were too many Australians and not enough New Zealanders. Mawson wrote Thomson a most sympathetic letter saying that he felt his work on Cape York was more important than the work he could do for the expedition in Antarctica and encouraged him to continue with it. The negative factor related to money and accounting for his expenditure to the ANRC. Throughout the first expedition to Cape York there had been minor problems occasioned mainly by distance, poor communication and organisation. In particular, much was made by the treasurer of the ANRC of the fact that one receipt appeared twice in Thomson's accounts. The treasurer, clearly put out by what he considered Thomson's peremptory demands for payment of the funds allocated to him and, as it turned out, by other factors, developed a strong dislike for him.

The problems were not enough to stop Thomson applying to the ANRC for a second grant to return to the field and receiving it, although Radcliffe-Brown wanted him to spend a year writing up and working on fellow field worker Ursula McConnel's material before he returned. This Thomson was not keen to do as he planned to leave in May 1929. On Thomson's arrival in Sydney the treasurer demanded that all the negatives of the first trip be handed over immediately to the ANRC as they were the council's property. Thomson refused and resigned his grant, but he set out as planned, accompanied by his wife and supported by his income from newspaper articles. This precipitated a major crisis in the ANRC, which called a special meeting to discuss the matter.

It was four years before the matter was resolved, during which time the treasurer continued his insinuations and accusations against Thomson's integrity and honesty. Radcliffe-Brown became less supportive and voiced criticism of Thomson for spending so much money on photography, which he felt was an extraneous subject and in danger of becoming the focus of his work. He pointed out that workers such as Warner and McConnel had handed over their collections of artefacts to the ANRC. Sir David Masson, vice-president of the council, put up a strong defence of Thomson, describing him as a 'young man with genius and some of the faults of genius'. Nothing was resolved but happily Thomson was away from it all, continuing his field work.[6]

A year later Sir Thomas Lyle, president of the ANRC, circulated a long letter to the executive committee for anthropological research, setting out Thomson's side of the case and suggesting that a complete retraction of all allegations by the treasurer be demanded and sent by letter to Thomson. If this were not done, he pointed out, or if Thomson were not given the chance to refute the accusations, 'it is obvious that his career in Australia as an anthropologist is ended, seeing that the members of the Australian National Research Council and of its Anthropological Committee are the scientists who will control future anthropological research in this country for some time to come'.[7] Although the matter of the negatives was resolved, and Thomson could keep them, he never received the apology.[8] However, on the death of the treasurer all became clear. He himself had been misappropriating the ANRC funds and had destroyed many of the Council's records to cover his tracks.[9] Thomson was thus cleared: difficult he may have been, but dishonest he was not. Even so, the whole affair had not only turned Thomson off the Research Council but also made it difficult for him to get funds from the Anthropological Research Committee that controlled anthropological research in Australia until 1955. As Sir Thomas Lyle had foreseen, Thomson became alienated from the Sydney clique, which dominated professional anthropology well into the 1960s, and chose to seek funds elsewhere. Until the end of the war he financed his research with grants from Melbourne University and by the publication and syndication of more than 900 articles in magazines and newspapers. Many of these articles appeared in the Melbourne *Herald*, with which he sought to ally himself for influential public support, support that he duly received in the subsequent years.

On his return from the second expedition to Cape York late in 1929, Thomson joined the staff of the Walter and Eliza Hall Institute of Research in Pathology and Medicine in Melbourne for two years to work on the development of an anti-venom for tiger-snake bites.[10] In 1932 he joined the University of Melbourne, where he became a research fellow attached to the Department of Anatomy. It was the beginning of a staff association with the university that lasted, with a few minor interruptions, until Thomson retired as Professor of Anthropology in 1968.

With the move to the university and the completion of his doctorate of science in 1934, Thomson established his switch from the natural to the social sciences, although he never lost interest in zoology or botany, making collections of considerable value both in Arnhem Land and later in the desert while on anthropological field work. His publications reflect the switch.[11] His earliest academic publication was on birds in *The Emu*, the journal of the Royal Australasian Ornithologists Union of which he was briefly associate editor when he was twenty-one. From the period 1930 to 1935 he was publishing both in zoology and in anthropology, including (in 1935) his first book, *Birds of Cape York Peninsula*, and three long and well-illustrated papers on his anthropological work in Cape York, one of which cost the Royal Anthropological Institute the significant sum of £130 to print because of the number of superb photographs included. More significant anthropologically, however, were two shorter papers published in the *American Anthropologist*, one on joking and obscenity and the other on fatherhood.[12]

In 1932 the university financed Thomson's third and final expedition to Cape York by making him a Bartlett research scholar. Once again his wife accompanied him. During the expedition he spent considerable time in the vicinity of the Presbyterian Mission at Aurukun. He himself had been brought up a Presbyterian and was an active churchgoer until that time. His attitude was changed dramatically, though, during the course of the year – in particular as the result of an event in December that can be seen retrospectively as a watershed in his life.

For many years, indeed into the 1960s, Aurukun was controlled with a rod of iron by a superintendent of long standing. Under his regime and by his hand Aboriginal people were summarily punished by complete or partial head shaving, flogging, chaining and imprisonment. The prison was a galvanised iron building, seven by twelve feet, divided into two compartments and containing as many as six adult prisoners at one time. For such a trivial offence as late delivery of the milk to the white staff's holiday camp on Archer Bay, miles from the mission, an Aboriginal man, Billy Blowhard, was threatened with gaol. Worst of all, in Thomson's eyes, was the power of the superintendent to have people exiled for life to Palm Island simply on his own word, and without any trial. On Sunday 11 December 1932, police troopers arrived from Laura to remove two women and three men forever to Palm Island. Not even waiting to conduct the afternoon service, the superintendent seized a rifle and led the police party up river in the mission launch to capture the five people. They were eventually caught. Back at the mission there was not even the pretence of a trial. On Thursday 15 December, the three men, each carrying a blanket, were chained neck to neck and, although the police had packhorses, were dragged off on a 240-mile walk to Laura at the height of the tropical midsummer. The previous year, when another party had been taken away by the police, one man died on the road from the cruelty and privations.[13]

Upset as Thomson was by witnessing such criminal proceedings at the mission, it was the reaction of the Presbyterian Church in Melbourne that firmly consolidated his distrust of most missionaries. On return to Melbourne he deliberately did not make public any of the details of the many injustices he

The harsh treatment of these Aboriginal people brought to a head Thomson's concern about the lack of justice at Aurukun Mission. Thomson commented on this photograph: ' Terrible though this picture is, it gives no idea of the misery of the scene, with the relatives of the prisoners wailing and weeping and screaming good bye to their kin who they know from long experience they will never see again.' 15 December 1932.

witnessed, nor the photographs he had taken, but instead asked to address the Presbyterian hierarchy behind closed doors so that they could know of the situation there and put their house in order discreetly. They refused to hear him.

It was in this context that Thomson, while still at Aurukun, first learnt of events at Caledon Bay, Arnhem Land, and the suggestion that the killing of five Japanese and three whites by the Aboriginal people there should be met by a punitive police expedition to teach them a lesson they would never forget. It is not surprising, therefore, that he was moved to write to the chancellor of the University of Melbourne offering his services through him to the government to go to Arnhem Land to seek a peaceful resolution of the conflict there. Of course, his motivation was surely reinforced by his feeling for the bush, by his love of exploration and by a somewhat romantic view of himself living with the unknown people of eastern Arnhem Land.

This book is the story of what happened there, but it is in Thomson's own words and from his own point of view, glossing over a number of conflicts and issues that lay behind the events described, and naturally includes few of the details of the government's side of the story.

The exact sequence of events is not entirely clear but from September 1933 onwards the Chancellor of the University of Melbourne, Sir John MacFarland, and the Master of Ormond College, D. K. Picken (both privately through letters and conversations), along with Professor Wood Jones, now at the University of Melbourne (via newspaper articles), urged the government to take up Thomson's offer.[14] The secretary to the Department of the Interior, however, was urging his Minister to postpone any action on the offer in December 1933 on the grounds that there existed in the Caledon Bay area a missionary expedition, the so-called Peace Expedition sponsored by the Church Missionary Society of Victoria and Tasmania, and that it was undesirable that another party should be sent there at the same time. He did suggest, though, that Thomson's offer could be accepted 'with advantage' when conditions improved.[15]

When nothing had happened by February 1934, Wood Jones wrote an article in the Melbourne *Herald* commenting on the government's rejection of Thomson's invitation and criticising the missionary party on the grounds that it was a part-police, part-missionary enterprise, a point he could very well have been persuaded to emphasise by Thomson after his experiences at Aurukun. Wood Jones argued that a long period of research was needed to establish the cause of the killings and that both a proper government policy and a Department of Native Affairs were required.[16] The next day, the issue was taken up by the Melbourne *Herald*, the paper Thomson had worked for, which was most critical of the Minister and supportive of Thomson and the university:

It is very disheartening to the University and to the cause of unselfish scientific research that such an offer should stupidly be received with cold discouragement by the same Minister who was prepared to subsidise and assume responsibility for a missionary expedition into the unknown area which the most experienced missionary leader in the district described as 'conceived by people who have not the faintest idea of the conditions the party have to face. It would not succeed and it would be next door to suicide for those who took part'.[17]

The Reverend T. T. Webb of Milingimbi Mission strongly supported Thomson but was critical of Wood Jones's view that there should be complete and rigorous segregation of the people inside the Arnhem Land reserve, which would rule out the need for Thomson to go there.

The Department of the Interior's advice to the Minister was that it would be unwise to vary his decision in view of the press and university criticism. But within two days of this advice the Minister indicated that he was going to meet the Assistant Treasurer who had some new proposals to make to him.[18] Exactly what these proposals were and why they persuaded the Minister to take up Thomson's offer after all is not clear but within two months detailed negotiations were going on between Thomson and the Department on the terms of his appointment. One factor seems to have been, as Thomson himself suggests, the incompetence and bias of Judge Wells who heard the case against one of the men involved in the Caledon Bay killings. So bad was this that the secretary of the Department of the Interior suggested to the Minister that 'very serious consideration must be given to the removal of Judge Wells' and commented, in the conclusion of his two-page memo, that strong representation from professors, societies, organisations and highly placed individuals indicated the 'feeling existing against the present Judge is very pronounced in the southern States'.[19]

Thomson met H. C. Brown, the Secretary to the Department, and outlined his proposals to him. The Minister felt them to be too anthropological and therefore not conducive to solving his problem of law and order or stemming public criticism.[20] It is interesting that as early as 18 July 1934 Thomson was requesting that the three men from Caledon Bay who had been imprisoned for the killing of the Japanese should be released to him and return as crew on his boat.[21] Thomson saw the Minister on 8 August 1934 and received a letter from him dated 23 August with details of the position of Patrol Officer that he was being offered. The model for his appointment was explicitly the duty statement of the New Guinea patrol officers. Thomson wrote back three days later rejecting the terms of the appointment. In particular he objected to being under the Administrator of the Northern Territory rather than directly responsible to the Minister in Canberra; nor did he feel it possible to work in conjunction with the Chief Protector of Aborigines, since this would be incompatible with making investigations. Further, he objected to any ethnological specimens coming into his hands being regarded as the property of the Commonwealth. Finally, he asked to be endowed with the powers of Special Commissioner and reiterated his desire to take the three gaoled men back as crew on his boat.

The Department was not prepared to make Thomson a Special Commissioner and found that it could not make him a patrol officer unless under the *Northern Territory Public Service Act*, nor could they make him a Protector of Aborigines unless under the Chief Protector.[22] The upshot was that, despite the absence of a rewritten commission, which he did not receive until 4 March 1935, he was given the go-ahead. In between times Thomson was finalising arrangements for a boat and making other preparations for his departure as soon as the wet season was over. Thomson did ask in September, however, that nobody be granted permission to enter the Arnhem Land reserve and that proposals to establish new missions by the Methodists at Yirrkala and the Church Missionary Society at Caledon Bay be delayed until reports had been received from him upon which a policy might be determined. He had no immediate success; although the Caledon Bay Mission was never established, the mission at Yirrkala went ahead early in 1935 and no complete bar was placed on entry into the reserve.[23]

Thomson departed for eastern Arnhem Land on 16 March 1935 and all remained quiet on the official front while he was in the field. The first batch of film of life in Blue Mud Bay, shot on his Zeiss cinecamera, created quite a stir at Melbourne University and provoked the Chancellor to write to the Minister of the Interior in October 1935 trying to arrange a viewing. Finance posed a minor problem because Thomson had underestimated his expenses at £525 per annum plus £225 salary and proposed that these two sums be allocated to expenses with the salary added on top.[24]

After submitting his first 'Interim General Report' to the Minister on 9 April 1936, difficulties arose about the conditions under which Thomson was prepared to return and continue to work. They all boiled down to the same issue of seeking to be completely independent, responsible directly to the Minister. Some of the reasons for this he does not make clear, but they emerge in correspondence between the Minister and Wood Jones. During Thomson's first trip certain enquiries had been instituted in Darwin about Aboriginal people under his control; in his mind these enquiries raised fears of interference. As it turned out they were simply the result of the Department of the Interior trying to work out the correct wage levels for various Aboriginal and Islander men employed on Thomson's boat. The secretary of the Department also believed that Thomson feared physical attack from white trepangers in the Caledon Bay area, although in the secretary's view these fears were quite unfounded. Finally, there was the original and important issue that working under the Darwin administration could be embarrassing in view of the possibility that he might criticise the administration. Thomson's colleagues at the university supported him strongly, saying they would not let him return to Arnhem Land unless the issue was clarified and writing, in the person of Acting Vice-Chancellor Professor D. B. Copland, to the Minister urging that Thomson be made a Special Commissioner so that he had freedom of action. It was, Copland suggested, as much a matter of status as power, especially in the context of acting in an emergency when he needed the authority of the government behind him if he were to preserve life in the remote areas. To make Thomson a Special Commissioner would have required that the government pass a special ordinance; this it declined to do, bringing the matter to an impasse until a clever compromise was reached. The government was prepared to recognise that eastern Arnhem Land was not under the control of the Northern Territory Administration in practice even if it were in theory. So the terms of appointment were reissued with minor but significant alterations, italicised here, on 10 June 1935: 'You are hereby authorised to enter the Aboriginal reserve, Arnhem Land, and entrusted with a commission to carry out *in that area subject to the Minister* the duties herein enumerated'.[25] This new agreement was widely heralded in the press, which in the previous months had also been carrying popular articles by Thomson on his time in Arnhem Land.[26] The news of his return provoked at least two letters to the Minister of the Interior. The secretary of the Northern Territory Pastoral Lessees Association wrote complaining about Thomson's kangaroo dog, Tiger, on the grounds that he might mate with the dingoes, to which the Minister replied that he was a well-trained dog that stayed close to Thomson and that it was too late anyway to do anything since he had already gone. The other letter was from Gray, a trepanger working in and around the Blue Mud Bay area, who after reading an article about Thomson's travels wrote in to comment that it was 'bunk' to say there were 'real wild bad' natives down in the area – a point of course that Thomson himself would fully have agreed with even if he may have coloured his newspaper stories a little to give added interest. Gray pointed out that anyone could come and go in safety as long as they did not molest the people: 'The white man is quite safe here and only the native who breaks the tribal law is in danger.'[27]

It was during this second expedition to Arnhem Land that Thomson carried out his most important anthropological work. Contact with the Department was largely limited to a spate of telegrams in 1937 in which he drew the Minister's attention to financial matters as well as to the number of Japanese vessels off the Arnhem Land coast and the frequency with which they were infringing the regulations prohibiting them from putting ashore. Apart from continuous petty accounting problems, all handled through Thomson's well-connected firm of Melbourne solicitors, Arthur Robinson and Co., there was the matter of continued applications for extension of his time and grant to stay in Arnhem Land. These were granted by Cabinet on 15 January, 21 April and 5 August but greatly irritated the Department, which felt that the total cost of his work in Arnhem Land was somewhat expensive at £3175.[28]

Thomson felt that the Minister for the Interior, Thomas Paterson, had shown little inclination to make use of his knowledge of Arnhem Land and its people since Thomson had had less than twenty lines of written and telegraphic information from him during the thirteen months to May 1937. Thomson's main correspondence throughout the period of this expedition was with Wilson, the solicitor who was looking after his affairs and conducting negotiations with the government about his applications for extensions of his stay in the field. Wilson also liaised with Thomson's brother-in-law, who was secretary to the Department of the Air, and other members of the Air Force to organise the visit of an amphibian aircraft for survey work to try to sort out the confusion in the river systems of the Glyde, Goyder and Woolen rivers in particular. This was only partially achieved, with the Goyder and Woolen rivers remaining confused on his own and some official maps well into the 1950s.

The other matter that Thomson raised with Wilson was in response to news from his wife that the film footage he was sending back was turning out very well. He was shooting silent film, which, as he told Wilson, he much regretted. He was particularly keen to record singing, music and the calling of the sacred names in ceremonies, which would, he said, transfer the finished film from a pageant of silent figures to a living record of Aboriginal life. Much to his disappointment, obtaining a suitable recording machine proved an insuperable problem and he was unable to carry out either this plan or a final resort plan to transport a number of singers to Darwin for a recording session there.

Despite a reluctance to leave the field, a deadline was imposed on him by a grant from the Rockefeller Foundation to study at Cambridge. As he was keen to take this up he had to leave the field in July. The departure was not without its difficulties, particularly in connection with some live animals he had collected and the trouble he had getting them from Darwin. This problem was eventually solved, partly with the assistance of a good friend, Colonel White, Minister for Trade and Customs, who was most sympathetic towards the Aboriginal people and supportive of Thomson. This contrasted, in Thomson's view, with the Department of the Interior, where Thomson felt that the Secretary's attitude to him was the source of the antagonism he had met there and part of the reason why Paterson had failed to take up his recommendations and develop a meaningful policy.[29] Thomson anticipated with some satisfaction that Paterson would lose his seat in the elections in 1937 – as he did, to be replaced by John McEwen.

With his family, Thomson set sail for England early in the New Year to take up his fellowship at Christ College, Cambridge. It was evidently a most stimulating year for him. He published four papers as a result of his time there, was appointed to a Standing Committee of the Royal Anthropological Institute on Applied Anthropology, received the Institute's Wellcome Gold Medal in 1939 for the 'application of modern scientific methods to problems of native administration' and spoke and showed his films to the Royal Geographical Society. Julian Huxley was so impressed by the films when he saw them at the British Association for the Advancement of Science meetings that he wrote directly to Robert Menzies, who had just been elected Prime Minister, urging the Commonwealth Government to turn the footage into an officially sponsored film.[30] This was not the first time direct representations had been made by or on behalf of Thomson to Menzies. Back in 1936, when Menzies was a rising star, the vice-chancellor of Melbourne University had promised to try to put Thomson in touch with him so that Thomson could interest Menzies in the plight of Aboriginal people. Thomson did not see Menzies then but they did meet in London in July 1938 to discuss Native Affairs policy. The immediate result of the meeting was that Thomson went to Copenhagen as the Australian representative at the International Congress on Anthropology and Ethnology being held there in August but it did not result in the realisation of his secret hope that the government might make him Director of Native Affairs.[31]

One of the first things Thomson did at Cambridge was to sketch out the chapter headings for the anthropological report on his work in Arnhem Land and send it to the Department for their approval to secure the funds to prepare it. The outline, which was approved as submitted, is set out here.[32] That it was never completed remains a tragedy.

Material to be included in proposed Anthropological Report or Bulletin on work carried out in Arnhem Land, Northern Territory, during the years 1935, 36, 37, which it is proposed to publish for issue to public, for guidance to officers of Administration, and members of Public Service concerned with native affairs.

1 *Introduction*
   The country and geographical features as a background in which the
   Aborigine lives, with account of the general nomad life of the people.
2 *Native Tribes of Arnhem Land*
   Tribes and other territorial, linguistic and social groups.
3 *Social Organisation*
4 *Totemism*
5 *Mythology*
   The place of myth in native life from a functional point of view
   and a number of typical myths from this area.
6 *Initiation*
7 *Culture Contacts* (see also section 10)
8 *Magic and Medicine*
   Secret killing, cannibalism, rain making, the cult of the medicine man.
9 *Legal and Moral Codes*
10 *Tribal Economics*
11 *Ceremonial Life*
12 *Malay Influence etc*
13 *Mourning and Burial Practices*
14 *Material Culture*
   i Weapons and implements ii Domestic utensils iii Ornaments and personal
   adornment iv Hunting and food capture v Fishing methods vi Food preparation
   and cooking vii Houses and house building viii Canoes and watercraft
15 *The Child in Native Society*

This must be regarded as a preliminary outline only, the chapters, their content, and
especially their order, must be regarded as elastic and to be fixed as the work takes form.

On 3 June 1939, with the threat of war looming, Thomson's wife left by sea for
Australia with their twin sons while he travelled to the United States at the
invitation of the Rockefeller Foundation. There he was visiting a number of
Indian reservations and anthropological colleagues when war broke out. He
returned immediately to Australia, enlisted in the RAAF as a flight lieutenant
and was posted to the Solomon Islands via No. 11 Squadron Port Moresby,
investigating possible flying boat bases and carrying out preliminary work associated with the setting up of a coast-watching system. After fourteen months he
was recalled to Victoria and almost immediately launched into planning and
organising the Special Reconnaissance Unit of Arnhem Land Aboriginal people

to defend the eastern flank of Darwin at the 7th Infantry Training Centre, Wilson's Promontory. Although there is no specific evidence as to how the idea originated, it has obvious parallels with the many coast-watching groups organised in New Guinea and elsewhere. Once initiated, the whole project bore the indelible stamp of Thomson's personal knowledge of Arnhem Land but it is of more than passing interest that Lieutenant Colonel W. J. Scott, the director of special operations, who was in charge of the whole operation, has been identified as the model for Callcott in D. H. Lawrence's *Kangaroo* and was directly involved in the organisation of right-wing paramilitary groups in the 1920s and 1930s.[33] But only somebody with Thomson's knowledge of and respect for Aboriginal people's abilities would have suggested that they be used as infiltrators in the Malay Peninsula, something of which many of those around him remained sceptical throughout the whole episode. Today the children of this fifty-strong Aboriginal guerilla force are airborne observers in the coastal surveillance program operating along the coast of northern Australia.[34]

When the direct threat to the northern coast of Australia receded and the main battleground moved northwards, Thomson was posted to Dutch New Guinea to the First Australia Army and Merauke Force in 1943. From Merauke he made two patrols into the endless swamplands of the region. He was physically tired from the time in Arnhem Land and frustrated by not being completely his own commander. Nevertheless, he carried out his two patrols under severe conditions. After the first patrol he was able to recruit Sergeants Ritchie, Egan and Kapiu, all of whom had been in Arnhem Land with him. The second patrol took them up the Wildeman River and down to the estuary of the Eilanden where they established a base only twenty miles from the Japanese lines, among peoples in touch with them. Early one morning as they were breaking camp 200 villagers attacked the small party en masse with steel axes, knives and machetes, severely wounding Ritchie, Kapiu and Thomson. The sheer number of the attackers impeded the assault after the first blows, allowing the three men to reach their machine guns and turn these on the attackers.[35] With his left arm and shoulder badly damaged by three wounds, Thomson got their motor launch under way and they retired upstream to their base hideout. Forty hours later they were picked up by a Catalina and taken to hospital in Merauke. The six weeks he spent there were dominated by memories of being hungry. He was then transferred to Australia where he spent a year in hospital, having developed diabetes in addition to his wounds. He refused to be hindered. To stop people treating him as a partial invalid, and for fear that his illness would prevent him receiving grants for field work, he kept it secret. For his military service in New Guinea he received an OBE in 1945.

The war not only affected Thomson's health but, coming on top of the long absences from his family in the previous years, eventually led to the end of his first marriage in 1954. On his return to civilian life, a number of his supporters at Melbourne University urged the Federal Government to find a place for him in the administration of Aboriginal affairs in the Northern Territory. However, this was strongly opposed by the relevant departmental officials in both Canberra and Darwin.[36] In the same period Thomson was offered a lectureship in anthropology at Cambridge University but in the end he decided to return to Melbourne University to work on his anthropological material. There was an inauspicious beginning to this period when a major slice of his life's work was lost. On the night of Monday 25 March 1946, a fire at the Commonwealth Cinema Branch of the Department of Information in South Melbourne destroyed the unique 23,000 feet of black and white film from Arnhem Land that had so excited Huxley and all other viewers. This event, in particular, underlay Thomson's concern in later life not to let the care of any part of his collection pass out of his hands and resulted in few people ever seeing it until after his death.

The major difference in his situation at the university now was a greater isolation than before. Wood Jones, whose commitment both to the Aboriginal people and to Thomson had been so strong, had left Australia in 1937, removing his main support; although others, such as Professor G. L. Wood and D. K. Picken, remained. Nevertheless, he was most productive in the years following the war. He wrote the two long accounts of his time in Arnhem Land on which some of this book is based, in 1948 received the Cuthbert Peak Grant of the Royal Geographical Society for geographical work in Arnhem Land and the following year received the Harbison-Higinbotham Prize of the University of Melbourne for his book *Economic Structure and the Ceremonial Exchange Cycle in Arnhem Land*. In 1950 he received his doctorate in anthropology from the University of Cambridge. The following year he received the Patron's Gold Medal of the Royal Geographical Society, London; in 1952 the John Lewis Memorial Gold Medal from the Royal Geographical Society of Australasia, both for his contribution to the geographical exploration and knowledge of Arnhem Land; and in 1953, on the nomination of Radcliffe-Brown, the Rivers Memorial Medal for field work from the Royal Anthropological Institute.

While he was receiving official recognition for his work in Arnhem Land, Thomson himself was already turning his attention away from the tropical north to the desert heart. His interest in the desert began shortly after the war when, late in 1946, he wrote a series of articles for the *Herald* on the state and treatment of Aboriginal people, urging the Commonwealth to take over responsibility for Aboriginal affairs and pressing for land rights and the freedom of Aboriginal people to live an independent life.[37] He was critical of government and mission treatment of Aboriginal people and this provoked a response from the Professor of Anthropology at Sydney University, Professor Elkin, who accused him of drawing on a prewar state of affairs. This initial disagreement developed into a permanent opposition over the matter of the establishment of the Woomera rocket range for the testing of guided missiles in South and Western Australia. Thomson and Dr Duguid, a leading Presbyterian advocate for Aboriginal people, strongly opposed the intrusion this would involve into the lives of 1,800 desert dwellers largely living beyond the frontier in reserve lands. The roads, scientific experiments, detonations and patrols would be highly disruptive and destructive of these peoples' way of life, they argued, so the range should be established elsewhere. Elkin acted as the government's apologist, arguing that the intrusion would cause no harm and thus completely reversing the views he had expressed about intrusion into this area before the rocket range was mooted. The rocket range went ahead.[38]

Undoubtedly, this debate focused Thomson's attention on the desert people; as they were now the only Aboriginal people in Australia living beyond the frontier he determined to work with them. It was ten years, though, before he was able to realise this ambition and take his first expedition into the area. In the meantime he had to overcome a great many obstacles in which he was ably assisted by his second wife, Dorita, whom he married in 1955.

Between 1957 and 1965 he led three expeditions into the Great Sandy Desert to make contact with the last few groups of Pintupi people there.[39] His field work there was focussed almost entirely on material culture and economic life, resulting in some important articles (but not on topics that were of central concern to most anthropologists), supplemented by colour cine film. Consequently he was not drawn into dialogue with the rest of the profession about them, although a handful of prehistorians recognised their significance. He was, however, involved in the setting up of the Australian Institute of Aboriginal Studies and served on its council; and in 1964 he was elected to one of the ten personal Chairs at the University of Melbourne. At the same time he was actively engaged as a member of the Aborigine's Welfare Board of Victoria, to which he had earlier been appointed as a special member by the Governor in Council but from which he resigned after ten years of frustration in 1967. Despite these involvements he remained isolated from the rest of his profession – partly because of the absence of a full-scale Department of Anthropology in the university, partly because of his interests and partly because of his health. As a result, when he died in May 1970, leaving behind three daughters and a son from his second marriage as well as his twin sons from his first, few people had any idea of the richness and scope of his ethnographic collection and field work. This became evident only after the university placed his collection, donated to it by Mrs Thomson, on loan with Museum Victoria, where it is now the crowning jewel. Its importance resides not only in its size and comprehensiveness – 7,160 artefacts, 10,580 negatives and 5,300 pages of field notes – but in the superb documentation of the items and the interrelationships between objects, photographs and notes which make it unique among collections from this period and a rich resource both for anthropologists and archaeologists and as an historical archive for the people of Cape York and Arnhem Land.

No introduction would be complete without a brief assessment of Thomson as an anthropologist. Although his book on ceremonial exchange was widely read and well regarded, little attention has been paid to his work in more recent years, except by prehistorians. The profession typed him as an ecological anthropologist mainly interested in the unfashionable areas of subsistence economics and material culture. Yet, even from his published work, he could have been equally well typed as interested in social life since he also wrote on kinship, religion and the use of language. But because of his isolation from the anthropological establishment, his reputation for being difficult and the publication of many fascinating articles in non-academic journals, he was ignored. The only anthropologist with whom he was in regular correspondence about the analysis of his material, in the postwar period, was Radcliffe-Brown. While Radcliffe-Brown was prepared to engage with the detail of Thomson's kinship material from Cape York, he did not offer the same level of advice on the Arnhem Land material, despite Thomson's explicit request for guidance in the analysis.

Thomson seems to have had two other problems, just as important as academic isolation if not more so. Methodologically he was before his time, although there is no clear indication that he recognised this. His anthropological training had been exclusively in the structural functionalist tradition, which placed great emphasis on describing, from the observer's point of view, the more formal features of social organisation such as political, economic, kinship and legal institutions and their systematic interrelationships. Thomson himself, however, was much more interested in understanding how life looked to Aboriginal people and in comprehensive documentation, probably as a result of his training in the natural sciences. Although this orientation made him a superb field worker, concerned to record exactly what Aboriginal people said on any subject in their own words and language, and to make uniquely detailed recordings of specific events with notes and camera and often by collecting the actual material objects used on any occasion as well, it created a rich body of information that could not be easily presented within the structural functionalist framework.

That this was so is evident from two sources: what he wrote and, more significantly, what he did not write. In his published work explicit theoretical statements are few but when they appear they relate mainly to myth, seen simply as a charter for behaviour, and ceremony, as an integrating force in society affirming the bond between members of the group. Beyond these simple Durkheimian- and Malinowskian-inspired views there was little other reference to sociological theory. When one comes to his field notes, of which there are approximately 3,000 pages on the life of Arnhem Landers, there is a great surprise. The man publicly seen as an ecologist is privately revealed as a person whose overwhelming anthropological interests were mythology and ceremonial life: almost all of the 3,000 pages deal with these topics. Why, then, did he not write on these topics more extensively?

Thomson had a natural facility as a linguist which allowed him quickly to pick up the various dialects he worked with and to make impressively accurate transcriptions of linguistically unknown languages. The importance he attributed to the mastery of the languages and the collection of texts comes out in a newsy letter to his solicitor, Athol Wilson, written by way of compensation for the stream of business communications with which he had flooded Wilson from the field. It was written in February 1937, at the peak of his anthropological work, and is most revealing of his approach.

> Just a few lines – perhaps a bit more – to add to what I have just written in my business letter, I always feel ashamed when I write to you from the field. I am working desperately hard – from early morning until eleven or twelve at night in a hard attempt to cover the whole field of work and I lose touch with outside things

altogether. . I spen[t] Christmas day inland s.w. of the Derby River where important ceremonies were in progress, and I eventually came in to stay at the Mission here about mid-January. I had a pretty grim time in the bush when it rained. The heat was appalling – and yet one had not only to get under the roof of a hermetically sealed bark humpy – but to erect therein a mosquito net under which one lay – devoid of pyjamas it was so hot – sweating. However, I have got a great deal of work done – and tons and tons of valuable material. At present I am working on mythology which forms the background to all the rest of the culture; working in the language getting down twenty and thirty foolscap pages of native text and then translating. *It is the best way of studying not only the mythology but grammatical construction – grammatical rule, conjugation and verbs, declension of pronouns (which are a nightmare) and also native psychology – for the text gives somehow, real glimpses of their minds working.* [Emphasis added.]

By the 1960s, when this style of linguistically oriented anthropology became established, Thomson had not only long left the field but he was also out of touch with mainstream anthropology so that he did not have a chance to benefit from this development, which might have provided him with a framework to write up his work. Instead he gradually abandoned the attempt to grapple with the social and religious life of the people of Arnhem Land and switched back to his interest in natural history as the focus of his researches in the desert.

The other issue was that, in the very year during which he was getting some of his richest material on ceremonial life and mythology, Lloyd Warner published his Milingimbi-based ethnography *A Black Civilization* (1937), over half of which is devoted to ceremonial life. Although Thomson nowhere says so, he must have felt to some degree that the basic descriptive inventory of eastern Arnhem Land Aboriginal economic and ceremonial life that he had been planning had been pre-empted by Warner.

Thomson's notes, photographs and collection of material objects made in Arnhem Land, Cape York and the desert form by far the single most important ethnographic collection made in Australia. But it was only after his death that the anthropological profession and Aboriginal people from these regions discovered this and only belatedly, therefore, that Thomson's work carried out so long ago has started to receive recognition. A renewed interest in material culture among anthropologists and a concern for local history among Aboriginal people have fuelled this recognition.

In the last thirty years many people have consulted the collection at Museum Victoria, and articles and theses that draw on it are beginning to appear. The collection is now an important part of the heritage of both black and white Australians and the only sadness is that Thomson is not alive to receive his due recognition.

Prelude

Late one afternoon towards the end of 1933, after almost twenty months of anthropological fieldwork on Cape York Peninsula, north Queensland, my wife and I were sitting on the beach near Cullen Point, at Mapoon Mission looking out on the wide empty water of the Gulf of Carpentaria, watching the sun set. The western shoreline of the Gulf is low and flat, the water generally muddy and great rollers break a long way out in the shallows of an emerging shoreline, marked in many places by a succession of raised beaches that extend inland for up to half a mile. We were talking of going home when suddenly our attention was attracted by a single masthead appearing over the horizon. Soon the mainsail of a small cutter stood out against the sunset.

The cutter dropped anchor outside the line of breakers and put off a boat which came through the surf. The craft proved to be the *Oituli* from Groote Eylandt on the opposite side of the Gulf. She had just come from Groote and her Aboriginal crew brought news of serious disturbances and interclan fighting at Caledon Bay in Arnhem Land.

They told of the killing of the Japanese crews of two luggers that had been fishing for trepang or *bêche-de-mer* at Caledon Bay; of the death of two white men, Traynor and Fagan, at Woodah Island in Blue Mud Bay; of the spearing of Constable McColl at Woodah Island and of the rout of a police party travelling from the mainland to Groote Eylandt by motor launch. It was fantastic to think that a party of armed police, with Aboriginal trackers, and a motor launch, had been driven off the mainland and isolated on an island by a handful of Aboriginal men using only spears and with no more than a dugout canoe for transport. Later we learnt more of these events from the wild news reports circulating throughout Australia. It was said that the people of Caledon and Blue

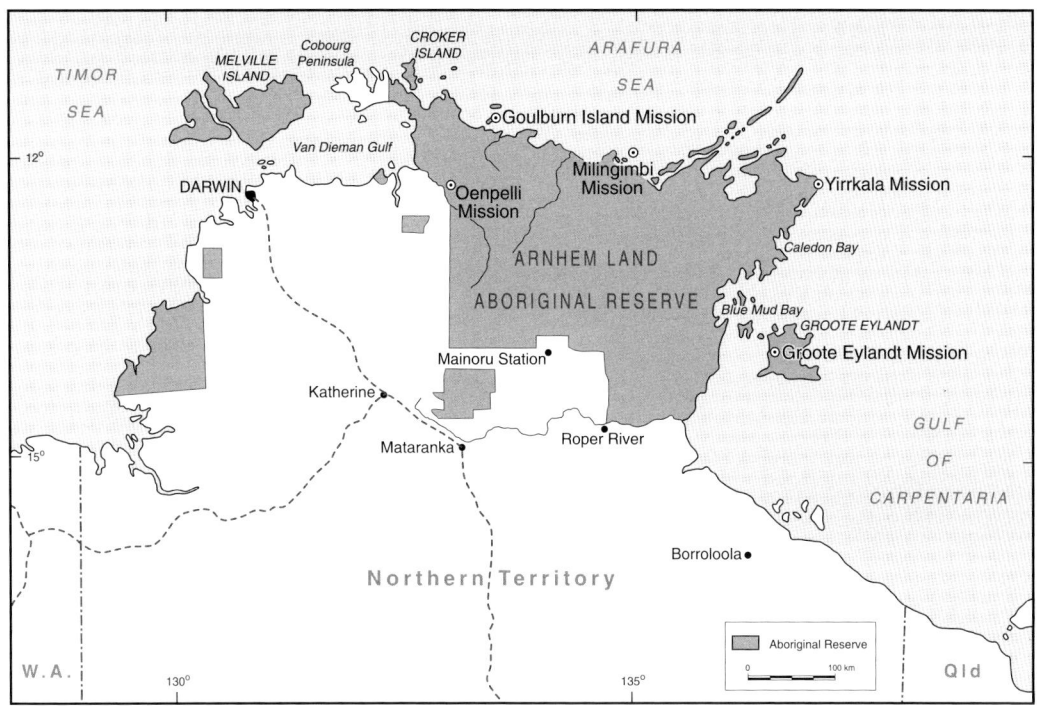

The Arnhem Land Aboriginal Reserve was established in 1931. In 1977 it became Aboriginal land under the *Aboriginal Land Rights (Northern Territory) Act 1976*. The total area, including islands, is 95,000 square kilometres.

Mud Bays were massing for an attack on the Mission at Groote Eylandt. An appeal was made for protection of the Mission by a strong police party and broken glass was actually scattered about the Mission buildings as a deterrent to bare-footed attackers.

A report published in the Melbourne *Herald* on 29 August 1933, reflects the state of panic that prevailed in Darwin:

> The Administrator, Col. Weddell and the Superintendent of Police (Mr A. V. Stretten) are planning another and strong expedition to capture the murderers of Constable McColl and of the five Japanese. They consider that unless prompt action is taken to punish the natives, it will be unsafe for any white man or trepangers to call on any part of the north-eastern portion of Arnhem Land.

Another press announcement at this time declared that the Government proposed to send a party of twelve white men with an equal number of natives to Arnhem Land:

> CANBERRA, Sunday. Cabinet will decide finally today whether a punitive expedition, requested by the Administrator of the Northern Territory, Colonel Weddell, should be authorised to proceed against the Caledon Bay blacks, murderers of Constable McColl. Latest information is that the Woodah (Groote) Mission Station is in danger of attack. The Minister of the Interior said tonight that the proposal was to organise a party of twelve with an equal number of natives, and all would be sworn in as special constables. It is reported that since the murder of Constable McColl who was sent at the head of an expedition to arrest those responsible for the killing of Japanese trepangers a year ago, the natives have got completely out of hand. Flushed with the success of their outrage they have threatened death to any other white party to penetrate their district.

The Minister of the Interior (Mr Perkins) who was responsible for the administration of the Northern Territory declared: 'The Government is convinced that it is necessary to uphold the prestige of the Administration by a display of force', but in the same breath, mindful no doubt of the record of earlier police expeditions in this area, the Minister added: '... nothing even remotely resembling an organised massacre has ever been thought of by Cabinet' (*Age*, 15 September 1933).

This statement was made to allay rising public indignation at the administrative handling of the events and to placate the missions, which had organised a 'Peace Expedition' to the area to befriend the people. The Peace Expedition ultimately betrayed them by luring some of the Aborigines to Darwin ostensibly for reconciliatory talks, but in fact to be arrested. Finally it became necessary for the Attorney General Mr (later Sir John) Latham, to declare in Parliament: 'A legend has arisen in other countries that Australia was about to begin a war in North Australia, and the Federal Ministry had to remove several misapprehensions'. A state of affairs unprecedented in the history of Australia occurred, and the Commonwealth Government was at a loss. Not only did it lack any objective, critical information on the situation in Arnhem Land, but it had no trained officers who could be sent to this area, having previously relied on police patrols, generally of a more or less punitive nature.

I followed these events as closely as I could from Cape York, becoming increasingly disturbed by the popular estimate of the Caledon Bay peoples as

How Blacks Speared Policemen

Above: A native holding a spear of the type used by the Caledon Bay natives and (right) the striking head of a Groote Eylandt native, a friendly tribe whose fishing grounds adjoin those of the Caledon Bay tribes.

FIRST OFFICIAL REPORT OF JUNGLE BATTLE IN N.T.

Natives Driven Off After Running Fight

GROOTE Is. WHITES REPORTED TO BE IN DANGER

SWIFT ACTION URGED BY N.T. ADMINISTRATOR

NO WORD FROM MISSION

PUNITIVE EXPEDITION.

RESTIVE CALEDON BAY BLACKS.

Administrator's Request.

The level of hysteria and the reality of a punitive expedition are indicated by these newspaper cuttings.

treacherous 'murderers' and appalled at the idea of the punitive expedition. Although I was tired from a long sequence of expeditions in Cape York, I realised that here was an opportunity which would not occur again in a life-time, to demonstrate the practical value of an anthropological approach, to avert disaster for the Aboriginal people of eastern Arnhem Land and to pave the way for a completely new policy in administration.

By living first with the seafaring people of the east coast of Cape York and later with the more strongly nomadic peoples of the interior, I had served my apprenticeship as an anthropologist. Was this work of academic importance only, or could it be used to bring about a complete overhaul of existing policy? I had lived and hunted with these people, accompanied them on their nomadic wanderings and learned their customs and their languages with the result that I understood and believed in them and resented the injustices under which they had suffered for so long at the hands of the white man and other invaders of their territory. To me they were warm, kindly and friendly people who I knew well and in whose camps I was at home. Yet at the time, not only were the Aborigines generally treated as outcasts, but a white man who liked and understood them was regarded as an eccentric.

I wrote to the Chancellor of the University of Melbourne, Sir John MacFarland, from which I was working as research fellow, told him what I had heard of the disturbances in Arnhem Land, and asked him to offer my services to the Commonwealth Government to go alone into the troubled area to make friends with the Aboriginal people and to report the true facts.

I offered to establish myself with these people, to live with them, for years if necessary, so that I could understand the real causes that were responsible for the frequent fighting that had raged about Caledon and Blue Mud Bays for so long, and so to endeavour to restore peace in this disturbed area. Above all I wanted to avert a punitive expedition and all that it would mean to these people.

It is true that I did not know the Arnhem Land Aborigines but I was confident that the methods which I had used to win the confidence of the Aborigines of Cape York would also be successful there. Aborigines are normally of a peaceful and genial disposition and their attitude towards aliens is generally friendly unless greatly provoked. I was convinced that there must be a very real cause underlying the constant conflict reported from Arnhem Land. I did not believe they were the aggressors, but rather that they had been so wronged that they had been goaded into retaliation. To me their actions were an indication of exasperation at the periodic invasion of their territory and the interference with their women by Japanese pearlers and other outsiders. They were a people holding onto their heritage and daring to defend their territory against violation and aggression.

Brief historical research later confirmed this. The European discovery of Arnhem Land is credited to the yacht *Arnheim*, commanded by Van Colster or Van Colsteerdt in 1623. The ship's name was given to the north-eastern corner of what is now the Northern Territory east of Van Diemen's Gulf and north of the Roper River. It is a region of great ethnographic and historical interest but for more than a century after the mapping of the coastline in 1803 by Matthew Flinders, the eastern portion was shunned by Europeans and remained a vast unknown land to them. However for many generations voyagers from Indonesia paid annual visits to the coast of Arnhem Land in their *praus* in search of trepang, pearls and turtle-shell. They came with the north-west gales that heralded the approach of the wet season in late December and returned in March or April of the following year when the winds swung round to the south-east.

Flinders had met a fleet of six *praus* from Macassar in the Celebes in a sheltered strait he subsequently named the Malay Road. The *praus* were under the command of one Pobasso, who told him that there were no less than sixty of their craft on the coast of Arnhem Land at that time, all owned by the Sultan of Boni, and that these vessels carried a total of around a thousand men. Pobasso also told Flinders that he had made six or seven such voyages to Arnhem Land over the past twenty years and claimed to be among the first to have come. If correct, his claim would set the time of the first visits by these Indonesian voyagers at about 1780. However the evidence of Asiatic influences on this coast suggests that such visits had taken place much earlier and over a longer period than was indicated by Pobasso.

Curiously, in the light of my experience in Arnhem Land, Flinders came to the conclusion that the Aborigines did not hold the Asian visitors in much regard. Although there were sometimes clashes with the Indonesians, the impression of their relationships with the Aborigines given to me was one of respect, amounting almost to hero-worship, which the Europeans have never been able to achieve. This respect was based on the pattern of behaviour which included recognition by the Macassans of the territorial and other rights of the Aborigines and respect for the integrity of their women. There is no doubt that the failure to appreciate this long history of Asian contact and failure to understand the relationship which had existed between the two peoples, was responsible for much of the hostility which the Japanese and Europeans met with in the Gulf of Carpentaria and for the reputation for savageness and aggressiveness which we attributed to these people.

My own experience in Arnhem Land was to show that they were in reality more sophisticated than other Aborigines, a fact that had impressed Matthew Flinders at Caledon Bay. He remarked on the bold, independent, almost blasé air of the people he met there. Of the meeting of these people on Thursday 3rd February 1803, with Lieutenant Fowler, whom he sent ashore to make contact with the natives Flinders remarked: 'They staid to receive him, without showing that timidity so usual with the Australians …' (1814/1966(2):205). And a few days later he wrote again:

> That this bay [Caledon] had before received the visits of some strangers, was evinced by the knowledge which the natives had of fire arms; they imitated the act of shooting when we first landed, and when a musket was fired at their request, were not much alarmed … The propensity shown by the natives to steal, especially our axes, so contrary to all I have known and heard of their countrymen, is not only proof that they have been previously visited by people possessing iron implements, but from their audacity it would appear that the effect of fire arms was either not very certain in the hands of the strangers or had seldom been resorted to in the punishment of aggression (Flinders 1814/1966 (2):213).

By the time my offer was made so much publicity had been given to the disturbances in Arnhem Land, and such a picture had been painted of the numbers, hostility and treachery of the natives of Woodah Island and Caledon Bay that the Chancellor was told that my proposal would mean certain death. But he asked me to return to Melbourne to discuss the matter. When I did return he was sceptical at first, but at last he understood the value and importance of this work and the long experience that I could bring to bear on it. Once he was convinced he gave me his whole-hearted support. The proposal was also supported strongly by my friend Professor F. Wood Jones, FRS, and the Acting Vice-Chancellor Sir Douglas Copland.

Further months were wasted however as the Government came under increasingly heavy fire for its handling of the Aborigines and it was not until a crisis was precipitated by Judge Wells passing a death sentence on Dhaakiyarr, a man from Caledon Bay, in the Darwin Supreme Court, that action eventuated. Dhaakiyarr was found guilty of the 'murder' of the policeman who, according to evidence of witnesses at the time, had first handcuffed and later raped Dhaakiyarr's wife and then emptied his revolver at her husband who had come at her call for help. If he had been a white man his action would have been self-defence and on other grounds, justifiable homicide.

Three other Aborigines, all sons of Wonggu, grand old man of the people of Caledon Bay, had also been sentenced to life imprisonment – to twenty years' hard labour in Fanny Bay Gaol. Their crime that, provoked beyond endurance, they had attacked the Japanese crews of two luggers who intruded in their territory and stole their women. My own experience in the years I spent later with them and their neighbours showed that violation of women among the Balamumu of

Caledon Bay and their neighbours of Woodah Island and Blue Mud Bay, the Dhayyi would inevitably bring reprisals.

Despite evidence at the trial of the three Caledon Bay prisoners that the Japanese had built a smoke-house on shore in their territory to smoke trepang, had mounted an armed guard and had taken and held their women in this house and had beaten the men who attempted to rescue them, the Aborigines were charged with murder. It was not these matters that precipitated the crisis so much as the remarks of Judge Wells which probably made judicial history for their partiality and impropriety.

In his summing up, he remarked that international resentment might result if the Aborigines who killed the Japanese trepangers were not punished. Yet these people were poachers illegally in the Reserve and their trespass was aggravated by the fact that Caledon Bay was an uncontrolled area, whose people had established a code of behaviour to which strangers were expected to conform.

In its review of the death sentence pronounced on Dhaakiyarr, the High Court of Australia, quashing his sentence and ordering his release, ruled that the very remarks of the judge had precluded any possibility of a fair trial. The public outcry that followed the sentence of twenty years' hard labour by Judge Wells on Wonggu's three sons, Natjiyalma, Maaw and Ngarkaya for their part in the Caledon Bay affair, followed by the High Court ruling on Dhaakiyarr, stirred public indignation in Australia as it had never been stirred before, and the Government was forced to act.

I was summoned to Canberra. I remember still my dismay when I arrived there to confer with the Minister of the Interior, Mr Perkins, on the situation in Arnhem Land and my offer to go into the disturbed area to make friends with the people. I had not been back in civilisation very long and faced at last with the cold and formal air at Canberra, so remote from the problems of the people of Arnhem Land, I felt embarrassed and bewildered. This was a world, bleak, soulless, far from the friendly warm-hearted people for whom I had come as advocate and I experienced a great depression of spirit – a feeling that I was never able to overcome in any of my subsequent visits to Canberra. It was compounded by an event that took place just before my visit. I received a letter from Sir Colin McKenzie, Director of the Institute of Anatomical Research in the Federal Capital, asking me, if I undertook the mission that I had volunteered to carry out in Arnhem Land for the Government, to make a collection of skulls for his Institute. I replied that it was inappropriate, and incompatible with the spirit and the gravity of the delicate task that I was to undertake for the

Commonwealth Government to avert disaster for the Aborigines. My shock can be imagined, therefore, when I was ushered into the ante-room to the office of the Minister and met Mr H. C. Brown, the permanent head of the Department of the Interior, with Sir Colin McKenzie seated beside him! I probably showed the surprise that I felt after my passage with Sir Colin, but before he took me to the Minister, Mr Brown made a new proposal that I could scarcely believe.

'Sir Colin McKenzie', he said, 'is most anxious that you should collect skulls for his Institute when you are in Arnhem Land.' If it had not been for the previous request directed to me, I would not have believed that I had heard correctly. At first the utter incongruity of such a request from the head of the Department that had invited me to Canberra to assist the Government in handling the crisis that resulted from the sentence of death passed by Judge Wells on Dhaakiyarr, stunned me. My heart sank at the utter inequity of such a request and I was close to withdrawing my offer but I remembered the people and the attitudes that still faced them if I did not go.

I turned to Mr Brown, and in a moment of sudden inspiration replied: 'I have already told Sir Colin McKenzie that I am unwilling to collect skulls in Arnhem Land. As a matter of fact, I feel that Judge Wells is in a better position to collect skulls for the Commonwealth Government than I am'.

The shot went home. A brittle, tense silence reigned, and then I found myself with the Minister.

Once again, I regretted my shortcomings as an advocate for I felt that here was a chance, the first occasion on which I had ever had a hearing from one who had the power really to help the Aborigines. I tried to tell him in simple terms of the life and background of these people, of the way in which the European rode roughshod over them.

I explained to the Minister that although I knew the people of north Queensland well, I did not know the people of Arnhem Land. But from long experience I knew how to approach them, and would not be in any danger provided that I went alone and had time to establish myself with them.

At first the Minister was sceptical. Remembering how the police party had been driven out he regarded the proposal as suicidal. Finally I believed I had convinced him that there was nothing either heroic or suicidal in my offer, but when I met him later he was still undecided. This experience was repeated over and again, even when I was at last in the field. I did not know then that the Government was almost committed to a punitive expedition, but the publicity given to the offer that I had made and the growing public opinion had delayed action.

Meanwhile, the immediate release of Dhaakiyarr, the man who had killed McColl in defence of his wife, had been ordered by the High Court. Dhaakiyarr was taken out of the cells and held in the compound in Darwin. But suddenly he disappeared. Dhaakiyarr, who would have been in no danger in Darwin, never reached home. Significantly, no high-level official enquiry was ever made as to his fate. But the Aborigines are unanimous about this. 'Policeman shoot 'im', was their verdict. And nothing escapes them, least of all the fate of a lone Aboriginal five hundred miles from home, who has killed a policeman.

Finally after further months of delay I was granted a commission to go to Arnhem Land to establish friendly relations with the people, to restore peace in the area, and to study and report on the problems of these people. More than a year had elapsed since I had returned from the field and during that time I lost faith in the task which I had set my heart on: I now felt tired and dispirited, particularly as all other efforts by the Government and the Administration had ended in failure.

In the interval, my twin sons were born and after all these years in the field my heart was in the home where the river ran at the foot of the garden, and the sound of water breaking over stones could be heard in the long watches of the night, where I could rest and write of the things we had seen and done.

I had made the offer to avert disaster for the people and in the belief that if I succeeded it would pave the way for a new approach to the administration of the Aborigines and the recognition of their rights as human beings.

At length, in 1935, after more discussions with the Minister, I was handed the following commission. He voiced the opinion of the Government that I carried my life in my hands, as is evidenced by the benediction with which the official document ends.

You are hereby authorised to enter the Aboriginal Reserve, Arnhem Land, and entrusted with a commission to carry out the duties herein enumerated:

- To make contact with and establish, as far as possible, friendly relations with the Aborigines.
- To encourage the natives, as far as possible, to realise the gravity of the major offences of murder, robbery and the like, both in respect of fellow natives as well as white men.
- To report cases coming under notice of serious illness, such as leprosy, tuberculosis, cancer etc.

- To study and report upon the language, ceremonies, customs, moral codes, etc. of the various tribes, such report to be forwarded to the Minister for the Interior.

With every good wish for your safety and success in this enterprise.

Thus began an involvement with the people of north-east Arnhem Land that lasted until 1943. During these years I lived with the people as nobody had before and, travelling by foot and boat, learnt much about their way of life. With the outbreak of war came an ironic twist to my involvement with them. I was asked to return to the self-same people, so nearly destroyed by their attack on the Japanese, to establish a guerilla force to help protect Australia from Japanese invasion. In the pages that follow I try to pass on some of what I have learnt about these peoples' way of life during my travels and work in this then unknown part of Arnhem Land.

To Caledon Bay

On March 16th 1935 I left Melbourne on SS *Ormiston* for Cairns, where I took over the auxiliary ketch *St Nicholas*, which had been given to the university for my use by A. M. and G. R. Nicholas.

The vessel, which was to have been handed over to me ready for sea, proved to have only one ton of ballast in her. We sailed her down the harbour and with the permission of the local harbour authorities, loaded some three tons of heavy stone to trim her.

Fuel supplies for the auxiliary motor and stores sufficient to last many months, as well as several caddies of tobacco, coils of heavy gauge wire for fish spears, fish hooks and other trade goods were obtained. Then followed several days of stowing cargo in the sweltering hold.

The Harbour Master, in whose care the craft had been left, proved helpful and friendly. He was particularly interested in my navigation equipment. This was a source of some embarrassment to me, for at that time I knew nothing of navigation and was anxious merely to put to sea. I did not know what the powers of a Harbour Master might be, but I did not want to expose my ignorance, and so maintained a discreet silence. I enlisted three local people – a man of mixed descent and two Aborigines – to serve as crew on the voyage to Torres Strait. At last the vessel was ready for sea and on the afternoon of April 4th I sailed from Trinity Bay on the run to Thursday Island, about five hundred miles away. This was my first voyage on the open sea in charge of a ship and the voyage up the Barrier Reef was a notable one, with many anxious moments. The sight of the mountains of the Lockhart River, 350 miles north from Cairns, was like a glimpse of home, for there I had spent some of the happiest years of my life with the dugong hunters and seafarers, living as nearly as a white man can, the life of a nomadic hunter.

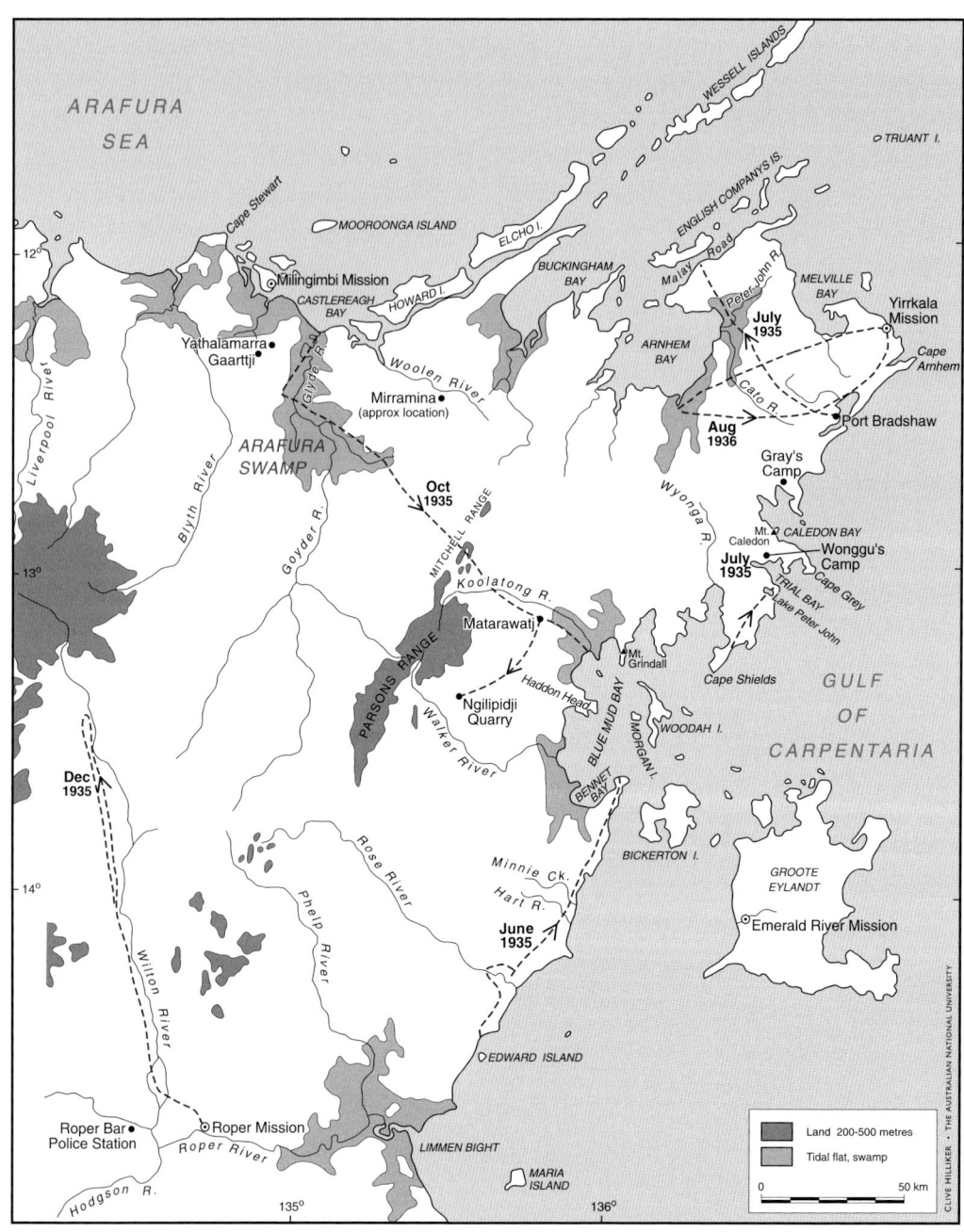

Lines of travel on land, 1935–1937.

At Lockhart River I found Tommy Tjamindjinyu, who had been with me on all my previous expeditions on Cape York Peninsula and whose language I knew well, waiting for me. Tommy was eager to accompany me, and recruiting two other Aborigines who had also been with me on previous expeditions, I left behind the men I had brought from Cairns, to be returned home from Lockhart River. We sailed northward to Thursday Island, where I had intended to 'sign on' the crew of Queensland Aborigines to serve with me in Arnhem Land. But after a few days, even those men whom I had known for years came under the spell which had been following me all the way up the coast – the feeling that I was bound for a place whence no man returns. They were told that I would certainly be killed in Arnhem Land. At length Tommy, in the capacity of spokesman, sidled up to me and after two or three preliminary coughs – always a prelude, with Tommy, to a momentous announcement – said tentatively, in a sepulchral voice:

'*Main pa*!' (My sister's son)

'Yes *Kala?*' (Mother's brother)

'More better me die home!' (It is better that I should die at home in my own native land.)

The white man's magic was at work again.

Following the defection of my Queensland crew I obtained three Torres Strait Islanders to man the *St Nicholas* on the voyage to Arnhem Land. Lack of funds, however, made it necessary to return two of the three men on arrival at Groote Eylandt and to depend on bush Aborigines recruited casually, to work the boat in the almost uncharted waters of the Arnhem Land coast.

It had been my plan to work slowly around the coast to Blue Mud and Caledon Bays. I had, however, been warned repeatedly of the danger of having my boat raided by the people of the coast of Arnhem Land, and this, coupled with the fact that I had to depend on a single Torres Strait Islander, Kapiu, whom I did not yet know, and who did not know me, and for the rest to employ inexperienced Aborigines rendered advisable a change of plans. I was anxious especially, to avoid the possibility of a clash with the Arnhem Landers even before I had had the opportunity of establishing myself with them. The greatest care therefore, was necessary in making this first approach.

Finally, I decided to send the *St Nicholas* to Groote Eylandt, where it was to remain within call of the mission pedal wireless set, until I had made some contact with the Caledon Bay peoples. My plan was to go to Darwin and thence to approach the Caledon Bay area by an overland patrol. In this way I would be

able to establish friendly contact in the disturbed area without the risk of exposing my boat, loaded with nearly ten tons of stores and equipment, to a raid,
before I had made myself known.

After completing the loading of the *St Nicholas* at Thursday Island, I sent her
to Groote Eylandt and travelled by the steamer *Marella* to Darwin. On arrival
there I found that the *Maree*, the store vessel of the Methodist Mission at Milingimbi in the Crocodile Islands, on which I had arranged to travel to Arnhem
Land preparatory to starting my overland patrol, was held up indefinitely
through engine trouble. Weeks had already elapsed since I left Melbourne and
as I was unwilling to risk any further delay, I signalled to Groote Eylandt
instructing the *St Nicholas* to sail for the Roper River and to meet me there.

My visit to Darwin was however not altogether in vain, for I visited Fanny Bay Gaol and made friends with Natjiyalma, Maaw and Ngarkaya, the three sons of Wonggu of Caledon Bay, whose death sentence for the killing of the five Japanese at Caledon Bay on 17th September 1932 had been commuted to life imprisonment. When I left Darwin I carried with me a message stick, accompanied by an oral message from these three brothers for their father, 500 miles away in Arnhem Land. This was the first step towards securing the liberation of these men who were sent back to their country in my custody just a year later.

On the 29th of May I left Darwin for Mataranka en route for the Roper, and reached the Roper Bar Police Station on June 1st.

When I arrived at Roper Bar the *St Nicholas* had not yet arrived in the River; and as the pedal wireless set at the police station was out of order, it was not possible to communicate with Groote Eylandt direct. The police depot at the Roper Bar is about a hundred miles from the mouth of the river, above the junction of the Hodgson and Wilton Rivers, and while waiting for the boat I moved to the mission station about twenty miles down-stream, transporting my gear in canoes. Several more days passed without any news, and as the Roper is strongly tidal and the vessel was only under sail I decided to go down to meet her. I obtained the loan of a small dinghy, into which I loaded the cameras and more valuable items of scientific equipment, and with the aid of three dugout canoes to carry the heavy stores and gear, set off down the river.

It was a memorable journey. I shared a dugout canoe with five Aborigines of whom two men formed the crew – wielding the bow and stern paddles respectively – and an old woman, a young woman and her child, four dogs, our swags, and a quantity of stores. When fully loaded, we had a freeboard of only a few inches. The canoes leaked badly. We placed sticks and branches crosswise to keep the cargo off the floor, bailed frequently to prevent the water rising to the level of the gear, and at intervals pulled into the banks to caulk the cracks with tea-tree bark. On the upper reaches of the river, where the stream was fresh and less strongly tidal, we made rapid progress, but on the lower reaches the crew flagged and with the heavily laden canoes we found it economical to travel only when the tide was running out, and to call a halt when it turned.

The wooden canoes of Arnhem Land are all built on the same lines; they have a rounded bottom with no keel whatever nor outrigger, and unless very carefully loaded, trimmed and handled, are easily upset. These canoes are a legacy from the Macassan voyagers, whose *praus* brought eight or ten canoes which served as tenders for the trepang fishing; when the *praus* were about to return home, the canoes, with other presents, were generally given to the Aborigines in whose territories the trepangers had been operating.

On the voyage down to Roper it required constant vigilance to keep the little convoy together. No sooner would we get under way after a halt than someone would sight a water 'goanna' or monitor lizard (*Varanus*) sunning itself on a mangrove limb overhanging the water. Our paddlers would exercise a deft manoeuvre, almost precipitating disaster, to swing our canoe backwards – and so give full scope to the hunter in the leading canoe – standing up now, tense and rigid, with spear poised awaiting his opportunity when the quarry came within range. It was useless to protest. Food was plentiful, and at the wayside camps we employed our time in hunting geese, ducks, wallabies and kangaroos. Crocodiles were also numerous and were seen frequently. When I went down the bank of the river to drink, one of the men would stand behind, throwing a log or branch into the water in front of me to frighten away reptiles that might be lurking near. From long experience the Aborigines are much more vigilant in these matters than the white man, for although deaths from crocodiles are infrequent, almost every river has its record of victims.

On the night of June 9th, shortly after we had made camp after a long day of paddling, the *St Nicholas* appeared around a bend of the river. Early on the following morning we loaded all our equipment aboard, took the vessel down to the mouth of the river, and anchored in the estuary off a large Aboriginal camp.

This camp consisted, at that time, chiefly of members of the Nunggubuyu tribe, with a few members from the Wandarang, Mara, Yukul, Ngandi, and other tribes of the Roper River area. The territory of the Nunggubuyu, generally known as the 'Rose River' tribe, lies to the north of the mouth of the Roper, and extends from the mouth of the river opposite Edward Island to Cape Barrow on Bennet Bay, at the southern end of Blue Mud Bay. There were about eighty or ninety people in the camp at that time; they had gathered in preparation for a ceremony, and were subsisting by dugong hunting in the Limmen Bight to the south of the mouth of the Roper River.

Kapiu, the Torres Strait Islander who had brought the *St Nicholas* from Groote Eylandt, had secured from adjacent Bickerton Island, two men of the Ingura (Groote Eylandt) tribe as crew. I collected a number of men including a crippled youth 'Smiler', who had been brought, in early childhood, from the northern end of Blue Mud Bay and a Nunggubuyu man named Mardi, of very powerful physique; two or three others from this coast also attached themselves to our party.

On the following morning we ran out through the mouth of the Roper River northward bound. Conditions at sea were not favourable, for a south-east wind had arisen soon after daybreak and was rapidly growing in intensity. The mouth of the Roper River forms a narrow channel that threads its way through a series of sand bars and banks, with shallow waters on which the yellow, discoloured seas break heavily in the south-east monsoon season. These banks extend for about five miles into the sea towards Maria Island. As we negotiated the bar the wind was freshening, and through the morning both wind and sea continued to rise. Conditions were growing steadily worse. By 1 p. m. we had cleared the banks off the mouth of the river, and were running northward on our course. But the wind had attained the force of a gale and the *St Nicholas* was rolling in a heavy sea that took her on the beam.

The only possibility of shelter now lay in making for Edward Island off the mouth of a small river, a little to the north of the Roper. The waters here are quite uncharted, the island is surrounded by shoals, and owing to the rough sea the water was yellow and discoloured. We were obliged to feel our way inshore with the leadline, make for the best shelter available, and at length dropped anchor on the south-west side of the island in two-and-a-half fathoms of water. Throughout the night the wind continued to blow strongly and the vessel rolled heavily with a cross wind and sea, and took on a good deal of water. On the following morning the wind increased in velocity and as these conditions appeared to have set in and seemed likely to last for some days, I decided to employ the time in making a reconnaissance on foot to locate the main camps and to make contact with the people between this river and Cape Barrow, away to the northward, leaving the *St Nicholas* to follow as soon as the weather had moderated sufficiently.

Taking two men, Joshua from the Roper River, and Mardi, the Nunggubuyu, I set out early on the afternoon of Wednesday, June 12th. We landed on the north bank of the river, prepared for a journey of three or four days, which I calculated would easily take us to Bennet Bay. In order to travel light we cut our loads down to the bare minimum. I carried a single blanket with a sheet of Birkmyre canvas, a tomahawk, a few short lengths of heavy-gauge fencing wire for fish spears, a shot gun and a few cartridges, about twenty pounds of flour, a small piece of bacon, a little tea and sugar, and tobacco as gifts for the people. I wore, instead of boots, only a light pair of sandshoes, without socks, and shorts and shirt.

We expected to reach Bennet Bay by Saturday night. Mardi knew the country well, having travelled with his people in their seasonal movements up and down the coast from the mouth of the Roper River to the Rose River and Bennet Bay. We planned to follow the coast and to reach the mouth of the Rose River that same night; to cross by canoe in the morning and thence to strike northwards.

We walked hard all through that afternoon and into the night, traversing miles of flat, dry salt pans fringing the coastline, and late that night, in the moonlight, we reached the wide estuary of the Rose. Although the mouth of the Rose River appears on the charts with a single channel, a small island or delta lies at the entrance, to which I have given the name Mardi Island. The guides were insistent in their desire to cross over to an old camp site on the delta at the mouth of the river. We were able to reach this island at dead low water by walking out across the sandbanks, wading the intervening channels and threading our way through the banks of soft treacherous mud, possible even in daylight only to one possessing intimate local knowledge. The island was surrounded by dense mangroves and we camped on an open sand spit on the seaward side, where the wind from the sea drove the mosquitoes away. The men went off in search of water, and by excavating a disused well, eventually obtained a small quantity, but it was very foul, with a foetid smell and taste. Much of the water in these deep wells on which the Aborigines of the coastal areas depend, and which we had often to drink, was like this – stagnant and smelling evilly from the decaying vegetable matter with which it was impregnated, and just brackish enough to be nauseating.

The night was bitterly cold with a keen wind off the water, and although we were all dead tired we slept only fitfully.

I awakened Mardi and Joshua early; they made up the fire and squatted over it like two lizards basking in the sun. The tide was now high and the island was isolated from either shore by a wide span of water. To the north lay the main course of the Rose River, which was here from half to three quarters of a mile wide, with a deep channel in midstream. The southern channel which we had crossed the previous night to reach the island was obscured from view by a dense wall of mangroves.

There was no sign of a camp. Mardi had 'thawed' a little and went off in search of dry logs and driftwood. He returned with two or three light logs, and bound them together with the creeping stems of *Ipomoea pes-caprae*, a plant with a wide distribution on tropical beaches, that sends its sprawling vines abundantly over the sand hills. Then, carrying this crude swimming raft into the water, and clinging to one end of it so that it supported part of the weight of his body, he swam across the wide estuary. At this season of the year the water is extremely cold and the Aborigines suffer severely if they are in the water for long.

In the meantime Joshua lay prostrate with a heavy 'cold sick' – a condition which affects these people frequently at this season of the year. It comes upon them quite suddenly; last night he had been quite normal, but all through this morning he lay face down on the sand. He was quite unfit to work and too morose to speak except in monosyllables. Quite suddenly he had completely lost interest in everything and for hours lay as if he were dead.

There was nothing to do on the island, and the hours of waiting seemed an eternity, but early in the afternoon Mardi returned alone, the way he had come – without any canoe – swimming with his log raft. He reported that the camp was deserted. The tracks indicated to him that the people had all moved north to Cape Barrow on Bennet Bay. Subsequent events proved that he was right, but the fact very nearly cost two of us our lives.

Mardi emerged from the water after his long swim, cold and sullen. He had been so certain that there were people here who would accompany us north. I gave him food and tobacco, and turned to make some hot tea. I put aside the billy for the two men, and then it occurred to me suddenly that I had not seen them for some time. I turned to look for them. They were nowhere to be seen. I knew at once that something was amiss. I went first, however, to see if they were searching for better water, or if they were out on the flats looking for a crossing, for it was evident that we should all have to swim. But there was no sign of them. At length I met Joshua alone – coming back to tell me that Mardi had run away. He had suddenly gathered his possessions, dived into the dense mangroves and swum across the south channel of the river. Already he was on his way back to the camp at the mouth of the Roper river.

I sat down and took stock of the situation. I was stranded on an island, separated by about half a mile of water from the north shore, with an Aboriginal whom I did not know – a man who was not only too sick to travel or to hunt, but who did not even profess to know the country between us and Bennet Bay, where the boat would be waiting for us. He had made one trip there – but that was more than twenty-five years before, when, as a boy, he had been sent to muster men for the ceremony at which he was to be initiated. We had no reserve stores, almost no water, and the *St Nicholas* would certainly have sailed northwards out to sea, so that we should not be able to signal her.

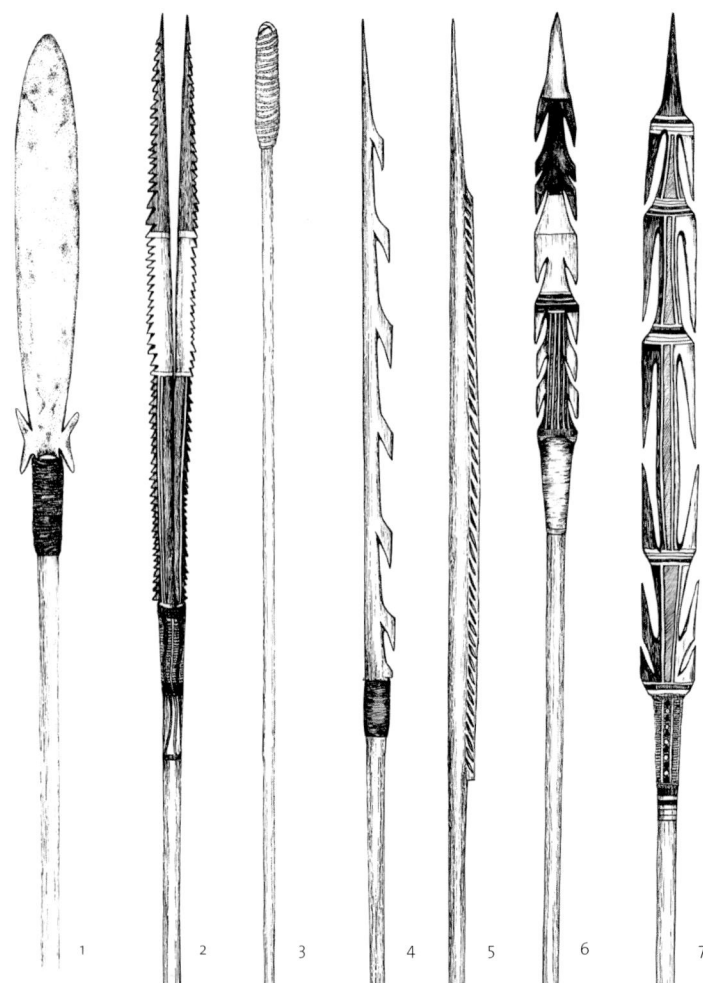

A large variety of spears were made by the Yolngu. Part of this variation was due to different uses: animal hunting, fighting, fish and bird spearing, play or training games and ceremonial exchange and display. Other variation was due to the wide variety of materials used – including wood, bone, stone, metal resin and fibre – and some variation was due to certain forms being identified with particular clan or regional groupings. This variation gave spears exchange value and may have encouraged the proliferation of spear variation.

1 This metal bladed spear is known in English as a shovel-nosed spear. The blades were most commonly made from pieces of metal piping or parts of old vehicles.
2 A Djambarrpuyngu fish spear.
3 A play/training spear. This is a spear shaft, with the blunt end wrapped in paperbark, used by boys to throw at each other.
4 & 5 These spears probably come from the area north of Port Bradshaw.
6 A Wurlaki spear from the Gaarttji area.
7 A Djambarrpuyngu spear. Those spears with barbs along one edge only are known as yininya and those with barbs on both sides are known as miliyarr.

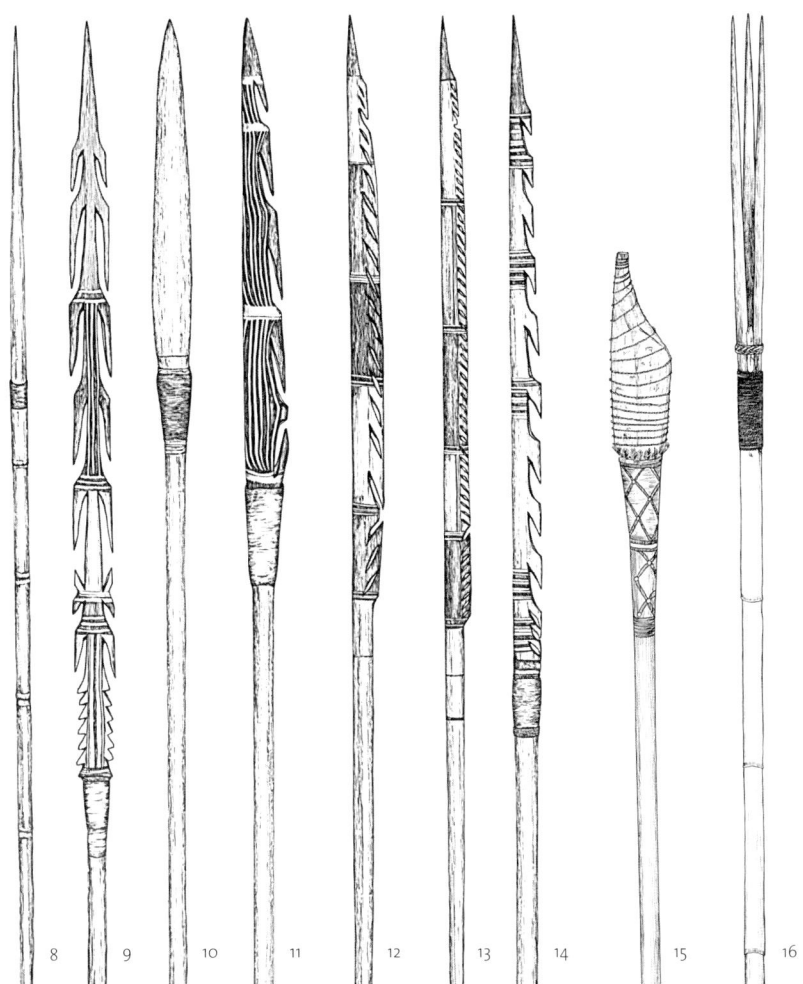

8   A bamboo-shafted spear from the Arafura Swamp, with a heavy hardwood point,
    that is used for hunting birds and fighting.
9   Another Djambarrpuyngu spear.
10 Another form of hunting and fighting spear, but with a wooden blade.
11 A Ganalbingu clan spear
12 A Warramiri fighting and ceremonial spear called baaarti.
13 A Djambarrpuyngu fighting spear.
14 A Ritharrngu spear.
15 A spear with a stone head from the Ngilipidji quarry wrapped in paperbark to protect it.
16 A three-pronged fishing spear from the Arafura Swamp.

I was anxious to get away from the island and to find good water, but Joshua had thrown himself down on the sand again and for hours I could get no response from him. Late in the afternoon he seemed to get a little better and began to take an interest in life. Our first object was to get clear of the island, and to find water.

While we were waiting for the tide to fall, we searched the island for stones which we could use to sharpen the wire that I had brought, to convert it into a fish spear which would be a valuable implement for getting food on the journey ahead. We found only a single large stone, but this served as an anvil and we used the tomahawk to draw out the wires, and then ground the points by rubbing them on the stone. We could mount them later, as soon as we found a suitable shaft.

It was now late afternoon, and as the tide, which had turned some time ago, was now falling rapidly, we made ready our loads and prepared to leave the island. We did not know the country ahead, nor whether we should find water easily, or if it would be necessary to make a long journey up the river course in search of it. There is a very large area of coastline and although there is abundant water inland, the Aborigines living on the coast depend chiefly on deep wells, some of which are very old. These wells are few and far between and local knowledge is needed to find them.

Joshua took the loads on his head, headed north and waded out across the mouth of the river, hoping to find it sufficiently shallow there to enable us to ford across to the sandbanks, leaving only the comparatively narrow main channel to swim. But at a distance of only twenty yards from the shore he was up to his armpits, with half a mile still to go, and he had not yet reached the deep channel. Night was approaching, it was already bitterly cold with a keen south-east wind, there was a strong tide, and I was unwilling to take the risk of the long swim under these conditions in a place that we knew to be infested with crocodiles and sharks. I called Joshua back and abandoned the idea of crossing the north (main) channel of the river. By wading from bank to bank we eventually retraced our steps to the south bank of the river, which we reached before dark. Our first objective now was to find fresh water, and on the following day a place to ford the Rose River without having to waste energy by travelling far inland.

We set a course westward, and by moon and starlight we walked for many hours that night. A little distance from the estuary we crossed the tracks of Mardi, making south towards the mouth of the Roper Rivers. The low-lying salt pans near the coast had been flooded recently and were reduced to a great expanse of deep sticky grey mud in which we sank at every step. It was heavy going. Again we crossed miles of salt pans interspersed with ridges of slightly higher ground, densely clothed with low xerophilous scrub, very dense and prickly, which tore our clothes and scratched us severely. Very late, just as we were about to abandon for the night the search for water, we ran into a series of low rocky outcrops, and following up the dry gulch, we found a fair pool of water – slightly brackish, but better than the water in the well that we had left on the delta some hours before. We made camp close to the pool, on hard reddish ironstone ground. We were astir early, boiled the billy in the dark and set off again, as soon as it was light enough to see at all.

The journey northward, for which we had originally allowed a bare four days, occupied eight long, heart-breaking days – and was nearly a disaster. For the most part I shall depend upon extracts from my journal made during the journey to tell the story.

'Friday 14th. Fair night, not so cold as last night; awoke very early, made up big fire and wrote this journal.

'Hope, but do not really expect, to cross the Rose River today; Joshua says it is deep and infested with crocodiles, so we shall have to go far up. Living on black tea, dry damper with an occasional slice of bacon.

'Miles of arid salt pans interspersed with sandy or gravely ridges, sometimes with heavy outcrops of stone. Camped eventually on a chain of lagoons to the north of the Rose River mouth but still on the south bank, after one of the hardest and most gruelling days of my life. On the south side of the river we saw much "Cyprus pine" (*Callitris*) from a few inches to about a foot, in diameter; many fine wattles, and a splendid shrub known as the "Turpentine bush" (*Calythrix microphylla*) – a blaze of rich purplish hue like heather.'

We left camp on the following morning soon after 6.00 a. m. and walked steadily. Joshua did not complain of 'cold sick' today but of his tired legs and aching back. After about two hours travelling the river began to narrow and we saw two or three places where it looked possible to cross. Keeping our eyes open for dry Pandanus or other material for a raft or swimming log we watched for a suitable spot. Fortune favoured us, and soon we came upon an outcrop of stone dipping steeply, that formed a ridge right across the river, parts of which projected above the water. At these fords, however, caution is necessary for crocodiles are in the habit of watching such places for dingoes, kangaroos and other prey. Soon after nine, about three hours after breaking camp, we were safely across. As we did not know the country now that our guide had deserted, and as our stores were short, I decided to make for the coast again, and so set a course east-north-east. The country was rough and stony, and after we left the river, water was very scarce again. Although at this season of the year the nights were cold, it was intensely hot all day, and I learned much about the occurrence of water, and of the Aborigines' methods of getting it. When we were very hard pressed we tapped the great nodular swellings on melaleuca trees, which some-times provide a little water – though bitter and highly mineralised. That night we had a fairly comfortable camp, with abundant water.

On the following morning, the fourth day, we set off again after daylight. Joshua talked constantly of a 'Lake Mary' which he described as a great camping place, and where he hoped to find people. No recent tracks were seen and we skirted this without sighting it, and struck east, to return to the beach, where travel would be less severe. After some hours of walking we caught a glimpse of sand dunes, and knew that we were approaching the coast at last. In the early part of the morning we passed within a few feet of the finest specimen that I have seen alive of *Pseudechis australis*, the King Brown Snake known as *daarrpa* in many Arnhem Land dialects, one of the largest and most aggressive of the venomous snakes of northern tropical Australia; he was sunning himself at the foot of a termite mound, a fine showy snake, rich copper–brown in colour, about seven feet long and very thick and heavy. When we passed he reared his head high in the air, flattened his neck, and lashed his body about from side to side – his orange–red eyes gleaming wickedly.

We steered east towards the sandhills. My left thigh and calf were now sore and swollen, and I had a big hard swelling behind my left knee that made every step an effort. Just before we reached the sand dunes the country opened out into a wide plain on which were several lagoons and marshes – all salt. Wading birds were numerous and Joshua took the gun and went ahead to try and stalk a Plain Turkey or a Jabiru, which were seen feeding ahead. But the birds proved too wary.

Our spirits had risen when we saw the white tops of the sandhills gleaming in the distance, and we struggled on, hoping and expecting to look down on the sea again from the top of the dunes. When we climbed the first sandhill we were dismayed to see that this was but the outer tier of a series – and to find ourselves confronted with lines of similar hills, the lower slopes and foothills between covered with dense, almost impenetrable, thickets of spiny and prickly shrubs and tangles of creeper. We rested a little; then we started to fight our way painfully through the dense tangles; sometimes erect, sometimes crawling on hands and knees. We had nothing with which to cut the tough, yielding, spiny brushwood. The sweat streamed down our faces. I called a halt again and we tried to fire the scrub, but it was still green and would not burn readily.

At last, after what seemed hours, we arrived, torn and bleeding, and utterly exhausted, on the open sandhills, and looked out across the empty sea. But luck was with us for just at this spot there was a group of she oaks, and a soak, with fair water. We limped to the trees and threw ourselves down gratefully in the shade. A glance southward showed us something familiar about the headland, close to the sandhills that we had just crossed. We were once more close to the mouth of the Rose River only a few miles from the delta that we had left three days before.

The journal reads: 'Made tea and damper. Made another damper to conserve water later, and also because Joshua is now so weary that he cannot yet be persuaded to go on. He now throws down his load repeatedly and says that he must rest. Got him away again early in the afternoon, but he was tired out. After a little distance he decided to abandon his blanket – which he rolled up and left in the fork of a she oak.

'After what seemed another long walk, but when in reality we had covered only a mile or two, we camped on a small but deep creek where there was a dugout canoe moored on the far side. Joshua swam over, got the canoe and ferried me across. Paddles, dugong rope and all the paraphernalia of the dugong hunter were placed for safety in a tree at the mooring place, and there we found also a deep little well scooped out of the shell bed.

'Decided to camp, partly because we were exhausted and partly because Joshua discovered a mark which he declared indicated that the owners of the canoe were not far away, so that it was probable that they would come if we made a fire. Tiger (my kangaroo dog) game as ever, was in a bad way from hard travel and no food, weak and emaciated. Joshua shot him a silver gull, which, somewhat to my surprise, he ate. I felt that this would help to carry him on. Joshua says that he will sail the canoe up tomorrow if the owner does not come along this evening.

'We burned the only grass that was dry enough and set fire to a patch of dry scrub near the beach, but it did not burn well and made very little smoke.

'We went upstream with the canoe and got firewood, also collected hermit crabs and oysters. Hermit crabs bitter, but the oysters good, though small.

Cooked them blackfellow fashion, the mangrove roots to which they were attached cut off and roasted whole.

'We made a fish spear this afternoon, but throwing it at a fish from the canoe, it was carried away, Joshua says because he speared the fish in the body and not in the head or neck. Tonight he made another spear with the remainder of the wire – a much better effort with a lighter handle.

'Joshua was uneasy and during the night, as we were sitting by the fire he cried out at intervals, in a loud voice, his name and that of the country he had come from. It was the custom, he explained, if strangers were present to prowl around the camp and to attack without warning, but if they knew who he was and what he was doing, it would set their minds at rest. During the next four months whenever I was travelling in country that my companions regarded as hostile, they observed the same custom.

'This may also account for what transpired about the canoe. He had undertaken to sail it north, but late at night he cried out that he was a fool and that he had forgotten to take the canoe and moor it out before the tide fell, and asked me, not very convincingly, to wake him up.

'I did so, but he said that there was too much wind and sea and that the canoe would be broken up. As he was very dour and sullen there was nothing to be done, but I guessed that he was afraid to take it. We had agreed to leave tobacco for the owner and later to return it. Bad night; at 3. 30 a. m. I gave up trying to sleep and boiled a billy of water and bathed my swollen and painful left leg. Soon after 6. 00 we left camp and pushed on northward.

'We followed the beach for a short distance, and then struck across a headland, where Joshua believed there was a short cut, but we found our way barred with a wall of mangroves. For several hours we struggled through dense thickets, sometimes of mangroves, sometimes of dry salt-water scrub. It was impossible to see out, or to tell what progress we were making or where the direction we were following was leading us.

'After a long, desperate struggle through this tangle – very painful for both of us – we found our way barred by a wide creek or inlet, its deep green water fringed with mangroves. We climbed up into these and saw that this barrier extended away to the northward and to the westward. We passed for two terrible hours through scrub so dense that part of it had once more to be traversed on hands and knees. I felt despair very near that morning.

'At intervals, we climbed trees to see how the land lay, but the trees were all too small and gave us a view only of a sea of dense seemingly impenetrable thickets. At length I decided to strike west, and climbed a low hill to survey the country. We saw the mangrove-fringed river swing away to the west and beside it lay wide, open, salt pans. There was still a long stretch of dense undergrowth to traverse, but we knew our direction; we knew now, at last, where we were heading. Rough stones, weathered to a series of sharp points and partly covered with long grass, outcropped on the low intervening hills, and cut our feet badly – for I, too, had been barefooted since the previous morning.'

When we emerged on the plains, tracks, all heading north, and all converging in one direction, were noted and became so numerous that we followed them and at length reached a point at which they disappeared into the river. This proved to be a ford and we crossed the river in water just up to our armpits. A hard struggle followed again through dense wattle and prickly scrub that further lacerated my bare legs and feet, but we were rewarded at last by striking the beach just at a point where there was a fine well. We filled a water bag, boiled a billy, and also made a damper to conserve the water that we carried. The tide was falling and we made the best time we could northward to cross the Hart River, a creek just to the south of the Minnie. Here, at this creek, we secured a Burdekin duck and two silver gulls and called a halt to cook them. To Joshua's great disgust I ate the livers of the gulls raw and also of anything else we killed – to offset the effect of the diet of black tea and dry damper. We had crossed the Hart about five o'clock, and reached the Minnie itself just after dark – clouds obscuring the moon.

The struggle of these days, the effort to keep going, and to keep Joshua from giving up, will live with me for a long time. I remember how on this and the succeeding two days, we dared not look far ahead at a distant landmark; the effort that we knew would be needed to reach it seemed more than we could stand; instead, we fixed our eyes on a tree or something on the beach, and concentrated only on reaching that.

My journal of that day, written at the Minnie, reads: 'For the last few miles I was so tired and in such pain that I felt half anaesthetised to the touch of the sand. I had great blisters on the soles of both feet – the one on the left much worse than the one on the right. These had burst and were giving me serious pain, and I found that the blisters were packed full with sand. Cleaned them out by removing the skin and tied the feet with some old rag that I had had for cleaning the gun. Lay down aching and very cold.

'Joshua made a half-hearted attempt to find a crossing, then we huddled under the lee of a great rock, and made a little fire; we were far too spent to do much foraging for firewood. First, he had told me that the river was knee-deep, now he reported that the tide was not low enough. I woke him again later – but the tide had turned and was then running in; it was too late to cross. A day lost; all this day's effort seemed to be in vain. Had no sleep; cold, stormy, overcast night with high wind; breakers booming all night.

'June 17th. Am writing this after the worst day yet. Joshua announced that we could not cross here but that we had better go up and around the Minnie. Tide high now and rising. He also says that he believes that there is a tributary on the south of the Minnie that winds for long way westwards. Painful to stand on my feet much less to walk. Struck tracks and followed them south-west through sandhills and found good water near a tributary creek about a mile back from the mouth. Decided that we could cross here, and we settled down to wait all day for the tide to fall. Today, the last two or three teaspoonfuls of sugar that I had kept, finished; did not use it yesterday but held it over. Cooked a damper and tried to make a raft – at least Joshua did; I could give little help as I can only walk with difficulty. Shot a bar-shouldered dove – our only fresh meat for the day – a few mouthfuls each, and had a little bacon. Went to inspect the mouth of the river. At the mouth saw a crocodile just slide into the water as we got there and it seemed the last straw. It was very "cheeky", it just partly submerged, and the long and perfectly still head, a little of the back, and the big upstanding scutes of the tail, all above water. Decided to push on up the river and try to get over. We laboured along an Aboriginal path over terrible country for what was probably only two or two and a half miles, and then climbed a tree and saw that after all the river ran south more and more, and broadened into a wide maze of mangroves. Decided, to Joshua's disgust, to return to the mouth and try to cross that way. He says it is dangerous; the alternative – miles of travel by night to cross the Minnie or get around it – to me, barefooted and scarcely able to walk, impossible.'

'We decided to wait until nightfall when the tide would be low. Tiger very emaciated and coat staring, but still game. Gave him some more damper, bacon rind, etc. – just enough to keep him alive. If we get over tonight I shall be more free with the cartridges.'

The hours of waiting seemed an eternity. Joshua collected a bundle of dry branches and lashed them together with strips of bark. The tide fell very slowly. It was late at night, the moon obscured by clouds, and bitterly cold. Just as we were ready a shadow seemed to pass in the water; we waited, but in the dark depths there was nothing to be seen. After a little, we went on. Pluckily, Joshua made a crossing first, reached a sandbank and stuck a fish spear there, then with the aid of the rough raft on which I laid my swag, I crossed to the sandbank. With my stiff and swollen leg I was not much use for swimming. He made another journey and this time Tiger swam too.

We landed on the outer fringe of a dense tangle of mangroves, muddy underneath, with high roots like stilts – and of an impenetrable blackness. We climbed on top of this tangle and groped our way through foetid ooze and a confusion of roots. When we reached the far side Joshua was exhausted, and his teeth were chattering violently. We walked across the open plain on the outer edge of the mangroves to the edge of a strip of scrub, made a fire, and lay down.

Before daylight in the morning – the seventh day of the journey to Bennet Bay – we were away again, making north. We returned to the beach, and the going was not at all bad. Ordinarily it would have been reckoned easy walking – but we were very weak from long travel and from want of food and rest. My own great trouble that day was to keep Joshua going; he wanted to give up and lie down. He asked me to leave him to die.

Always in my mind and spurring me on, was the worry lest Kapiu, the Torres Strait Islander in charge of the boat, might become anxious, and I was afraid he might then sail for Groote Eylandt, where there was a wireless set to ask for help. This would have meant defeat for me, a disaster far worse than anything that could have happened on the journey.

I cannot describe adequately that journey. We were both by this time in a desperate state; the pain of the sand on our now skinned and lacerated feet, and swollen legs, brought a feeling of numbness, and of intense cold. There was about us a vast space that seemed suddenly to have closed in, like a material, substantial thing. It was as if at each step we had to force our way through a solid nothingness. So had the sense of unreality become fantastic.

Joshua had long abandoned his blanket. I tore mine up now to make band- ages for my feet, but these filled with sand which added to the pain of the wounds, and after many attempts, the idea had to be abandoned. After a while we did not talk much. Our pace was reduced to little more than a crawl. Joshua insisted on lying down at frequent intervals, but for me these halts only made matters worse. Before the day was out we had some difficulty in getting on to our feet after a rest, and the pain of walking again was intensified by each halt. We walked as close to the water's edge as possible, for the sand was harder there and progress less painful. But it was an intense effort even to move up the width of the beach. Early that morning I noticed what appeared to be a dead turtle at the water's edge – so shrunken and emaciated that it seemed at first to have been long dead. It proved to be a small green turtle, thrown up on the beach in the storms of the past week, injured too badly to regain the water, but still alive. It provided us with some meat which we needed badly, very pale in colour, for it had little blood; almost like fish. A little later in the morning we saw turtle tracks across the beach and found a nest of fresh eggs. We dug these out, broke the soft parchment-like shells, and greedily swallowed some of them raw. The remainder we carried.

Early in the day, we came abreast of Bickerton Island which lies between Groote Eylandt and Cape Barrow at the head of Bennet Bay. But by nightfall, after a full day's walk, we had made such little progress that we were still miles from Cape Barrow. This was the worst day of the journey. Joshua lay down at frequent intervals and when I tried to get him on to his feet he begged me to leave him behind. I knew that we could not now be far from Bennet Bay. If I could find water we could live for several days on the turtle eggs.

During the day we saw fresh human tracks. They were still moving north-ward, but they were obviously recent and indicated that the people had passed since the storm, and therefore, were not far ahead of us. Towards nightfall, we reached an old camping place, which my companion remembered having touched previously in a boat that put in for water.

We found two lagoons in both of which there were water-lilies, and close to one of these lagoons, we made camp. The water-lilies meant food in emergency – for the seed capsules and the rootstock form an important part of the Aboriginal diet but Joshua was now too spent and too cold to swim for them. Here we boiled the last morsel of bacon that we had cherished, carefully conserving the liquid in order to cook the pieces of turtle meat that we had carried since morning. This, with as many turtle eggs as we could eat, made the best meal that we had had since leaving the vessel. Another cold night followed.

On the following morning – June 19th – we were much refreshed. but Joshua was very weak, and I was now suffering so much pain from my feet and legs that I could stand only with difficulty. It was impossible for us to carry our loads if we were to make any progress. Before leaving camp we dug a hole and buried most of the remaining turtle eggs to preserve them in case of need. My other possessions, a sheet of canvas and the tomahawk, we also abandoned, placing them in a tree close to where we had slept. We were now a little to the south of Cape Barrow, and leaving the beach here, we turned west and set a course for the north of Bennet Bay, where the *St Nicholas* should be waiting for us. We knew that she should not be far off, or failing the boat, we should find a camp. But although we again started early, we made little progress and after several hours we had covered only a short distance. During the morning we saw smoke and evidence of recent fires and we burned what dry vegetation we could, hoping to attract the attention of hunting parties that might be about. Much of the skin had now gone from the soles of my feet. Stones, sticks and sharp grass stems made the journey a painful one so I again bandaged my feet to protect them, with the remaining rags of blanket. But during the morning we had to wade through a wide, shallow swamp and the heavy, clumsy bandages dragged so that I could scarcely lift my feet, and again the bandages had to be abandoned.

Early in the afternoon we came out on a grassy plain, and thence emerged on a salt pan. In the distance a green wall of mangroves marked the vicinity of salt water. A little later, we sighted what appeared to be a group of people. This was no mirage or vision that mocked at us but proved to be men of the Nunggubuyu tribe – members of the group whose tracks we had been crossing from time to time during the past week.

I remember the sight of those figures, and how they affected us, as if it were yesterday: the sight of other human beings. Only eight days had elapsed, but there are occasions when time cannot be measured. A mist shimmered before me and a dry lump rose in my throat. I had to swallow hard. We could not relax at once. I knew that I could not talk. There was the need to retain control and to present outwardly only a mask of indifference. I remember our formal greeting. It was as if they had been old friends from whom we had been parted only a few hours. I know that I must have seemed unfriendly, even callous, for I could not trust myself to speak.

These men guided us to the *St Nicholas* which lay at anchor close at hand in Bennet Bay. Later, they went back over our tracks to pick up the gear that we had abandoned at the last camp.

There was a big camp on the eastern shores of Bennet Bay at this season, numbering approximately ninety men, women and children. They had concentrated in this sheltered place following the stormy weather that had prevailed for some weeks past, and were engaged in dugong and turtle hunting and in fishing. They were a happy, friendly people. Most of them had already made contact with white men at trepang camps at the mouth of the Roper, or they had made visits to the missions at Groote Eylandt and the Roper. They hunted and fished industriously, and each morning, soon after sunrise, a fleet of five or more canoes would set out from camp for the fishing grounds a mile or two off shore. Besides dugong and turtle, fish and game were plentiful, and the people were in splendid condition, well fed and happy. Children, who were conspicuous by their absence under civilised conditions, were numerous in this camp.

During my absence from the boat, the two Bickerton Island men whom Kapiu had taken to the Roper on the *St Nicholas*, had deserted when the ship returned to Bickerton for water on the journey north. Subsequent enquiries showed that they had been on bad terms with Mardi, who ironically enough, had himself deserted at the mouth of the Rose River, and that there existed between them a feud of long standing, connected with women. It seemed that the two Ingura men had been afraid to meet Mardi again at Bennet Bay, where he would have had the backing of his own people. This desertion had left only the cripple 'Smiler' (who later proved to be suffering from nodular leprosy in an advanced form) and a Ritharrngu man, Marrilyauwuy, to assist in bringing the boat to Bennet Bay, so that Kapiu had run the ship almost single-handed despite the rough weather.

When we reached the *St Nicholas* I gave Kapiu one instruction, which he was never to forget. No matter what happened, or how long I might be delayed on any later patrol, he was never to ask for help. And although he had many anxious times, he never forgot this instruction.

We remained at this camp for two days in order to make friends with the people and to have a short rest before proceeding with the most important part of my mission. Both Joshua and I were suffering severely from our injuries. For several days I was scarcely able to stand, but had to content myself with crawling about the deck on hands and knees. At the time of our arrival the camp had been situated on a rocky part of the shore, strewn with boulders and stones covered with oysters. But to enable me to visit them the people moved their camp a little distance along the coast to a sandy beach, which I could reach easily in the dinghy, and from which they carried me ashore.

The 'dry' or south-east monsoon season was now well advanced and I was anxious to proceed with the real objective of my expedition – to locate and make contact with the people of Blue Mud Bay.

The people in the camp at Bennet Bay knew nothing about the Blue Mud Bay people or their movements, although they lived within sight of Woodah Island and must frequently have seen their canoes. But the anomaly is explained by the fact that a distinct cultural break occurs just here and the Nunggubuyu cannot understand the language of their northern neighbours of Woodah Island and the hinterland of Blue Mud Bay, so that there is a minimum of contact between the two peoples. It was impossible, therefore, to find out anything whatever about the people of whom I was in search, or even to obtain a guide to assist in the quest. All the southerners regarded the peoples of the northern end of Blue Mud Bay as enemies, and were very unwilling to venture into their territory.

On June 21st we bade goodbye to our Nunggubuyu friends and sailed from Bennet Bay along the western side of Woodah Island. We failed to find any people and that night we anchored under Morgan Island, named by Matthew Flinders in 1803 after Thomas Morgan, a marine on the *Investigator*, who died of sunstroke there. It was also on Morgan Island that a crew member was speared leading to the death of an Aboriginal man.

No fires were to be seen, or any other signs of life, and on the following morning, June 22nd, we set a course WNW, and anchored behind an unnamed

The *St Nicholas* at Caledon Bay in June 1935.

headland between the mouths of the Walker and Koolatong Rivers, which I have called Haddon Head, in honour of Dr A. C. Haddon, FRS, father of the Cambridge School of Anthropology.

During the day the wind freshened from the east and south-east, bringing a sea from which we could obtain no shelter along the entire western shoreline of the bay. Conditions at the anchorage became rough and uncomfortable, and continued so for almost the whole of the period during which I was working in Blue Mud Bay.

The water was always yellow and discoloured, light rain squalls started to blow up, and visibility was so bad that working in inshore waters, even with a vessel drawing barely six feet of water, was possible only by almost constant use of the lead line. The waters of the whole of this bay are shallow and the bottom is chiefly of blue mud, after which Flinders named it, and there are many uncharted shoals and reefs.

In the south-east trade season there are very few safe anchorages even for small boats along the coast, and frequently we were obliged to lie for days in waters where there was a cross wind and tide, so that the vessel lay broadside to the swell. At such times the *St Nicholas* rolled to such an extent that the water ran across the decks from rail to rail. To live, and to try to cook food, under these conditions was extremely unpleasant and was at first a matter of some difficulty.

At Haddon Head I landed two guides, 'Smiler' and the other young Ritharrngu man, Marrilyauwuy, sending the younger off to look for signs of a camp, or for fresh tracks. He had been to Blue Mud Bay previously, and he set out northwards towards the Koolatong River. But before nightfall he returned, unable to cross the intervening rivers, and complaining that his foot, into which he had run a stake of mangrove wood at Bennet Bay, was too painful for him to continue the journey.

It was clear that there was nobody in this vicinity. The weather was growing steadily worse, and as the anchorage in which we were lying offered so little shelter and was likely to prove dangerous in bad weather, we sailed across the bay, sounding with the lead, and dropped anchor behind Roundhill Island, a few miles to the north of Woodah. Easterly weather prevailed for the next three days (June 23rd to 26th) so that at times we had difficulty even in getting the dinghy ashore, for long seas came in from the east by Cape Shields, and swept around this little island. From Roundhill Island dense clouds of smoke from hunting fires were visible to the eastward and northward. I sent the two men again to search for a camp, but on each side of the headland on which Mount Grindall stands, their way was barred by saltwater creeks, and they again returned without making contact. But they reported having seen fresh tracks which indicated that the people had moved towards the big camping site at a place called Matarawatj, on the south side of the Koolatong River not far from the mouth.

On June 26th, therefore, we sailed across to the westward of Grindall Point, and anchored in an inlet outside the mouth of the Koolatong River in the best anchorage that we had made in Blue Mud Bay. To this I have given the name St Nicholas Inlet and to the neighbouring point, Point Kapiu. Rain squalls were becoming more frequent, and although the dry season was now well advanced, heavy rain amounting to several inches fell over the next few days, and the wind was cold and penetrating. The decks were constantly wet with rain and with saltwater and the crew suffered severely from colds, which reduced them to a very dejected state. This cold snap was to me as unexpected as it was acute, enduring in a more or less severe form during the remainder of the month, and into the early part of July.

Soon after our arrival at this anchorage, a violent storm broke, that lasted with almost unabated violence for two days. The mud bottom was too soft to make very good holding ground, and the anchor began to drag so we put out a second and heavier anchor, with a four inch coir line.

The night of June 26th was an anxious one, and seemed interminable. The shriek of the wind in the rigging rose to such a pitch that we could scarcely hear ourselves shout, and it was so dark and overcast that we could see nothing. Sometimes we could hear the thunder of the waves breaking on the rocky shore, above the noise of the wind. If the anchors had not held the vessel must have been driven on to the rocks or shallows about a mile away and pounded to pieces. The fact that the anchor had dragged during the day added to my anxiety for the safety of the ship.

Daybreak came in very grey and bleak, but we had held our position, and the wind had fallen a little. A small island, Fowler Island, lies in the mouth of the bay into which the Koolatong flows; it would have been impossible to have beaten out past this island and headland at the height of the gale, even if we could have seen anything, and behind us lay only shallows and rocks. The river mouth is very wide and shallow and although there is deep water inside the bar we failed, even on high tide, to get the *St Nicholas* across and abandoned the attempt, anchoring about a mile or two off in two fathoms of water.

The smoke of hunting fires was seen in dense clouds not far up the Koolatong River and whenever possible I landed Smiler and Marrilyauwuy to search for tracks which would indicate where the camp was. At last Marrilyauwuy found a group of people and although they were very shy and suspicious, since the events that precipitated my expedition, he was able to induce a number of the young single men to come down to the coast. None of these people were able, of course, to speak any English, and at that time I knew nothing of their language, but was obliged to depend for interpreters on Smiler and Marrilyauwuy, neither of whom had much English.

I have mentioned that both were Ritharrngu men – members of a group that occupies a very large stretch of country in the interior, behind Blue Mud Bay. This language differs somewhat in vocabulary, but not in structure, from that of the Dhayyi-speaking people of Blue Mud Bay, but they can understand one another and can converse in Ritharrngu. These people are the most strongly nomadic of all the Arnhem Landers. Their territory lies in the region of the upper Walker River and extends northwards, inland from Blue Mud Bay, but I found members of this group quite at home, and still making themselves understood in their own language, in localities as far separated as the Roper River and the Crocodile Islands. Their language, therefore, is understood over a wider area than any other in the whole of this country.

We learned from these people that Matarawatj was inland, some distance up the Koolatong River and, as I later found out one of the renowned, almost legendary, camping places of the fighting men of Blue Mud Bay. This was probably the very same camp from which they had come to attack Flinders' men at Morgan Island more than 130 years before. This was the camp of the Aborigines I had come to meet. I had now reached the critical period of the expedition. They would be anxious and suspicious after the troubles and clashes which had occurred, still fresh in their minds, but if I could succeed in making friends with this group, the most difficult part of my mission would be accomplished. In any case, it would be useless to proceed northward until I had established myself with them and won their confidence. I decided at once to leave the boat and to go inland to their camp, to meet them in their own country away from my vessel. I was to show them this time that a European was prepared to trust them.

For two or three days I camped ashore with the young Dhayyi-speaking men to get to know them and then returned to the boat for stores, tobacco and equipment for the inland journey. The first part of the journey lay up the

Koolatong River, and we set out in the dinghy. But the tide was falling, and we went aground on the mud banks at the mouth of the river, half a mile off shore. It was around two in the afternoon, and we remained stranded for about seventeen hours for there was only one full tide per day in this area, as Flinders had suggested. When we were first stranded we jumped out and attempted to push the boat off. But the deep soft blue mud of the bottom did not give any foothold and we sank up to our thighs and were still sinking at the same time cutting our feet nastily on sharp shells embedded in the ooze.

Two men from the shore, who were piloting us inland, set out to help us. They were evidently experienced at walking over mud, and appeared to have a technique of their own for doing it. After a long time, they succeeded in reaching us, but in spite of the cold and discomfort of the dinghy, they would not attempt to return to the shore. At first we had expected to get off on the evening tide, and we made ourselves as comfortable as we could. But evening came, the night wore on, and the tide did not come. We did not get off finally until after daybreak on the following morning. It was one of the most uncomfortable nights that I have ever spent with five of us lying in the bitter cold, shivering on the bottom of the eleven foot dinghy. Afterwards one of the men in the boat told me that he had been much afraid that one of the numerous crocodiles in the river might come up in the dark and attack us.

Early the following morning we floated off on the incoming tide, and crossed the bar into the Koolatong River. A few miles upstream we picked up Smiler and the others who were to accompany us and who had been awaiting our coming anxiously all night, and pulled on up stream. Once inside the bar, the Koolatong River is deep, and there are more crocodiles in this river than in any other that I have known. We saw many in the river, or slipping down the banks, and heard others, that morning, as we passed. At almost every bend of the stream we came upon their broad 'slides' by which they enter the water from the high banks on which they sun themselves. At this time of the year, the middle of the south-east trade wind season, these reptiles leave the water for long periods to sun themselves on banks sheltered from the keen winds, for the water is cold during the day but relatively warm at night.

The people had developed a special technique for crossing the crocodile-infested reaches of the Koolatong River near the mouth, which at this point is fringed with a dense wall of mangroves. When a large party wished to cross without the trouble of bringing a dugout canoe and of making several trips to ferry the party across, they climbed out as far as possible on the overhanging limbs until they looked like flying foxes. Then all dropped or jumped in together, splashing so that they churned the water into foam; making as much noise as they could, they swam quickly across. Even as they swam however the heads of two or three crocodiles could sometimes be seen just above the surface of the water a few hundred yards away.

Some miles up the river we tied up the dinghy and, making a pile of such gear as we could not carry, we set off behind our pilots across the salt pans, which were soft and muddy after the recent heavy rains. The country about Blue Mud Bay was low and flat with extensive areas of flood plains stretching inland from the coast, hidden from the sea by a dense wall of mangroves. We were obliged to travel very slowly. The thick, sticky mud on the salt pans made travel heavy, and my feet were still painful after the walk to Bennet Bay. About three miles of this travel brought us to a camp, situated in a clump of brush on a low knoll, close to a lily lagoon. The people had seen our approach a long way off. As we drew near, the men stood up close to their spears and waited. This was the critical moment of my meeting with the Aborigines. There was no loud exchange of greetings, no shouting, not a word was spoken at first, for the etiquette to be observed at these times is an important business and on one's behaviour at such a time Aborigines are apt to base their permanent attitude.

To those accustomed to regarding the Australian Aborigines as disorganised people it must come as a surprise to learn that custom, etiquette, good manners and good taste, much as we know them are nowhere more important. An ill-mannered person, a man who does not know how to behave himself, is regarded contemptuously by these people of Blue Mud Bay as raw, salt/sour or uncouth.

We stood up, my guides and I, some twenty yards outside the camp and waited as custom demanded. We had seen from a distance the stir and excitement that our approach had caused in the camp, but now all was quiet. Nobody spoke. To one who did not know the customs of these people in receiving strangers, these dour, immobile people standing in the camp must have seemed ominous. At last, two or three of the old men advanced, unarmed slowly towards us without haste and with a casualness that was too studied, too formal. They knew two or three only of those who were with me and these they probably had not seen for many years, but not the least interest, the slightest sign of emotion was betrayed outwardly on either side. A few words were exchanged, casually at first, the important news long ago communicated by gesture or sign language. Then a pipe was lighted by my companions and handed round with due ceremony.

Gumuk of the
Dharlwangu clan
on the right and
Kutnung on the
left at Matarawatj.

The tension was over, the reserve forgotten and in a few minutes the people poured out from the thicket in which the camp lay, surrounded us, and carried our loads back into their camp. Another party went back to the landing place on the river and brought up the remainder of our baggage.

They could see that I trusted them; that I carried no revolver. One white man, alone, on foot, away from the coast and from his boat, could not have seemed to them to be very formidable. They received me with the greatest friendliness.

I selected a little area of clean ground on the fringe of their camp and had a breakwind of boughs built there, to provide some shelter from the keen winds that were blowing across the open plains.

This camp was a very big one for a nomad group at this season of the year, numbering about 200 people from about seven different clans, speaking a number of named dialects. The dialect of the area of the camp was referred to as Dhayyi.

I shall refer to them therefore, throughout this account as the Dhayyi-speaking peoples of Blue Mud Bay. These people, it should be noted, include those who are commonly referred to as 'Woodah Islanders'. Woodah Island is part of the territory of the Manggalili clan, also Dhayyi-speaking people. There is not, and has not been in recent times, a permanent population on the island, which could not support a large group at all seasons of the year. But they visit Woodah Island at intervals for special foods, such as turtle eggs, and for turtle hunting, as well as for ceremonies which they sometimes carry out there. They reach Woodah in dugout canoes, from Grindall Point via Roundhill Island, thus avoiding wide stretches of open water.

The night of our arrival, a great dance was held in the camp. The 'sing man' who led the performance was Merara, one of the most renowned fighting men of the coast. These dances frequently take the form of exquisite little pantomimes which among these people are generally based on the dance or display of a bird or an animal, formalised or conventionalised. But this night the dance centred around a shallow circular depression scooped out of the ground, in which a little fire burned. On the fringe – just inside the shadows – the women danced apart; not the dance of the men, but a mincing shuffle from one foot to the other which they employ invariably on these occasions. Towards the end of the dance each of the performers took a leafy branchlet in his hand, warmed it in the fire and beat his head and body all over with the leaves. The women and the onlookers did likewise, then the leaves were thrown back into the shallow crater in the sand and the dance ceased.

At the time I thought this was just an ordinary dance, but afterwards I came to know it for what it was – a ceremony called *Manytjarr*, held whenever a death occurs, or when the news of death reaches a group – the leaves warmed in the

opposite, top: Merara and his wives and children at Matarawatj. The Mardarrpa woman on the left has recently passed away and sitting beside her is Gukguk. One of the young girls is said to be Shirley Gunumungu. Merara was involved in the death of Traynor and Fagan and was subsequently killed during the feud described in Chapter 6.

opposite, bottom: The brackish waterhole at Matarawatj.

fire drive away the spirit of the dead which may otherwise haunt his relatives and bring them 'bad luck' in hunting. While you may not yourself see the ghost that is following you it is visible to birds and animals when you are hunting, and will bring 'bad luck'. In the years that followed I was frequently present at and took part in, these ceremonies, and the people often gave me the leaves with which formally to beat myself.

This time the *Manytjarr* was Dhaakiyarr, for these were his people and we had brought news of his death. But the man I most wanted to see, Wonggu, father of the three men in the Darwin gaol, was not here. In this camp I met men like Merara and Djimbaryun, whose names were known far and wide for their fighting prowess and for the raids and ambushes they had carried out; men whose names were spoken with awe and fear in camps as far away as the coast of the Arafura Sea. These men were associated with Dhaakiyarr in the killing of the white men, Traynor and Fagan, and in the *mêlée* of 1933 in which constable McColl of the Northern Territory police was killed at Woodah Island. Here too was the widow of Dhaakiyarr, still waiting for her man who had been taken away in the white man's boat two years before, never to return.

The place bristled with spears. I noticed too, neat parcels of paperbark or baskets suspended from trees, or from forked branches stuck firmly in the ground; these contained the bones of deceased relatives which are carried from camp to camp for several years before their final disposal.

The camp was a very big one for this season of the year, when the people would normally have been scattered about inland in little groups of two or more families. The grass should have been drying off fast, after the months of the wet season, and the family groups would have been burning the grass in hunting drives to secure game – especially goanna, some species of snakes, bandicoots and other small animals. The smoke which we had seen earlier was from these hunting fires, but the heavy, unseasonal June rains had meant that the grass would not burn readily and the normal seasonal activities had had to be modified and the people were still subsisting upon lilies from the big lagoon, with some fish.

I had not brought with me sufficient stores for a long stay on this occasion. Moreover, I had been obliged to leave the *St Nicholas* in charge of only one man, and as the weather remained overcast and stormy, I was anxious for the safety of the vessel. I hoped, therefore, to be able to induce the people, when I had made friends with them, to accompany me back to the coast and to camp with me close to the boat. After being with them for two days, I was able to persuade

Djimbaryun of the Munyuku clan who was involved in the feud described in Chapter 6.

them to do this, and we moved down to the shore close to the mouth of the Koolatong River. In the meantime messengers brought in a number of small parties that were out hunting in the neighbouring country.

By this time I had established myself with them so they brought their sick to me and I gave many injections for yaws. Although their health was generally good, yaws (*Framboesia*) was prevalent here as it is throughout Arnhem Land, particularly on the coast. It causes ugly lesions and disfigures and deforms

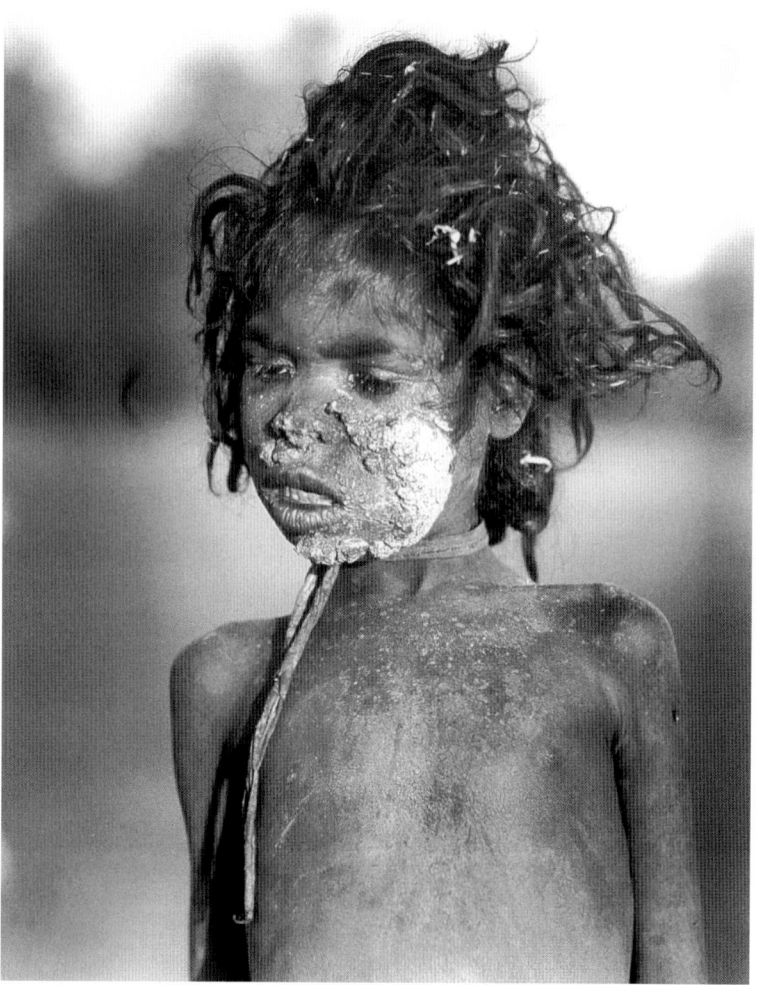

Thomson's treatment of yaws, seen here on Matina, responded almost instantly to injections and helped him to be accepted by the people.

the children, producing a condition known as boomerang-leg which the people themselves, however, attribute to a ritual visitation for the breaking of tabus on the eating of certain food at certain times. The lesions respond dramatically to injections of *neoarsphenamine* and clear up quickly after three or four injections.

Although this treatment necessitated the frequent sterilisation of instruments and involved much work it was gratifying to see the way in which the disfigured faces of the children healed up and it undoubtedly did much to win the goodwill of these warlike people.

above: A group of men resting
in camp at Matarawatj.
From left to right, Djunggi,
Ganbardatj, Maama, Bandulu,
Djimbaryun, Wawit, Mundukul,
Garrarrambu and Gumuk.

Djapari, the widow of
Dhaakiyarr, and her child.

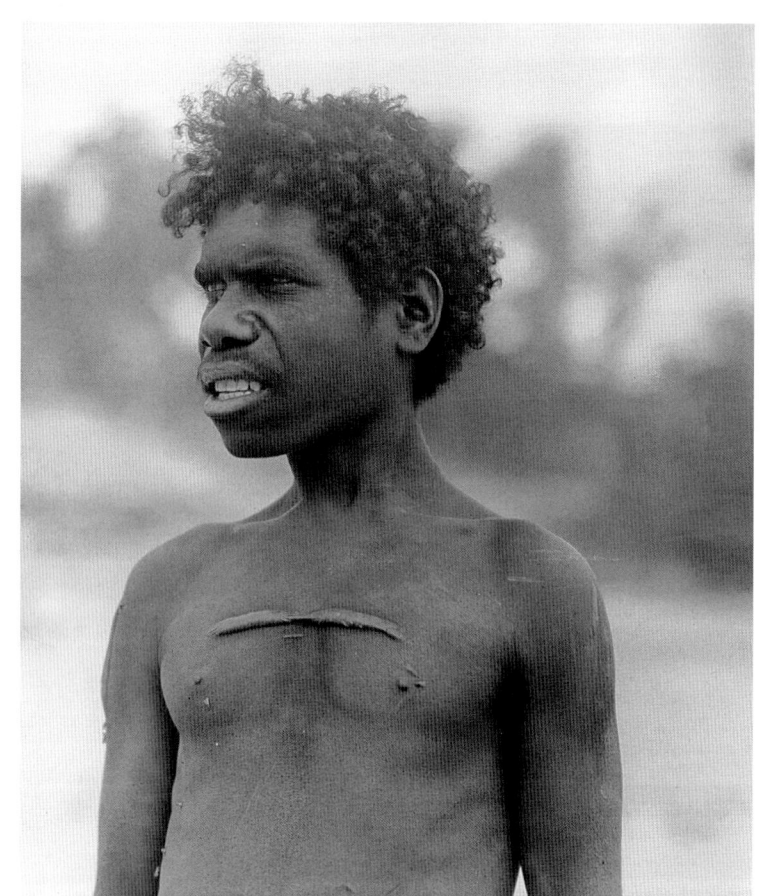

Mithili of the
Marakulu clan.

below: Wakuthi on
the left and Birrikitji
on the right, both of
the Dharlwangu clan.

I was able to start a study of the language and the social organisation, and, taking advantage of the friendly relationship that I had established, endeavoured to explain to them the reason for my visit and the purpose of the Government in sending me. I told them that I had not only come to speak to them of the white man's laws, but that the Government had, besides entrusting me with a message to them, sent me to learn their language and their customs, in order that we, in our turn, should better understand them; that the Government wished to introduce a 'new fashion' in dealing with them.

By July 6th, the weather was fine again. After making as liberal presents as I was able of trade tobacco, wire for fish spears, fish hooks, and also some flour (to mark a special occasion), I bade farewell to the group, promising the people that I would come back after I had found Wonggu.

Wuyulwi and Putjir of the Marakulu clan.

Wawit, son of Garrarrambu (see photograph page 67), a constant companion for Thomson at this period, with a wallaby killed with a shovel-nosed spear.

below: A hunting fire at Trial Bay, July 1935. People kept a constant lookout for other people's fires so that they knew where they were.

Four Aborigines from this camp accompanied me on the voyage north and one of them, Wawit, remained with me constantly until the following November, when he was returned to his own country in the *St Nicholas*.

From the Koolatong River we sailed east, anchoring that night on the north side of Woodah Island. The weather was now more settled, and, fine conditions, with calm seas, and a fair sailing breeze, set in, and continued for the next three weeks. I took advantage of them to make a further examination of Blue Mud Bay and carried out a short reconnaissance of Woodah Island (and of other islands in Blue Mud Bay) but as the people in whose territory these islands lay were still in the camp we had recently left, nobody was seen.

They had told us that Wonggu and most of the Caledon Bay group were camped in the vicinity of Trial Bay, for they had seen the smoke of their hunting fires. These must not be regarded in any sense as signal fires but because they knew most people were at Matarawatj it was simple to deduce it was him. Accordingly, leaving Woodah, we sailed to the northern end of Blue Mud Bay and landed at a point, east of Cape Shields, in the territory of the Arrawiya, the clan of which Wonggu and his sons were members. From here we made a patrol on foot across to Trial Bay; we arrived on the 9th July and camped on the southern side of the bay to await the arrival of the *St Nicholas*.

This short journey overland from Blue Mud Bay to Trial Bay was one of the most interesting and instructive of the expedition. Six men, including four from Blue Mud Bay accompanied me. We carried light loads, a small supply of food and a single-barrelled shot gun for game.

On this and all other journeys, which I carried out during the next two and a half years, I lived and travelled like an Aboriginal. At night we built a few breakwinds of boughs, with a fire between each two men, and on this occasion I shared one of these little fires with a man from Blue Mud Bay.

Each night, as we approached Trial Bay, my companions became more alert and uneasy. Before we settled down to sleep Smiler, who had established himself with the Dhayyi people, informed me that we were in hostile country, for a considerable amount of fighting had occurred between them and the Caledon Bay people, chiefly arising from feuds over women.

Each time I awoke during the night at least one man would be awake and sitting up watchfully at his fireside. Moreover, on all these patrols, one or other of the Aborigines, often the one best known to the people in whose country we were travelling, would call out at intervals, in a loud voice, generally in the Ritharrngu language, some variation of the following phrase: 'It is I (mentioning

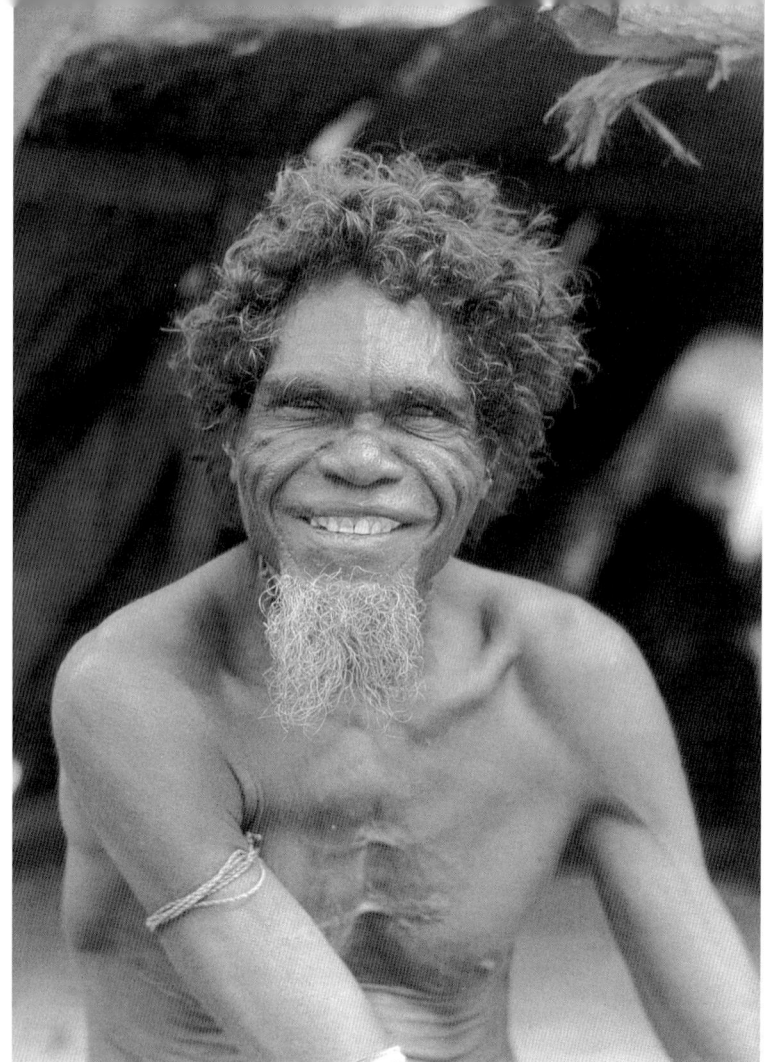

Wonggu – 'a tall, powerful man with intelligent face, deep set eyes and a heavy beard'.

his own personal name). I come from Matarawatj (or other well-known camp); I do not come to fight. I bring a good white man'.

The men told me that they do this when they believe they are in danger of attack in order that any enemies, or potential enemies from the country they are travelling in, will recognise their voices and so not take them for the scouts of a raiding party. If a party approach a camp unannounced they are likely to be taken as an enemy raiding party and to be attacked before they have an oppor-tunity to make themselves known.

It is the practice of the organised raiding parties, called *miringu*, to halt when they near their objective and to send out one or two scouts to spy out the land, locate the enemy, assess their number and strength, and to make themselves familiar with the layout of the camp they plan to attack. These men then return to the main body of men and they all smear themselves with white clay: this is said to make their numbers appear greater than they are, in the dawn half light. They then stealthily approach the sleeping camp, surround it and fall upon the people, killing as many as they can without even waiting to identify the victims. Before the confusion has died down they disperse, making long forced marches to meet at a pre-arranged rendezvous.

In the morning Tiger, my kangaroo dog, scented a big red wallaroo and chased it into the hills. When we caught up with him he had already pulled the beast down and was lying exhausted on top of it. It was a splendid achievement for any dog to catch and pull down single-handed such a full-grown animal and especially in hilly country, outcropping with rough stone. From this time on Tiger acquired great renown among the people. Although we were glad of the meat, the kill was a mixed blessing for me as it meant delay and the loss of several hours of travel. As is the custom of these people, we carried the animal to the nearest waterhole and sat down to cook it.

The approach to Trial Bay, where Wonggu's camp was situated, was a curious experience and I came to realise how seriously my companions regarded the prospect of and ambush. Some miles to the south of the bay we picked up the tracks of Wuluwirr, and Clara, of whom I shall tell later. Fringing the southern side of Trial Bay was a belt of dense scrub, to penetrate which we had to follow a footpath that wound in and out among the branches. While we were negotiating this narrow path, the men were expecting an ambush at any moment. They could not be induced to speak aloud, but would communicate with one another only with gesture language or in whispers. I tried to joke them out of this, and told them to speak at once if they saw anybody for I felt sure that if they insisted on creeping stealthily through the bush, accompanied as they were by one European, and we came unexpectedly upon a camp, the people would almost certainly, in their present state of mind, take us for a police party and attack us before we had a chance to explain. Fortunately there proved to be no camp at that time on the south side of the bay. The track through the scrub led us out, eventually, by sand hills and dunes, to the shores of the bay.

Trial Bay forms a good harbour for small boats: it possesses deep water and safe anchorages and is sheltered by hills and dunes on either side. I had hoped to find the *St Nicholas* already there, but when we camped for the night on a high sandy headland, she still had not arrived.

My companions had by this time identified the tracks of old Wonggu and of Clara, the woman to whom popular report has sometimes attributed much of the trouble on this coast, as well as many other people, and located their camp on the northern side of the bay, three or four miles away. From our camp on the southern shore we could see the fires in Wonggu's camp as night fell.

About sunset on July 10th we sighted a ship entering the bay. At first we took it for the *St Nicholas*, but as it approached we saw that it had only a single mast. As the vessel entered the bay I saw that she was a small cutter and concluded that she must be the *Oituli*, owned by the trepanger F. Gray, who had been at Caledon Bay when the Japanese luggers had been attacked. The cutter passed close to the headland on which I had camped, and anchored behind an island. Without raising a signal that might have been taken as one of distress, I was unable to attract the attention of Mr Gray.

As our own boat had not arrived we were short of supplies again, and had only the meat of the kangaroo that Tiger had killed on the journey, and a little flour and tea. My companions were uneasy again that night, and not only kept a keen lookout, but called at intervals throughout the night, on the name of Wuluwirr, whom I found, subsequently, to be one of the younger sons of Wonggu, and the most aggressive of that group. At daybreak the *St Nicholas*, which had anchored off shore during the night, moved into the bay, and we went aboard her and sailed across to the opposite shore. My surmise as to the identity of the cutter that had entered the bay after our arrival on the previous evening proved to be correct, and I met Mr Gray and had the opportunity of discussing with him conditions on the coast at that time. There had been some unrest at Caledon Bay and he had lost recently some of the stores from his vessel. Mr Gray remained in Trial Bay for two days, and sailed on July 12th for Groote Eylandt where he remained for the greater part of the year. He was at the Mission Station at Groote Eylandt when I left there for the Roper River in the following November.

While talking to Gray I sent the Dhayyi guides across to Wonggu's camp to tell of my visit. Later I went across myself and carefully observed the same

opposite, top: Wonggu (centre) with four of his sons smeared with mud to prevent their prey smelling their sweat. From left to right: Marrawata, Munguyuma, Matuwa and Wuluwirr.

opposite, bottom: Wonggu had the quite exceptional number of twenty-two wives at the time when Thomson visited. Most older men could expect to have between two and four wives.

customary etiquette of approach that I had gone through at Matarawatj a few days before.

Here at last I met Wonggu. Although he must then have been over fifty he appeared still to be in the prime of life – a tall, powerful man with intelligent face, deep set eyes and a heavy beard, trimmed almost in Van Dyck style. His cheeks were devoid of hair which, I learned, had been plucked clean by smearing with black wax of the native bee and pulling out the hairs. With him he had four of his warrior sons, Wuluwirr, Matuwa, Mawunbuy and an adopted son Munguyama and eight of his twenty-two wives, with their children. Djeriny, one of his older sons was absent at this time. I did not myself explain why I had come immediately because I wanted first to make friends with him and his people. I did however present the message stick I carried from his sons in Darwin and told him that I had spoken to them and that they were all in good health.

That night there was a great ritual crying – the lament that these people employ to give expression to their collective sentiments at times of loss, or, as on the present occasion, when something has occurred to prove that their kin were still alive, reaffirming the bond between the group and those separated from them. I remained with Wonggu for nine days.

In a few days I had established a firm friendship with Wonggu, who soon addressed me in his own language by the kinship term *gaminyarr* meaning daughter's son. When he used this term I knew that he had accepted me. He was frank and completely fearless, and each day my respect increased for this gallant warrior.

After a few days I told Wonggu why I had come to his country. That I had been sent by the Government in the Big Country to tell him that they were not pleased with what he had done. When I talked to him about his attacks on the Japanese, and later the killing of Traynor and Fagan, he did not deny that he had been responsible for these attacks, but told me what had occurred and claimed that he had defended his people and his country.

The period that I spent in this camp was one of the most interesting and profitable that I spent in Arnhem Land. I quickly established friendly relations with Wonggu, to whom it must have appeared very strange, at the outset, that a white man should have come to his country without desire either to make him

opposite, top: Wonggu with some of his family.

opposite, bottom: Djeriny, one of Wonggu's older sons, and his wives. From left: Manharr (Wanguri clan) or Bakurra No. 1 (sometimes more than one person has the same name, Wanguri clan), Gunygulu (Gumatj clan) or Bakurra No. 1 (Wanguri clan), Gunygulu (Gumatj clan), Djeriny, Dharrkiny (Madarrpa clan) or Ngupanyapa (Gumatj clan), Gulthana (Gumatj clan), Marrmiya (Madarrpa clan), Manharr (Wanguri clan).

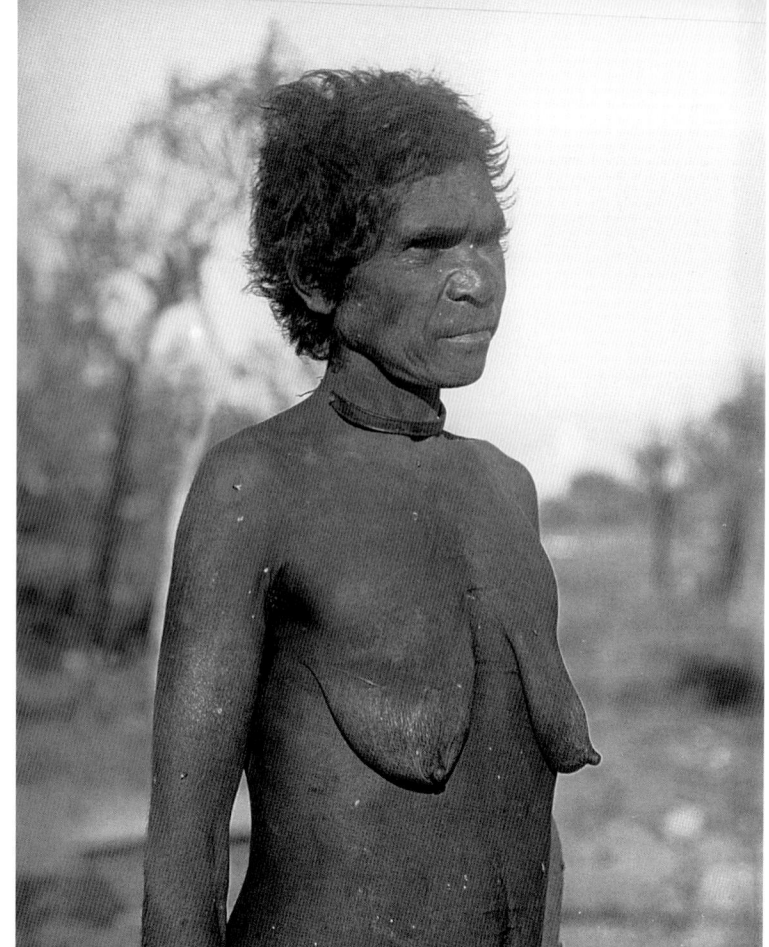

Ganiwa, also known as Clara. Her smattering of English, learnt from fishermen, is believed to have given rise to rumours that the Caledon Bay people had captured two white female survivors of the *Douglas Mawson*, which was wrecked there in 1923. These rumours were revived by the killings in 1933.

below: Thomson and his dog Tiger with some of Wonggu's family in front of the darkroom at Trial Bay.

work, to exploit him, or to interfere in some other way with his life, or that of his people. Wonggu proved to be a man of remarkable intelligence. Partly by virtue of his own personality, partly by the power that he derived from the backing of his sons, of whom there were, including the three now in custody in Darwin, at least eight, all strong, active fighting men, as well as a large number of children. Although he is often spoken of as 'king' or 'chief' of the Caledon Bay tribe, it should be remembered that kinship or chieftainship, or anything approaching this form of rule is entirely foreign to the organisation of Aboriginal people.

The state of affairs as it exists at Caledon Bay today was certainly not the traditional one. The group to which Wonggu belongs was far below its normal strength and he had in consequence many more wives than he would normally have been entitled to, or been able to hold. Further, his own clan land was not in Caledon Bay but at neighbouring Trial Bay. As for the term *Balamumu* it is only a general name applied to the collectivity of clans in the Caledon and Trial Bay areas by other Aborigines in the region. It is not what the people call themselves.

The other person well known, at least in name, to the outside world was Clara. She was represented by some to be a half-caste of great influence responsible for inciting and organising the people to raid the boats along the coast. In reality she proved to be a member of the Mara tribe whose territory lies far to the south, on the Roper River. She had been captured on a lugger which was attacked many years before and had been seized by one of the local men and taken in marriage. At the time of my visit she was an old woman, with no influence, who had just lost her husband in the intermittent feuding, looking after her two children.

She had so completely forgotten her own language that she could understand nothing when one of my party addressed her in Mara. But she knew some English, and to this fact is probably due the report, widely circulated, that she was a half-caste. The fact that this woman still remembered a little English may also have been responsible for the persistent rumours, which were still current, of the existence in this area of white women survivors of the wreck of the *Douglas Mawson* which was lost in a cyclone in the Gulf of Carpentaria in March 1923. During April 1924 a rumour circulated in Darwin that a white woman and her fourteen-year-old daughter, survivors of the shipwreck, were being held captive by the Caledon Bay people. So persistent was it that a party of twelve police and several trackers travelled by ship to Arnhem Bay and then overland by horse. They convinced themselves, after extensive travel, that there were no captives and that the source of the rumour was a visit to Caledon Bay by the family of the Rev. Warren the previous year from the Groote Eylandt Mission. Despite this in 1925 Constables McNamara and Bridgeland were dropped off just near Caledon Bay to spend six months in further investigation of the rumour. Just prior to the end of their time there yet another rumour circulated in Darwin to the effect that the two constables had been killed. HMAS *Geranium* happened to be in the area and was sent to investigate, only to find the men alive and well.

When I had made friends with old Wonggu I told him that he would be held responsible for the peace of his group, and that this time he himself, and not his sons, would undoubtedly be blamed by the Government for any further trouble that might occur. He took this very much to heart. He knew that I was his friend and he showed no resentment, but later he brought me a message-stick, and explained that the marks inscribed upon it represented himself sitting down quietly and maintaining peace among the people.

A few days before I left this camp, three of the four men who had accompanied me from Blue Mud Bay, ran off suddenly in the night. Two of them were Ritharrngu men, one of them named Liyawulpul; they had heard that I planned later to return overland to Blue Mud Bay down the Glyde River and across eastern Arnhem Land and it transpired that all four of them had taken part, during the preceding wet, in an expedition to recover and avenge the stealing of the wife of one of the Ritharrngu men, and that in the course of this excursion they had killed the aggressor. They were afraid, therefore, to pass through that country in so small a party, and had run away to Blue Mud Bay. The fourth man, Wawit, remained with us. Shortly before I left his camp, Wonggu became sick and called me over to help him. Two days later he sent two of his own sons, Matuwa and Wuluwirr, with me to act as guides on the overland journey that I made from Trial Bay to Caledon Bay itself. I could hardly have visited this place under better auspices although I did not trust Wuluwirr and watched him closely.

On July 19th I made the journey on foot across to Caledon Bay. Striking the beach to the westward of Cape Gray, I followed the shoreline, and camped that night at Mt Caledon. We had expected to meet the boat at Caledon Bay, but she was becalmed, and failed to arrive. I had shot a wallaby on the journey and this, with a quantity of turtle eggs and some fish, provided us with sufficient food, but we had no blankets, and the nights on this coast were still very cold. Although at that time I could speak only a very few words of the language of

Child's necklace from
Caledon Bay, made
of fish vertebrae strung
on a very fine twine.

below: The message stick
prepared by Wonggu for
Thomson to take to his
sons in prison.

Thomson and carriers on his overland journey from Trial Bay to Caledon Bay.

the Ritharrngu and Caledon Bay men who accompanied me and therefore could only communicate with them by mime, these four men prepared a breakwind and a bed of grass for me, and made my camp as comfortable as possible. I was anxious about the fate of my rifle, which I had used during the journey, and for which there was no oil, but we eventually made a pull-through by unravelling the binding from a fish spear, and used one of the wires as a weight. Early on the following morning the boat arrived, and going aboard, we sailed across to the camping place used by the trepanger Fred Gray on the other side of Caledon Bay – called by the people variously 'Ngandjiingun' and 'Ngandjipuy'.

Caledon Bay is one of the most picturesque regions on this coast. The water here and at Trial Bay was fresh and blue in pleasing contrast with the dull

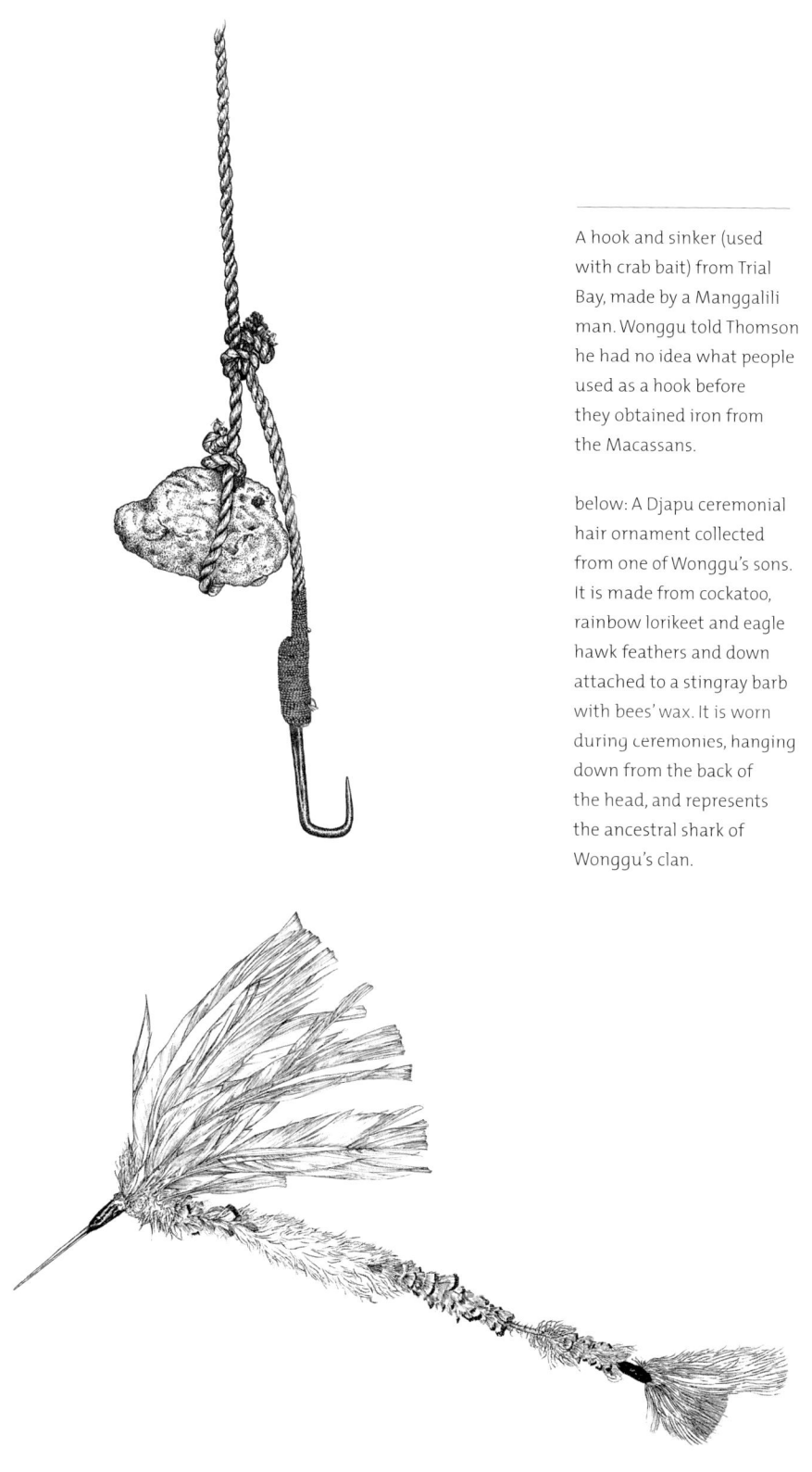

A hook and sinker (used with crab bait) from Trial Bay, made by a Manggalili man. Wonggu told Thomson he had no idea what people used as a hook before they obtained iron from the Macassans.

below: A Djapu ceremonial hair ornament collected from one of Wonggu's sons. It is made from cockatoo, rainbow lorikeet and eagle hawk feathers and down attached to a stingray barb with bees' wax. It is worn during ceremonies, hanging down from the back of the head, and represents the ancestral shark of Wonggu's clan.

yellow waters of Blue Mud Bay. The wide bay is surrounded by hills, and there are fine sandy beaches, which are a relief from the mud and the low shoreline fringed with mangroves, of the coasts further south. Many men came out to the boat to meet us in their canoes. Included in this camp was Wonggu's eldest son Dhangatji. Evidently they were told, by their countrymen from Wonggu's camp who were on board, of our mission, and of our reception along the coast, for they received me with great friendliness.

4

Travels in Arnhem Land

I had now achieved my first objective. Wonggu was warned of the Government's attitude in so far as I had been able to communicate it given my limited control of the language at that stage, and I had been accepted by his people who had been the main focus of the troubles. It was now necessary to patrol more widely inland and on foot, I felt, to convince the Aborigines that Europeans are not helpless away from their boats, or afraid to leave the coast but to impress upon them the fact that we had the strength and resourcefulness necessary to make long journeys through their country and were able to live as they lived. I think that the subsequent success of this depended largely upon the fact that my approach to them was different from that of any other white men that they had met. I did not live apart but camped with them, sat in the single men's camps at night to watch them dancing, shared in as many of their activities as possible and when travelling slept upon the ground, sharing a fire. I dispensed with almost all the usual European impedimenta; sometimes I carried only a tooth-brush and a sheath knife, no watch, no razor, mirror or cooking utensils. In this way, once I was on a journey, I was obliged to live the same life as the people themselves.

I was compelled to modify my plan of walking across from Caledon Bay to Arnhem Bay. The strain of the past month was now beginning to tell, and I had scarcely started to work at Caledon Bay when I went down suddenly with a sharp attack of fever. With my temperature at 103 and still rising, and feeling very sick, I was obliged to lie down, but I sent for the men, who came aboard to see me. I told them that now I was sick, I could not start at once on the journey that I had planned with them, but that I would sail the boat to Port Bradshaw, a day's journey to the northward, and arrange to meet them there and to travel overland with them to Arnhem Bay on the north coast. I was anxious for the

A paperbark dish used for holding water or honey and a honey mop stick with a frayed end that is dunked in the honey, then sucked on.

fresh air of the open sea, and impatient to proceed with my work. Twelve men brought me bark drawings, spears and dilly-bags but they had only a few spears since Webb and Yorum, missionaries from Milingimbi, had bought most of them on their recent visit. On the following morning, July 22nd, we sailed for Port Bradshaw. There was only a light breeze during the afternoon, and we made slow progress under sail. I could not afford to run the engine, as my fuel supplies were low, and I felt obliged to keep what kerosene I had for emergency, for the nearest port where I could replenish supplies was Darwin, more than 500 miles away.

Two of the men from the Caledon Bay camp accompanied us to pilot us through the entrance at Port Bradshaw including Mawalan, a Rirratjingu man, and in addition, a number of others promised to journey overland to meet us there. We reached Port Bradshaw after nightfall and I decided to risk running through the passage to make an anchor inside the bay. It was well that we did so, for by the following morning the wind was blowing almost a gale from the east and south-east, and set in for several days.

The vessel had been sailing slowly, and examination showed that there was a heavy growth of barnacles and weed on the copper sheathing. I therefore careened the vessel and removed the worst of the barnacles and weed, while awaiting the arrival of the men of the overland party to accompany me to Arnhem Bay.

No people were then living at Port Bradshaw; they had all gone away either to Caledon Bay, where we had met them, or to the English Company's Islands, where there was another big camp. The remains of Macassan camp sites, chiefly in the form of stones, where they had prepared their trepang or *bêche-de-mer* which I noted all along this coast, were an especially conspicuous feature of Port Bradshaw where there were also many Tamarind trees (*Tamarindus indica*) which were undoubtedly brought to this country by the Macassans. The presence of these camp sites, and of the groves of old Tamarind trees, as well as the evidence of the people themselves, show how well these voyagers stood with the Aboriginal population, and the permanent nature of the footing that they had established.

The fever had now left me, and after another day's rest I was anxious to proceed. On the day after our arrival at Port Bradshaw, one man arrived, accompanied by several women   his own wife and the wives of the men whom we had brought up on the boat from Caledon Bay. The man told us that the others had not come as they had promised because, when they had seen me lying sick at Caledon Bay, they had been afraid that I was going to die and they thought that the Government might blame them.

On July 24th I left Port Bradshaw on foot for Arnhem Bay with a group of people, some of whom belonged to the Melville Bay district and were returning northwards. This reconnaissance, undertaken before I was really fit to travel, was another severe ordeal and was nearly my last. I was still weak from the recent attack of fever and during the walk I developed slight dysentery. This trouble increased in severity during the journey, which became a very difficult ordeal, and I was soon passing considerable quantities of blood.

The country behind Port Bradshaw was the most rugged that I had so far encountered in eastern Arnhem Land. We crossed a series of low hills, with rocks and boulders outcropping on all sides, in the centre of which was a fine, timbered plateau, about fifteen miles inland from Port Bradshaw. This plateau, conspicuous from the surrounding country as far as Melville Bay, I called MacFarland Plateau in honour of Sir John MacFarland, then Chancellor of the

University of Melbourne. But if it was the most rugged and rocky country that we had so far encountered, it was also the best watered, and we crossed numerous springs and creeks, swiftly running, with fine clear water. This was in strong contrast with conditions in most other areas, where the sluggish creeks are generally reduced, quite early in the dry season, to a chain of more or less stagnant pools, which, except for deep lagoons, later dry up completely. At the end of the second day I reached the shore of the eastern side of Arnhem Bay, although at that time I was unaware of the fact, and actually mistook my position.

On the fringe of Arnhem Bay we descended upon a great grass flat, thousands of acres in extent, covered by a dense growth of blady grass fully six or seven feet in height. We were obliged to force our way through this for a distance of several miles, which, in my poor condition, was a slow and painful business. The men had expected to find a small camp somewhere in this vicinity, so with the dual object of clearing the way and of attracting the attention of any people who might be in the neighbourhood, we fired these grass flats. The result was the biggest fire that I have seen. It swept after us rapidly with an ominous roar and we had to halt and burn breaks to clear the ground ahead of us to ensure our own safety. Flames shot hundreds of feet into the air and dense clouds of smoke rose to the sky, obscuring the sun, so that for hours it shed only a pale yellowish light over the country. We learned afterwards that the smoke of that fire had been visible aboard the *St Nicholas* as far away as Melville Bay. To me the destruction was appalling, but the people were accustomed to these great fires for they burn the grass regularly each season to enable them to travel freely about the country and to assist them in hunting game.

We reached the shore of Arnhem Bay late in the afternoon of the second day at a point between the mouths of two big rivers visible only as two great walls of green mangroves to the left and right of the open salt pans on which we were walking. This was to have been my rendezvous with the *St Nicholas*.

Although we were on the east side of the bay and not far from the place at which I had arranged to pick up the boat, the only two rivers which appeared in this vicinity on my maps and on the Admiralty charts, were on the *southern* shores of the bay, much out of place, but in the same relative positions as the two that we now saw, and I assumed wrongly that we were now between these two rivers. None of the people who were with me at this time could speak English, and I could not yet cross-examine them on a question of this kind, so that I was uncertain that the place to which they were guiding me was the one that I had marked on the chart, and to which Kapiu was to take the *St Nicholas*.

A biting bag held between
the teeth while grimacing
when about to fight.
This was intended to
intimidate opponents.

below: A pipe made from
a piece of wood that has
been split, hollowed out and
joined together again. Pipes
were sometimes painted or
incised with powerful clan
designs so that only older
people of that clan could
smoke from them. This was
done deliberately to restrict
the sharing of tobacco. Such
designs were masked with a
sheath of paperbark or cloth.

I instructed the guides therefore, as well as I was able, to take us a little to the north to look for the *St Nicholas*. This later proved to have been a mistake. The country along the coast was quite impassable on account of the dense mangroves and deep saltwater creeks and waterways and we had to return inland to the grassy plains that we had burned, and then swing to the northward. Here, however, the men made me understand that on the following morning we would have to swim a big river.

We camped that night on the fringe of the plain. I was feeling very weak and unwell and knew that I should not be able to stand many more days of this travel. The food we were carrying could not last for long, and while it did last I shared it with the people who accompanied me. We had killed two wallabies, and I gave all of the party some flour and tobacco that night and again on the following morning to keep them in good spirits. For they, too, although they had been fresh when we started, were now tired, and it must be remembered that it is not naturally the custom of these people to make long or hard marches unless driven to do so by real necessity. I was not able to eat much food myself, but it was of the greatest importance to keep the others cheerful, since I was not sure of my position. In such country one is entirely dependent on local knowledge, for to follow a compass course is impossible in a terrain intersected with streams. I was dependent upon these people as guides and porters – and we had a deep wide river to swim in the morning. We saw no evidence of recent occupation, and it was evident that this great tract of country was now almost uninhabited – that people visited it only at rare intervals. A sure indication of occupation is the regularity with which the seasonal burning of the grass has been carried out for this is always done in occupied country, otherwise it would become impassable.

A long, almost sleepless night followed, for I was in some pain and weak from dysentery. In the morning I bound my leg, which I could flex only with difficulty, using an elastic bandage, but the limb was stiff and swollen, and this bandage only added to the handicap and had soon to be removed. Because I knew none of the people with me well I worried that if I waited to rest, they might slip away during the night as soon as the food was gone. Moreover, the dysentery showed no signs of abating, and it is not easy to lie still, alone, in far away places. The peculiar conditions of this work called for activity and hard work. I decided to push on while my strength lasted. I believed that the boat could not be far away.

I was now holding the party back. Hitherto I had always been able tire them out. When we reached the river the prospect did not look attractive. It was a wide, muddy estuary lined, as usual, with a dense unbroken wall of green mangroves standing above a bank of grey mud. It was low water but there was still about eighty to a hundred yards to swim, and all these rivers are infested with crocodiles. This river I named Peter John, after my sons who were again much on my mind. The river to the south of the Peter John has since been named the Cato by the Rev. T. T. Webb of the Methodist Mission at Milingimbi, who visited it in the *Maree*.

The Aborigines now took the initiative. They collected the dry buoyant driftwood that lay about and lashed it together with strips of the green bark of the cotton-tree (*Hibiscus tiliaceus*). This did not look very secure and as I could not hope to swim very far with my leg as it was, I took the straps off my canvas bag and strapped these around the bundle to supplement the bark. On top of this the men placed the sheets of tea-tree bark which they had obtained for the purpose, earlier in the morning, and stripping off my clothes, I lay flat on top. The women remained on the bank and the men swam with me, pushing the raft across, while I paddled with my hands. The people are accustomed to crossing rivers in this way, many of them swimming at one time, keeping close together and making as much noise as they can to frighten the crocodiles. They landed me safely on the north bank and then returned with the 'raft' for the gear. On later patrols when I became more accustomed to the way of life I was able to swim all the rivers with them, to live on their food and to travel barefoot. This stood me in good stead when in 1942 I returned to organise and lead a unit of these people in wartime for guerilla scouting and fighting.

While threading my way through the mangroves to the open salt pan beyond, I ran a stick into my left eye. Fortunately only the mucous membrane was injured, but I was unable to see out of it or to open it fully for several days and without a mirror I could not tell the extent of the damage. To add to my difficulties I now sprained one of my ankles, which commenced to swell badly.

Eventually we reached salt water again, once more between two walls of mangroves, which marked the courses of creeks on either side. Later reconnaissance showed that these two creeks formed part of a system of streams in the vicinity of Arnhem Bay which were unknown and unmapped. Our food was finished and the people with me were in strange country. Too sick to move, we camped for a few days to rest and to await the arrival of the *St Nicholas*. The only foods obtainable were the rhizome of a fern – the Swamp Fern (*Blechnum serrulelum*) called *dhulwarn*, which grew in abundance in the fresh running creeks in this region. These were about the size of a pencil. When roasted they looked like charred pieces of stick, but chewed thoroughly they provided some nourishment and were surprisingly good, though rough and very fibrous. We met a small group of people here. They gave me a few slender yams which supplemented the rough and fibrous diet of *dhulwarn* – not very digestible for one with the complaint from which I suffered. After two days I took stock of the situation and realised that I was not in Arnhem Bay at all but that when we swung to the north we had come up towards the English Company's Islands and that I was looking out into the strait called by Flinders, Malay Road. I checked my position and sent some of the men to the head of Arnhem Bay, close to Mallison Island. There, from the rocky heights, they sighted in the bay below the white sails, tiny in the distance, of a vessel which of course proved to be the *St Nicholas*. With the aid of smoke fires which marked our route as we descended painfully over these last few miles, we reached the shore at last and were soon aboard the vessel, very spent. It was now July 29th.

On the following morning I stood off Mallison Island at the head of Arnhem Bay in the *St Nicholas* and waited to meet a canoe from the camp in the English Company's Islands – the camp of the people who had brought food to us when we were in a bad way, and who had assisted me in the search for the boat. I rewarded the people liberally with presents of fishhooks, wire, tobacco, and flour, and then sailed westwards for the Crocodile Islands. We anchored that night in Cadell Strait, which separates Elcho Island from the mainland. Cadell Strait is shallow at the eastern end but navigable by small vessels drawing up to eight or nine feet of water. The western end is deep but the shores are rocks and very strong tides run there. On the following evening, after driving the boat all day with the engine, we reached Milingimbi in the Crocodile Islands, where I was received with every kindness and hospitality by the Rev. and Mrs T. T. Webb and their staff.

I reported to the Federal Government by wireless my safe arrival at Milingimbi and of the successful completion of the first stage of my undertaking.

After a few days at Milingimbi with fresh food and vegetables, I was well again although it was some time before I could walk very much. I careened the boat again, and replaced several sheets of Muntz metal close to the waterline, that were corroded badly. The Methodist Mission's auxiliary vessel *Maree*, which carried the stores for Milingimbi and Goulburn Island Missions, was out of commission at the time of my arrival, and both of these stations were becoming short of supplies. I therefore dispatched the *St Nicholas* at once to Darwin to

Milingimbi Methodist Mission, established in 1923, was the only mission in north-east Arnhem Land ministering to the people until the Methodist Mission at Yirrkala was established in 1935. There was an Anglican mission on Groote Eylandt established in 1921 for people of mixed descent. Milingimbi was the site of Lloyd Warner's anthropological field research carried out between 1927 and 1929 and published in 1937 as *A Black Civilization*.

bring back stores for Goulburn Island and Milingimbi Missions as well as for myself and settled down to make the mission my base for the next two months.

During this time I was able to carry out a good deal of anthropological work. With the aid of some excellent interpreters I was able to make a survey of the people in the area and obtain much general information on their culture and ceremonial life. I was also able to add to the cinematograph record that I had commenced at Blue Mud Bay.

On the 9th of October I broke up my depot at Milingimbi, and made the longest and most important patrol that I was able to accomplish during the course of this expedition – the crossing of eastern Arnhem Land on foot, from

Donald Thomson in Arnhem Land

above: These men are decorated with the finest paintings on the last day of the ceremony. The man on the left is of a Gupapuyngu clan and decorated with a honey design; the second man is of the Warramiri clan with a design relating to a fresh water swamp grass; the third man is decorated with a mangrove worm design; and the last man is of the Durili clan and decorated with a stone design. The top portion of this last design is undecorated because it is the first time he has been through the ceremony. It is versions of these designs that are usually painted on the barks produced for sale.

opposite: These two photographs indicate the diversity and complexity of the body painting associated with *Ngaarra* ceremonies. These are the most sacred of all ceremonies, each clan having its own version to celebrate its founding ancestor. They can run for many weeks before the climax is reached. The single band of painting indicates that it is early in the ceremony.

opposite, top (from left): Burrurrunyingu, Munonga, Dhimala, Nyarrang, unidentified, Gadatjiya, Gadhany and Ruwarrina.

Harry Makarrwala,
who was Lloyd
Warner's great friend
and assistant.

the Crocodile Islands to Blue Mud Bay and thence to the hills of the Walker River.

The objective of this patrol was to demonstrate to the Government once and for all that, despite official forebodings, I had been able to establish myself with the people and that this area was really under control and safe for a European who understood the Aborigines and who treated them as fellow human beings.

The chief difficulty was in securing sufficient carriers to take the loads. I had hoped to travel with horses, to lessen the hardship and to have made it possible to cover a greater area of country but enough equipment was not available. For the first two or three days I was accompanied by about thirty-five people, but these dwindled as soon as they got out of the territory that was familiar to them and only five finally reached Matarawatj at Blue Mud Bay.

Many remembered feuds of long standing – for blood feuds among these

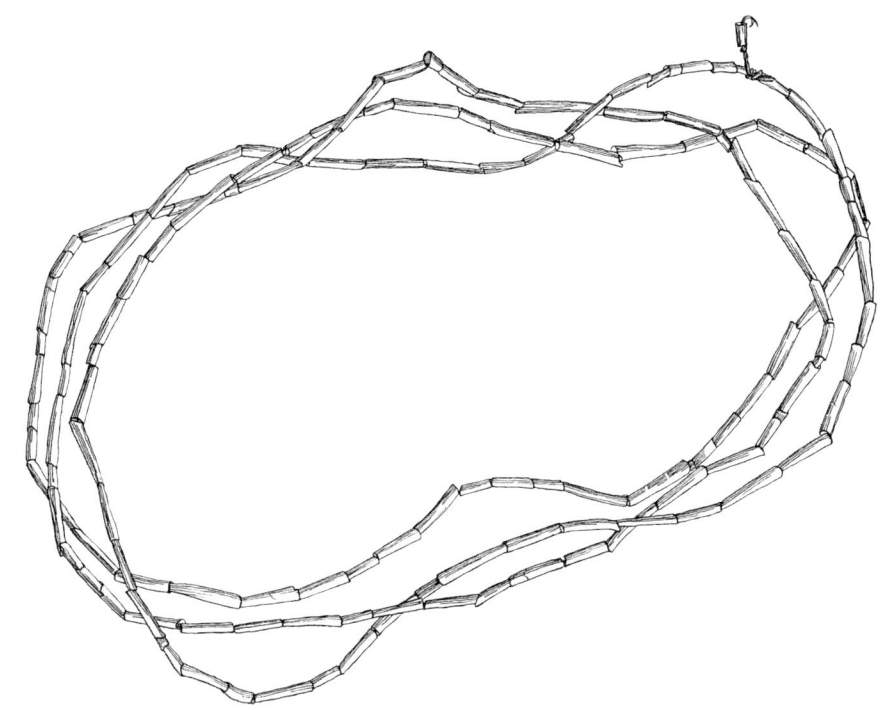

above: A grass stem necklace.

Harry Makarrwala's daughter, Bela, playing at being a mother, with moulded mud breasts and a mud doll lying on a sheet of paper bark.

people are carried on for many generations. The 'pay back' as they call it, may be delayed for years in order to catch a man, or a group, off guard. When they deserted they generally disappeared during the night.

Leaving my boat to the west of the mouth of the Glyde River in Castlereagh Bay we crossed through the wall of mangroves that fringe the coast opposite the Crocodile Islands and came out onto a bare salt pan which led, after two or three miles, to open savannah so like Cape York Peninsula that I could not have judged whether I was in Queensland or Arnhem Land by the appearance of the bush. On a little hill we passed four wet season houses, called *katawurdu* by the Mildjingi people, through whose territory we were passing. They stood six or eight feet high and consisted of a floor or table of sticks roughly roofed with stringy bark. At Burlingur, in Djinang territory, we reached a big camp where many of the Aboriginal people who visit Milingimbi live, and camped there. The next day we moved south to a second camp at Kallutngur, near the old Arafura homestead that lasted for a few years in the early 1900s. It is incomprehensible to me that the mission has never made use of this country to form at least an outstation for agricultural or stock raising purposes. It would be less convenient for them but undoubtedly better for the people.

On the morning of 12th October I set out with about thirty-six people. We came across some old buffalo tracks. While halted at a small billabong to catch long neck turtles a small family group of Djinba speakers appeared. The woman had a gash on her shoulder which I dressed.

We threaded our way among glades of swamp tea-tree, chiefly *Melaleuca leucadendra*, our footfalls muffled by the green sward of grass and dry peaty loam. This green park-like country formed a striking contrast with the bare arid country, with its leafless trees crying out for water, that we had traversed close to the coast, and some of the barren, rocky arid terrain that we were to meet during the latter part of this journey. Away to the east, south, and west, rugged hills and rocky outcrops showed in sharp relief above the low-lying, swamp bed, wherever we could see to the horizon. The people informed me that although

opposite, top: The group of carriers who set out from the Upper Glyde River at the beginning of the walk to Blue Mud Bay in the dry bed of the Arafura Swamp. It was on this journey that Thomson made friends with Raywala (the rear line of men, fourth from the right).

opposite, bottom: Some of the carriers on the walk to Blue Mud Bay who left when they reached their own country on the Upper Glyde River. Left to right: unidentified, Burumila (Mandalpingu clan), unknown, Mundjingu (Ganalbingu clan), unknown, Liyawulpul (Ritharrngu speaker), Dejewiy (Djinba speaker), Djimbun, Wagirr (Djinba speaker), Birriwun (Ritharrngu speaker), Kikirri (Ganalbingu clan) and Dhunupirri (Djinba speaker).

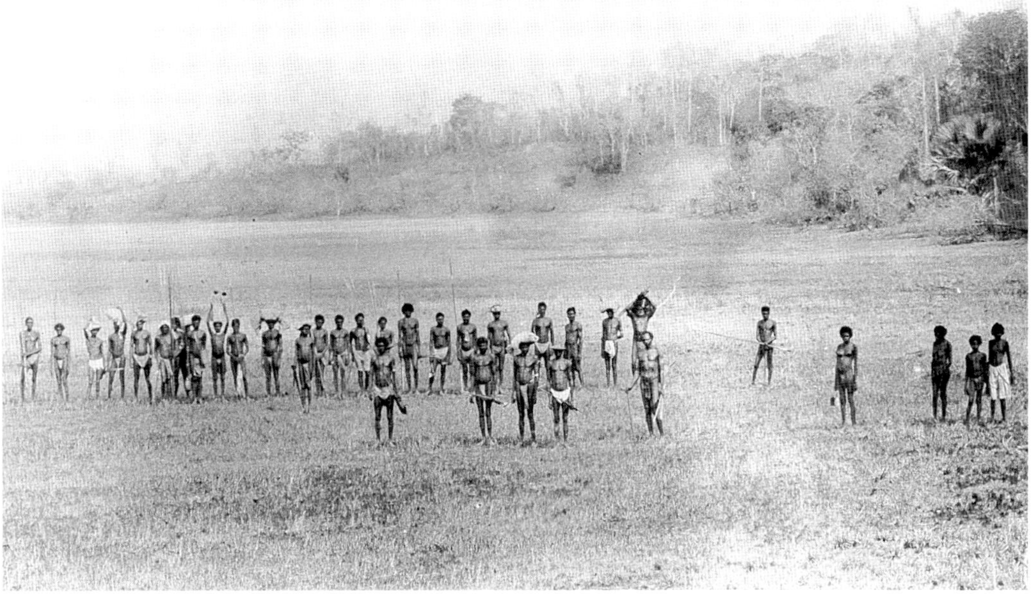

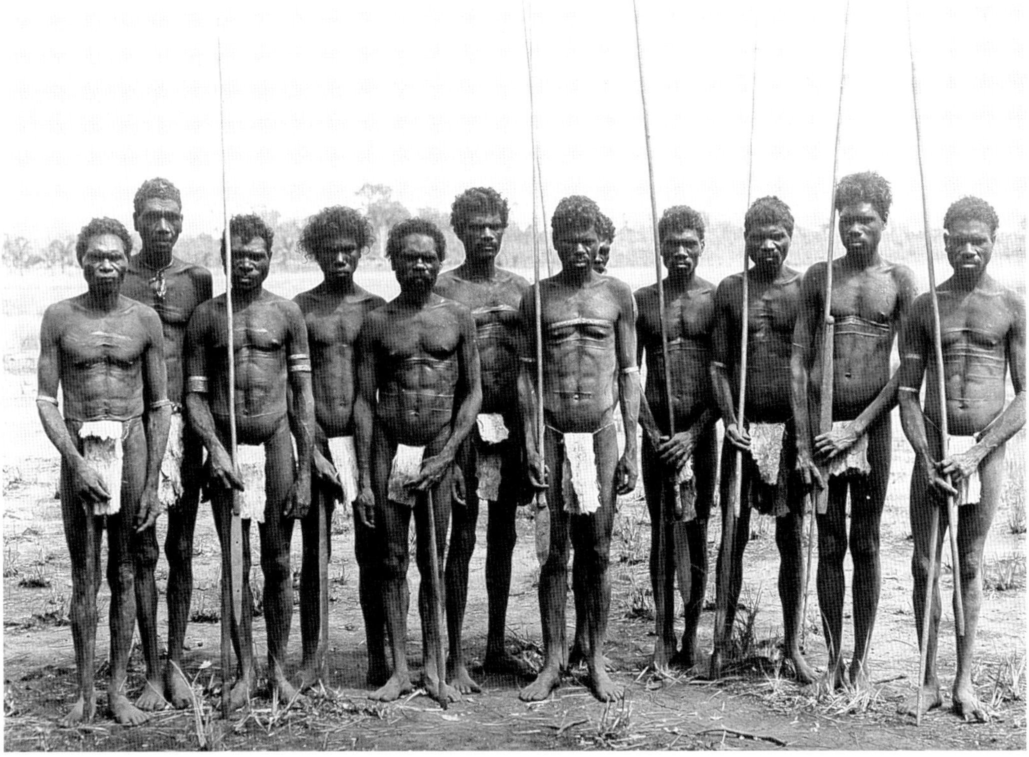

this great basin was now dry, towards the end of the 'wet' it became a big swamp, into which they journeyed in bark canoes of a curious type, which were quite distinct from those they used on the coast and in the river estuaries. I was greatly interested in this and resolved later to investigate this country for it promised to be of interest geographically, and also to provide information to untangle the river systems which were but poorly represented on the maps.

We traversed a total of about seventy miles of the park-like country before it gave place to uplands, and we ascended a series of low, rough, stony hills, excessively rugged, over which travel was difficult and slow. From time to time during this journey, we met with people of the Ritharrngu and other groups of the inland; sometimes in little hordes, at other times in family parties consisting of a man and his wives and their children; occasionally just a hunter or two, their faces and bodies smeared with grey mud or clay so that their quarry – red kangaroo or wallaroo – would not 'smell' them. There is something indefinable, a quality, a permanence, about the nomadic hunters that abides with one. They are so much a part of the landscape; they fit in without a single note of discord, and I for one cannot bear to think of their passing, these lithe, splendid, unspoiled men, from their last stronghold in the oldest continent. They came out of the bush, they appeared from nowhere, they did not need to speak, and they were friendly always.

Each of these men whom we met, carried a neatly made parcel of a special kind called *dabarr*, containing bones. These consisted generally of the bones of certain birds such as a jabiru, the emu, the native companion or even the long bones of the kangaroo intermingled with fire sticks. Such bones are called either *galngbuy*, if killed by a young man, or *tjambin*, in which case they are accumulated for ceremonial purposes. In their right hands these men carried a spear-thrower and a bundle of spears – hooked wooden spears with villainous looking barbs perfectly carved from ironwood, or stone-headed spears called *ngambi* from the famous quarry at Ngilipidji in the hills of the blue distance – a quarry that no European had seen. I had long know that the quarry was remote for very few, even of the oldest men on the northern coastline had even been there although they knew and cherished, lovingly, the flint spear-heads from it.

It was the hottest time of the year, the season called *wurlmamirri* (literally, with-thunder) or *ngurru waltjarn*, the nose/threshold of the rains. The days were scorching hot and our fingers became taut and swollen as we walked, our lips dry and parched, and the land shimmered under a mirage that was with us always. We broke camp very early and were on the way soon after daylight. At midday we called a halt and lay down in the shade near water, if any was to be

Thomson's constant companion and friend, Raywala (Thomson spelt his name Raiwalla), a Mildjingi clansman.

found, fighting off the flies that crept into our eyes, mouths, and noses, with such persistence that they intensified the discomfort of the heat during the day and the mosquitoes at night.

On October 15th, after traversing at very nearly the hottest time of the year, more than two hundred miles of some of the most rugged country in Arnhem Land we arrived at Matarawatj. The success of this journey owed much to the faithfulness and devotion of a man of the Mildjingi clan, of the lower Glyde River, Raywala, who, although he had never been in that country and did not know its people, accompanied me and stood by my side as faithfully as any white companion could have done. When the carriers were deserting at night, leaving us without sufficient men to carry our loads, at considerable personal risk and with very real tact, he always succeeded in persuading sufficient to go

The country inland from Blue Mud Bay which has been recently burnt, making the north–south oriented 'magnetic' ants' hills standout clearly.

just a little further to enable us to replace them, and so to carry on. When they tired and dropped behind, Raywala dropped behind with them and often himself carried the bulk of their loads. Throughout the whole of the journey he was always cheerful, keeping the others who were ill at ease away from their own territory, in happy mood, by his cheerful manner and jokes.

Weeks later when he left me on the Wilton River, whence he was returning to his own country, he turned his head away, and when I looked at him again, real tears were streaming down his face. He returned to his clan territory on the Glyde River and in the following year when he heard by wireless that I was coming back, he rejoined the *St Nicholas* and was waiting for me in Darwin.

Raywala was renowned as the greatest single-combat fighter in Arnhem Land, and although living in his own territory, had been sentenced to life imprisonment for 'murder' and had served some years of his sentence before he was released.

Thomson's shelter at Matarawatj, where he lived while the *Mundukul* (rock python) *Ngaarra* ceremony was going on. *Ngaarra* ceremonies are the most important of each clan's religious celebrations.

His case illustrates how ill planned Government interference in Aboriginal life creates unnecessary resentment amongst the people and was to influence some of my recommendations. According to the law of his own people, under whose legal and moral code (in the entire absence of any other effective Government control of this Territory) he can fairly be stated to have been living, he had done no wrong. The anomaly, and the injustice, of the whole of the punishment of tribal, and also of most other, offences for which the people of this territory have been penalised is the fact that they believe that they are still living under their own laws, and they have no reason to recognise the fact that a new regime has taken over their affairs, except that they know vaguely that there is, somewhere, an individual or a power, called the 'Gub'ment' that sometimes visits vengeance upon them. For that is all that white man's 'justice' has so far meant to the black man in Arnhem Land. The unhappy fact is that he can look back on the tradi-

Women gathering the corm of the Mat-Rush (*Eleocharis* sp.) which was in abundance in this area and one of the staples supporting the large number of people gathered for the *Ngaarra* ceremony.

tion established by the Indonesian voyagers and contrast this with the treatment he (and his women) have received subsequently, from the whites.

Some three months had elapsed since my last visit, and the people at Blue Mud Bay were very glad to see me again and proud of the fact that they had kept their promise to maintain peace in their country. No fighting had taken place on the entire coastline since our departure. Important totemic ceremonies were taking place and a very large number of people, approximately two hundred, were in the camp at Matarawatj on this occasion. I was able to be present at these ceremonies, and also to visit their burial place where the bodies of the dead are exposed for the purpose of cleaning the bones prior to presenting them ceremonially to their relatives.

In recent times Aboriginal people from over a hundred kilometres away have sought knives and spearheads from this quarry at Ngilipidji on the Upper Walker River. The older man is Dhutjuru of the Mardarrpa clan. The younger man is Marrilyauwuy, a Waagilak man and one of the men Thomson recruited at the mouth of the Roper River to help crew the *St Nicholas* and who guided him to the camp at Matarawatj.

After remaining for some days in this camp to rest, I gathered together a party of guides and carriers, and set out for Ngilipidji in the hills close to the Walker River. Ngilipidji is renowned throughout the whole of eastern Arnhem Land as the quarry at which the fine stone spear heads and knives are manufactured – and from which, for many generations, they have been circulated over a vast area of country. I had seen these spear heads in use as far south as the Roper River and northward to the Goyder, as well as at Caledon Bay. The journey to Ngilipidji and return to Matarawatj, which lies some forty miles inland, occupied four long days of travel, but I felt greatly privileged to see with my own eyes the quarry that had acquired a legendary renown.

At Ngilipidji the quarry covered many acres of ground. The stone was not quarried from a face of rock, as I had expected, but from the open ground, where a big overburden of earth had to be removed in order to expose boulders, which were then levered out, or fractured by the use of fire, into pieces that could be handled. Great heaps of chips and broken or rejected flints marked the sites of old working places. The actual manufacture of the flints is carried out only with a pounding stone of quartzite; a great deal of skill and experience is required, and only two or three old men remain who are considered skilful enough to make the fine heads and knives. We were fortunate in finding one of the most renowned of them, Dhutjuru, there. Of hundreds of flints struck off, all but a dozen or so would be rejected. These fine flints were wrapped separately, in bark sheaths, tied into bundles of a dozen or two to be given to people not only for tipping of spears but also for fighting picks and the knives which are still used in circumcision. I obtained a series of still photographs and a cinematograph record.

It was excessively hot in these rocky hills at this season of the year, flies were unbelievably bad and persistent and water was scarce; all this made travel very severe.

During my absence on this journey, the people from the camp at Matarawatj had taken charge of my depot in their own camp, containing food, equipment and personal belongings, and with a canoe they had also visited the *St Nicholas* which lay some miles away off the mouth of the Koolatong River, and had kept her supplied with water and firewood. In spite of the bad reputation of the people of this coast, and especially of this camp, as raiders of boats and plunderers of stores, I am able to record that not only did I lose nothing from my vessel or from any of my shore camps at any time, but that they guarded my stores and possessions faithfully in my absence. While I was inland at the Walker River, the large gathering of people at Blue Mud Bay were actually between me and my depot and vessel. They were all aware of where I had gone and that I must be absent for some days. It was difficult to believe that only two years before these people had attacked three separate parties all of whom were armed in this same neighbourhood, with considerable loss of life.

On my return from the flint quarry at Ngilipidji the important ceremony associated with *mundukul*, a mythical Rock Python, and one of the totemic ancestors, was still in progress.

These ceremonies are very sacred. Totemism forms the basis of solidarity within the clans, and ceremonies of the type called *mardayin*, which represent in pantomime the activities of the clan ancestors when they were 'finding' or creating

In the final stages of the *Ngaarra* ceremony the men, women and children ritually wash themselves in the Malarawatj waterhole.

the culture and way of life as it is lived today, are carried out at intervals. I delayed to attend this ceremony and then sailed south, visiting Bennet Bay again in the hope of finding my Nunggubuyu friends there. As the draught of the *St Nicholas* was too great to risk sailing close in to the mouth of the Walker River, I sent a dinghy to cruise off the shore and rejoin the vessel at Bennet Bay. Nobody was seen, and we learned later that most of the Nunggubuyu were camped at that time on the Phelp River, close to the mouth of the Roper.

On October 29th I left Bennet Bay, sailed round Barrow Point, and set a course for Groote Eylandt. In the Lowrie Channel, between Bickerton Island and the mainland, we sighted a canoe some distance ahead and still some miles off shore. The occupants had also seen us and began to paddle with frantic haste for the mainland. I was anxious to make contact with them and to show them that the presence of a white man's boat did not always mean trouble. Opening

Dugout canoes of varying sizes were common along the coast of Arnhem Land. Originally obtained by barter or theft from Macassans who started regular visits to northern Australia around 1720, people resorted to making them after 1907 when such visits were stopped by the government. Sails were made from pandanus fibre. Outriggers were never used in Arnhem Land. The introduction of dugouts, along with metal for harpoons, seems to have increased the importance of turtle and dugong in the diet. The man on the left is identified as a Liyagawumirr man, Nupurray Garrawurra.

opposite: Details of forms of hafting and four turtle harpoon points.

the throttle of the engine, we drove the vessel at full speed in pursuit. They redoubled their efforts to get away, but after about half an hour we cut them off from the shore and made them bring their canoe alongside. The party consisted of a man, three women and a number of children, with their dogs. When I brought the man aboard the *St Nicholas* he was shaking with fright and clung to one of my crew. We allowed the women to remain in the canoe alongside. After the crew had talked for a few minutes, the man began to be reassured. I asked him then what he had done wrong to make him try to run away. Then we gave

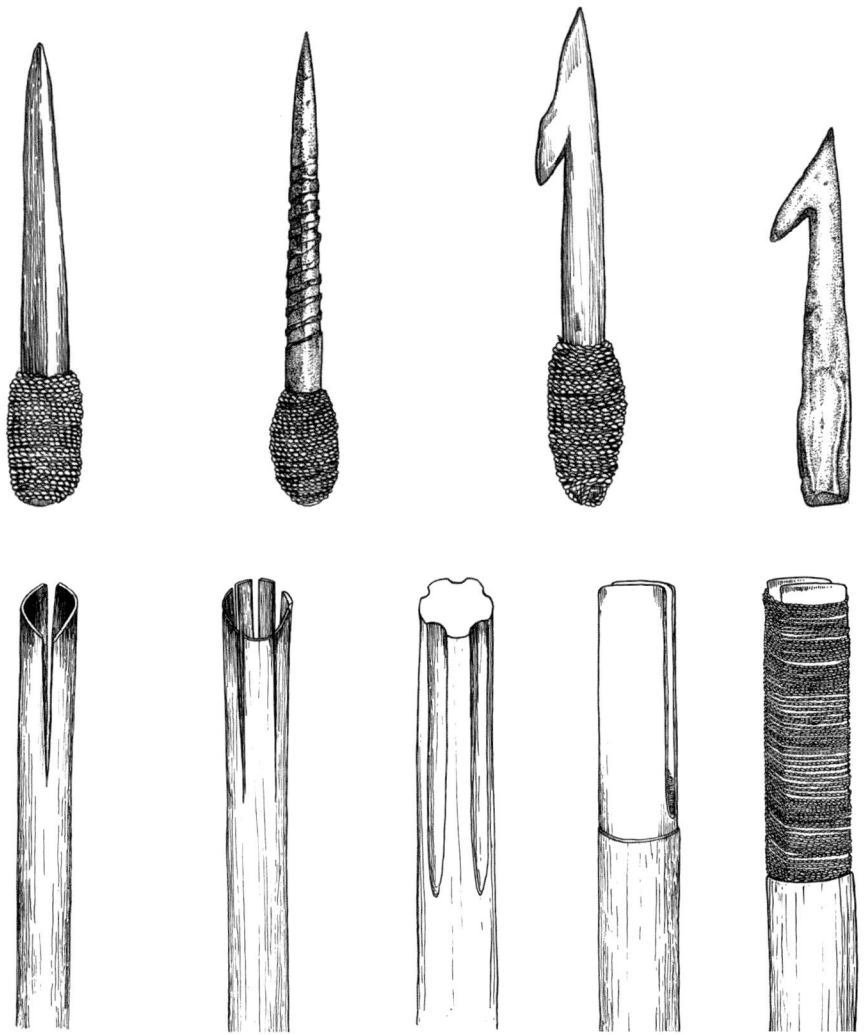

them all presents of fishhooks and wire, which are of great value since they help them to increase their food supplies, as well as some tobacco. They were delighted with their reception and after making us in return a present of turtle eggs, they pushed off and continued their journey to the mainland. In the afternoon we reached Groote Eylandt and anchored off the mouth of the river in which the Anglican mission was situated in a deep, sheltered bay, to which I gave the name Wood Jones Bay, in honour of Professor F. Wood Jones, FRS. The cape to the south, the south-western extremity of the island, I called Cape Agar in honour of Professor W. E. Agar, FRS, of the University of Melbourne. The bay which lies inside the point affords a sheltered and comfortable anchorage in the south-east season, for small ships.

The people of Groote Eylandt are of special interest, for they remained isolated and little known until about 1921, when a mission station was established there. But much earlier they too had come under the influence of the Macassan voyagers who established at least one camp on the island, in the north-eastern corner, which bears the name Djarrakpi, and here they set up a shore station for the boiling and curing of *bêche-de-mer*. To this site, as to other similar stations, the *praus* returned again and again. Their influence was considerable.

Of special interest was the emphasis on the seclusion of the women of Groote, which may have been a result of the contact with the Macassan seafarers. Until the mission influence in recent years altered their moral codes and tabus no visitor, and in fact no strange man, was permitted even to see a woman. The late W. McLennan, a bird collector who, in 1923, spent a considerable time on Groote Eylandt, told me that although he was out in the bush collecting birds almost every day he did not see a woman during all the months he was on the island.

On my brief visit earlier in the year I too saw no women, but this time I was able, without any trouble, to make friends with them and to make a study of their food gathering and domestic economy.

I found that the women of Groote carry a screen of tea-tree bark, neatly seamed together and hinged, so that it can be wrapped closely round the body or rested on the ground in a half-folded position to form a screen. A screen of somewhat similar type which is used in the same way, but made from Pandanus fibre, is found in parts of north central Arnhem Land, where it is used by the Djinang, Wurlaki, Mildjingi and allied clans.

At Groote Eylandt I waited to develop the plates taken at Blue Mud Bay, which I had been unable to process for lack of fresh water. Photographic work carried out on this expedition was extremely laborious on account of the difficult light, and severe weather conditions, and most of the actual photography had to be carried out in the early morning. Because of the heat and humidity, and the length of time that I was out of touch, most of the photographs had to be developed on the spot at night. A dark room for this purpose was therefore built at each main camp. But the biggest problem during the dry season was to obtain good water, water which had not been contaminated by decomposing vegetable matter, free from abrasive particles which would scratch the emulsion.

A principal purpose of these screens, carried by women on Groote Eylandt, is said to have been to conceal themselves from the Macassan fishermen who visited the area in the wet season. The Church of England missionaries, who arrived on the island in 1921, did not see an Aboriginal woman during their first four years there. This woman is Tumulapundha of the Bara clan.

All the water had to be carried, often from water holes or wells some distance away. It had to be strained, and finally cooled by exposure to the air, in wide, shallow vessels which gave the maximum evaporation. As a rule, developing, even when all precautions were observed, could only be carried out between midnight and daybreak, when the temperature of the water was at a minimum.

I remained at Groote Eylandt for five days, to carry out some work on the social organisation of these people. As I wished to continue this work and could not remain longer at Groote, I carried two of my informants with me to the

Roper River. They were returned to Groote Eylandt on the *St Nicholas* on her voyage northward in the following month.

On 4th November I arrived in the Roper River again, and anchored off the Anglican mission station there. I was anxious to resume work here on social organisation for comparative purposes. I also planned to carry out a survey along the course of the Wilton River, and to cross central Arnhem Land to Liverpool River in the north, then to Oenpelli on the East Alligator, which flows into the Van Diemen Gulf. With this journey in view I had requested the Administrator, some time before, to have pack horses and mules made available through the Northern Territory Police at Roper Bar Police Depot to await my arrival. Some delay occurred in sending down the required team, and I was not able to set out from the Roper for a month, by which time the heat was intense, the opening showers which herald the wet season had already fallen, the atmosphere was sticky and humid, and conditions were not favourable for long and hard travel. Flies, both the common house fly and the biting March fly (*Tabanus*), were numerous and very troublesome. But the breaking of the wet, although it meant there was a danger of being caught in the boggy, low-lying country that might become impassable during the rains, had one advantage, for it provided some surface water for the mules and horses, and a picking of fresh grass where the country had been completely bare during the long dry season.

While awaiting the arrival of pack animals I was able to spend the time in intensive work with people of the Mara, Nandi, Ngalakan and other tribes of the valley of the Roper River.

On December 9th I set out for the Liverpool River. I hoped to complete the journey across to the Liverpool River before the ground became too boggy for horse travel. On December 14th I passed Mainoru Station, and the following day passed Mt Catt, some forty miles to the northwards, and camped on the Upper Wilton River. At Mainoru I had been unable to obtain anyone who knew the country west of the Goyder to act as a guide. The local people assured me that to the westward, where I had set my course, there were dry sand ridges, which would mean a waterless stage of at least two days. In the light of this information and of the intense heat and humidity that would endanger the pack animals, I decided not to attempt the crossing until after the wet. Reluctantly, therefore, I turned back to the Roper arriving at the police depot on the 18th December.

While at Groote Eylandt I had sent a wireless message to the Minister for the Interior informing the Commonwealth Government of the completion of the first part of my mission. Now, on my return to the Roper I received instructions to return south to make a report on the work and explorations carried out. I was feeling the effects of the long strenuous months of hard work so I went south by sea. The rest and good food on the ship enabled me to recuperate before I reached Melbourne early in January 1936. I was able to tell the Government that although much fighting and many deaths had occurred prior to my arrival not a single Aboriginal was killed in eastern Arnhem Land while I was in the area. I had made contact with the most important groups and had carried out patrols of more than 500 miles on foot and by canoe through the worst of the territory, in addition to journeys by sea amounting to about 3000 miles. The whole area was now under control and I had accomplished the first part of the undertaking with which I had been entrusted, but I had much to learn before I could report on the customs and social life of the people.

My Report

Back in Melbourne I settled down to write an interim report for the Minister of the Interior. In preparing the report I endeavoured to show the facts from the Aborigines' point of view and to demonstrate that from their point of view they have not received fair treatment at our hands.

The most definite conclusion I drew from this initial expedition was the undeniable fact that the population was not only dying out rapidly, but already on the road to extinction. Extensive tracts of fertile country that formerly supported large populations were in many instances completely depopulated, and unless steps of a positive character were taken without delay, I was convinced that the fate of the Aboriginal was sealed.

It is evident, even to the casual observer, that at every point where the Australian Aboriginal has come into prolonged contact with a European or Asiatic population, his culture has commenced to decay, and degradation and racial extinction have followed. The most striking example of the rapidity with which depopulation can proceed may be seen in the valley of the Roper River. While it is impossible here, as in most other parts of Australia, to quote exact figures, since no accurate census could be taken at the outset, there is abundant evidence of the fact that the Roper River valley supported, until quite recent years, a very dense population. The organisation of the tribes that formerly occupied this area, and the evidence of the survivors, prove this fact. But in 1936 there remained only a few completely detribalised Aborigines who lived as hangers-on of the Europeans renting their territory from the Government, and employing, or to use a more accurate phrase, working the more able-bodied. Alternatively, they live as detribalised outcasts in the territory that all their traditional lore tells them to be the birthright of their ancestors.

Even in the Arnhem Land Reserve, the Aboriginal population had greatly decreased and large tracts of country are now completely depopulated. An example may be seen at Blue Mud Bay. There were formerly eight clans in occupation of the surrounding territory, including Woodah Island. By 1935, two of these clans were extinct, and all the others below strength, so that it could fairly be stated that the Dhayyi-speaking peoples were already at least three-eighths of the way to extinction.

It is generally assumed that north-east Arnhem Land carried a very large population. Yet as a result of the patrols, in which I made contact with the great majority of the population in this area, I concluded that including Groote and Bickerton Island, there were no more than one thousand, five hundred men, women and children in the entire area.

In June 1935 I had not seen an Aboriginal camp between the mouth of the Roper River and Bennet Bay. I estimated the population of this tract of country to be approximately one hundred and fifty, of whom about ninety were in the camp at Bennet Bay at the time of my visit. The Groote and Bickerton Islanders who speak one language and who constitute a single tribe, the Ingura, number about two hundred and fifty. There were approximately two hundred and twenty-five people in the Blue Mud Bay area. Most of these I had seen at the big camp at Matarawatj from which centre they dispersed to hunt over the surrounding territory. This was much the largest camp that I encountered anywhere in Northern Australia. I estimated the total population of the Caledon Bay district including Trial Bay, and Caledon Bay itself, at not more than two hundred. After leaving Caledon Bay there was only one large group of Aborigines on the northern coastline, east of the Crocodile Islands; at the time of my visit most of these people were in the vicinity of the English Company's Islands, and I assessed their numbers at not more than one hundred and fifty. There were probably about four hundred people in the vicinity of the Crocodile Islands and the Goyder River district, east of Cape Stewart; this figure includes members of numerous small clans from Elcho Island, Buckingham Bay, and the neighbouring areas, who went to Milingimbi when the Methodist Mission was moved there from Elcho Island in 1923.

Finally there is the small nomadic population, chiefly of the Ritharrngu and Waagilak groups, that wanders from the head of the Goyder River to the head of the Walker, and thence to the Roper River. I assessed the number of these people at not more than a hundred.

While the total figure must be regarded as approximate only, as even in large camps people are constantly coming and going so that exact enumeration is difficult, it gives a fair estimate of the numbers and is substantially lower than other estimates hitherto made, which have been arrived at by guess work.

Nunggubuyu and neighbouring peoples, occupying territory from Phelp River to Bennet Bay	150
Ingura of Groote Eylandt and Bickerton Island	250
Dhayyi-speaking peoples of Blue Mud Bay	225
Trial and Caledon Bays	200
English Company's Islands	150
Crocodile Islands and Goyder River district (east of Cape Stewart, including peoples from Elcho Island district, now at Mission)	400
Interior groups of Eastern Arnhem Land	100
Total figure	1475

Although at Blue Mud Bay, Trial Bay and in the English Company's Islands, children were numerous in the camps, I noticed they grew progressively less so with the approach to the fringe of civilisation. Therefore, if an attempt was to be made to preserve these people immediate steps had to be taken to safeguard them – not merely by leaving them in occupation of their territory, but since harmful contacts have already been permitted and have created such havoc on the coast, by taking positive steps to preserve their culture intact. I was convinced, by my experience in the field, and after examination of the factors that have led to the reduction of the population of Australia to its present level, that this could be done only by preserving the nicely balanced organisation upon which Aboriginal culture stands. Attempts to modify the social organisation and ceremonial life result in disintegration and destruction. I was to suggest that the retention of the whole culture be adopted as a policy in the administration of these people at least until the fate of the detribalised, and semi-detribalised, has been settled by the establishment of a settled policy. Each year, under the existing conditions, adds to the difficulty of preserving the culture of the few remaining tribes.

A female pubic covering made from plant fibre and possum fur string.

Most of the projects that have so far been advanced for dealing with Aborigines assume at once that their culture is to be destroyed; they aim vaguely at 'betterment' of the people and depend largely upon setting them up in agricultural communities. It is also generally assumed that their food supplies are inadequate, and that the necessity of gathering their own foods inflicts hardship upon them.

But as I now knew from my patrols there is an abundance of food available throughout Arnhem Land, and in fact, the food resources in this area are sufficient to support a population much larger than the one now in occupation. Moreover, it had been proved conclusively that they cannot be converted into gardeners, although they can be compelled, by bribery or force, to work in gardens under the supervision of others. The fact must be stressed that the difference between a nomadic race with its peculiar and specialised adaptations and social organisation, and a gardening people, with an established village life, is more than a matter of environment, it depends upon deeper factors, and has a definite psychological basis. This fact has long been recognised in countries where enlightened methods of dealing with the indigenous population are practised.

Another almost invariable assumption is that the first essential in dealing with Australian Aborigines is to curtail their wanderings, to settle them either in a compound or an institution, or to remove their children from their custody to these places in order that they shall grow up without any knowledge of the life and customs of their own people. Except for more or less casual work on stations there are no industries that could absorb the product of these institutions but, deprived of their own culture, out of touch with their own people, and despised by the majority of the white population, they become dependents of the cattle station, or cadgers on the fringe of civilisation. This is an exact picture of what is to be seen today in most settled parts of the Northern Territory, and in the far north of Queensland. Every 'useful' Aboriginal employed casually on a cattle station has involved under the present system, the ultimate degradation of many, who live in a state of beggary. It can truly be said that the road to progress of the white man in the Northern Territory is paved with the tombstones of the Aborigines.

I therefore concluded that the essential basis for an enlightened policy was:

1   Absolute segregation within the Arnhem Land Reserve to preserve the social structure *in toto* as an essential factor in the lives of the people
2   Acceptance of the nomadic habits of these people as an integral part of their culture. As they live extensively, rather than intensively, their seasonal movements enable them to draw fully upon the resources of their territories. The collecting of people into compounds or institutions should be prohibited. If it is desired to teach Christianity to these people it should be insisted that the Christian teacher or missionary be prepared to visit the people in their own country, and not to gather them about a station or mission school.
3   The establishment and maintenance of patrols to move among the Arnhem Landers to protect them from interference and exploitation, and to maintain a state of domestic peace. Many of the 'attacks' that have occurred in

this territory have undoubtedly been merely retaliatory measures to which the people have been goaded. A particularly unfortunate aspect of these incidents is the fact that vengeance may sometimes be delayed and fall ultimately upon an entirely innocent individual.

Such patrols should be entrusted only to men who are fitted temperamentally as well as by their special qualifications for the work. They should receive at least a thorough elementary training in anthropology and in the application of anthropological methods. They should be 'Protectors' in the true sense of the word.

4   The employment of a qualified medical officer to work exclusively among these people is essential. By this means a systematic attempt may be instituted to eliminate leprosy, yaws, and acquired diseases introduced since alien occupation of the country.

5   Abolition of the present anomalous system under which police constables act as 'Protectors' of Aborigines.

6   Adoption of a settled, uniform policy for the treatment of the whole of the Aboriginal population of Australia.

7   Immediate establishment of a Department of Native Affairs staffed by men selected solely for their special qualifications and sympathies for dealing with Aborigines and for controlling the organisation outlined above.

I felt that in the evolution of any policy aiming at the preservation of the remnant of the tribes of Arnhem Land, absolute segregation must be regarded as essential. Not only has it been shown that their culture cannot withstand the contact with advanced culture, but falls into decline. Further it is also well known that these people have no racial immunity to white man's diseases and that they succumb in great numbers to epidemic diseases which are of comparatively minor importance among Europeans. From the point of view both of culture and of health, segregation is necessary to the survival of the Aborigines.

I felt it was unjust and wrong for the Government that assumes control over this territory to permit any form of interference with, or exploitation of, the Aboriginal population, without first making a cultural survey of the region and establishing a permanent patrol to administer justice and to safeguard the people's interests

In particular, I pointed out that in recent years trepang or *bêche-de-mer* fishing had been carried on as far afield as Caledon Bay, without steps having been

Fred Gray, who was active along the east coast of Arnhem Land as a trepanger during the 1930s and was in the area at the time of the killings. In 1938 he opened a settlement on Groote Eylandt in Port Langdon due south of the flying boat base established there in the same year.

taken to protect the people or to prevent friction – following Aboriginal resentment at what they naturally regard as the trespass upon their rights. Nor has any attempt to prevent exploitation been made, although the fact is well known that the alien crews of these vessels have been using the people of this Reserve in their operations. Little explanation is needed for the trouble that has occurred, and there is no doubt that unless proper control is assumed, trouble will reoccur.

During the past season a trepanger, Mr F. Gray, again operated on the Arnhem Land coast, within the Reserve, and also on the coast of Groote Eylandt.

The presence of such casual visitors along the coast, who exploit the Aborigines without any control or supervision, is a source of irritation and of temptation to them. I drew the Minister's attention to these facts and stated that the presence of Mr Gray on the Reserve at this time was not in the best interests of the Aborigines. Mr Gray has assumed an unwarranted authority over the camps at which he has worked, friction has recently taken place and a serious situation may arise at any time.

I also drew attention to the disabilities, and gross injustice to which the Aborigines are subject under the present system of administration of native affairs, in the Northern Territory. Nowhere was this more evident than in the valley of the Roper River.

The anomaly of the situation in this area was brought home to me by the fact that whereas the European has taken the ancestral lands of the Aborigines, and left them as hangers-on in their own territories, by stocking the country and driving out the native game and assuming control of the water holes and billabongs, he has taken upon himself the right to poison or shoot the majority of the natives' hunting dogs. Thus while the Aborigines may not kill any of the Europeans animals, the European freely kills any native game as well as his own cattle.

The culmination of this injustice occurs at Urapunga Station on the Roper River, where the lessee has taken over the territory from the Aboriginal owners, occupied it for some time, and then apparently abandoned the station. The Aborigines see that there is no longer anyone in occupation, and that no attempt is made either to muster or to brand the stock but know they will be penalised if they should kill any of the untended cattle. It must be remembered too that the Aborigines have been given a taste for beef since they are fed largely upon it when employed casually on stations. Such, I pointed out, is the position today on Urapunga Station.

Just prior to my return to the Roper River in November, the Aborigines informed me that a number of their fellows had been sent to Fanny Bay Gaol on charges in connection with cattle. They appealed to me for help, yet they did not understand anything of what had really taken place. Charges of cattle killing are brought frequently against them and I wished, therefore, to take advantage of this opportunity to investigate the facts of one of these cases. Except that a number of Aborigines had been sentenced for 'illegal possession of beef' to terms of imprisonment, and had been sent under escort to Fanny Bay Goal, I was able to obtain no definite information. I was informed that although the alleged offences had been directly connected with the business of the cattle-men, the people were tried before a local Justice, or Justices, who were themselves cattlemen. The local 'Protector' of the Aborigines was also prosecutor. The meagre facts that I was able to obtain on the spot suggested that there was a travesty of justice so grave that it appeared to be merely fantastic; I relied upon the fact (as I then assumed) that the fullest evidence relating to the case must have been sent to Darwin, and must have been sufficient to satisfy the Crown Law Department. In Darwin, I was informed that no evidence whatever had reached either the Crown Law Department or the Superintendent of Police, although the Aborigines had been for some time in the Darwin Gaol.

I had not believed, at the outset of my inquiry, that it was possible for an Aboriginal, charged with an alleged offence in connection with cattle, to be tried by cattlemen who work these people on their properties, and who appear to them, therefore, to have power of life and death over them, with no possibility of appeal.

I submitted to the Minister that there appeared to have been the gravest miscarriage of justice and that an investigation of the facts was required, which would provide valuable evidence upon which to base new legislation.

Return to Arnhem Land

While I was in Victoria preparing the report for the Government, the University of Melbourne was trying to secure better conditions and more adequate funds to make it possible for me to return to Arnhem Land to complete the work. That we had at least one supporter in the Government is shown by the following letter from Mr W. M. Hughes, then Minister for Health and for Repatriation, to Dr J. F. Mackeddie, in the University's medical faculty.

> I shall be glad to do anything I can for Dr Donald Thomson. What can I do? How am I to do it? What salary – if any – is he getting or did he get from the Commonwealth? I want to help Dr Thomson: but I can't do much unless I have a definite objective. I think you and Professor Wood Jones should evolve a plan – a scheme – call it what you will. Do this and let me have it and I'll walk round Jericho like Joshua blowing such a mighty and ear-splitting blast on my trumpet as to reduce them to their lowest denomination – which, believe me, dear doctor, is pretty low – and hand out large chunks from their treasure chest.

In my report I had also made representations to obtain the release from gaol of the three sons of Wonggu who were serving life sentences in Darwin for their part in the killing of Japanese at Caledon Bay. Government officials at Canberra had foretold that I would be killed by the Aborigines and I now used this fact to urge the Government to free the men – as a reciprocal gesture for my own safe return.

I felt that the liberation of these men would be a very appropriate gesture following the excellent reception that I received at the hands of Wonggu and the people of Caledon and Blue Mud Bays. It would be appreciated by them not only as a reward for good behaviour, but as a gesture of goodwill and confidence on the part of the Government.

A press photograph of Thomson with Natjiyalma, Maaw and Ngarkaya after they had been released into his custody from Fanny Bay Gaol. They are pictured about to board the *St Nicholas* in Darwin harbour on 28 June 1936.

My suggestion was accepted and an order was given for the release into my custody of Natjiyalma, Maaw and Ngarkaya. In order to avoid the risk of possible recurrence of the incident that occurred when Dhaakiyarr was released, I made a visit to the gaol on the day preceding my departure, to establish myself on a friendly footing with the prisoners. I arranged with the Police Department to provide me with a car on the following morning to take the men directly to the boat. There Raywala, the Mildjingi clansman who had accompanied me on the overland patrol to Blue Mud Bay was waiting.

We left that morning, Sunday 28th June 1936. We took with us, too, to return to their own country near Milingimbi, eight other Aborigines – three men, three women and two children – some of the many who were then living derelict on the city's fringe, having walked in, some from three or four hundred

Looking south-west across the mouth of the Glyde River in the general direction of Gaarttji lagoon, where Thomson was to spend some of his most productive research time during this return visit. Gaarttji is just beyond the right-hand edge of the picture in the area where the two hunting fires can be seen. The Glyde River drains the Arafura Swamp, which lies off to the left hand side of the photograph. The open areas in the foreground are tidal salt flats edged with mangroves.

miles away, just to see Darwin. This was a symptom of the unrest, due to outside influences, which was having a very disturbing influence on the people of Arnhem Land.

We sailed first to the eastern side of the Van Diemen Gulf, to visit the Oenpelli area, on the East Alligator River, where I wanted to see the rock paintings. These are in caves high up on a rocky hill, which must have been the wet season refuge of Aborigines for countless hundreds of years. They were used too as burial places – under many of the ledges were scattered bones, some still with the bark or baskets that had held them.

The paintings were the most extraordinary I had seen – mammals, fish, lizards, snakes – including a fine picture of a fish seized in the talons of two sea eagles, showing that the artists drew upon their memories for incidents as well as for individual animals. Fish predominated, particularly barramundi: one of the biggest and best paintings showed a small fish inside a large one.

Here too I saw, under the over-hang of the rocks, little hollows, perfectly smooth, even and symmetrical, in which the pigments used in the figures on the walls and the roof had been ground and pulverised.

In one of the caves a wallaby (*Phascogale*) was actively hunting for insects and especially spiders. It was extraordinarily alert, running nimbly over the rocks in the dim light and jumping several inches into the air to snap up insects and spiders from the rock face above.

On our way across the Cobourg Peninsula to rejoin the *St Nicholas* and sail to Goulburn Island I camped with my carriers near a swamp where buffalo tracks were plentiful. As we lay down to sleep under some stunted trees one of them looked up at the tree above him and observed: 'Suppose buffalo come, this one belong me; I go climb up'. This led to a talk on their adventures with buffalo and Raywala told me that a man had been killed by a buffalo while out hunting on the Goyder some months earlier. He told me that although metal shovel-nosed spears were sometimes used for hunting buffalo, they preferred the stone head spears because they made a greater wound and caused such a loss of blood.

After about a week at the mission on Goulburn Island, studying the social organisation of the local tribes – Maung, Gunwinggu and Iwaidja – I worked down the coast. Leaving the eight people at Milingimbi, where I planned to establish a base, I went on to Yirrkala Mission which Wonggu was visiting at the time and returned his three sons to him.

During my absence in the South a raid on the Blue Mud Bay people, result-ing in the killing of two men and two women, had been carried out by a man of the Wangurri clan. This was Bindjarrpuma, known as 'Slippery', who, years before, had been with a police party in Arnhem Land and who now lived the life of a semi-outlaw with a large group of followers in the rugged country behind Arnhem Bay. I determined to find Bindjarrpuma and to try to discover the root of the trouble. At first I had difficulty in getting enough carriers for all were

opposite, top: Bindjarrpuma (on the right), a man of the Wanguri clan and the actual brother of Harry Makarrwala, who was central to the inter-clan feuding taking place in the late 1930s in eastern Arnhem Land. On the left is Banggaliwuy , a Djambarrpuyngu man.

opposite, bottom: Barratjuna, Mawalan, Wonggu and Baldarrpingu making rope for turtle and dugong hunting. The rope is made from the inner bark of the kurrajong (*Brachychiton* sp.). Wonggu told Thomson that the technique was acquired from Macassans.

Wurrguluma, a
daughter of
Wonggu's,
with her eldest
daughter Maliny.

frightened of venturing into his country as he had threatened to spear anyone,
Aboriginal or European, who approached him. But on the 15th August, the day
before we were due to leave Yirrkala, Wonggu's second son, Djeriny agreed to
come and immediately I had a number of volunteers. In the end I set out with
ten men of whom five were sons of Wonggu – besides Djeriny there was Maaw,
Wuluwirr, Mawunbuy and Matuwa – and a sixth, Gunuyuma, an adopted son
'grown up' by Wonggu. Others in the party were Raywala, Naanyin, Matjirri,
the wife of Raywala, the wife of Munguyama, two wives of Djeriny, and several
children. Our guide was Dhanyotjati, a youth from Bindjarrpuma's group, who
had come into the mission recently.

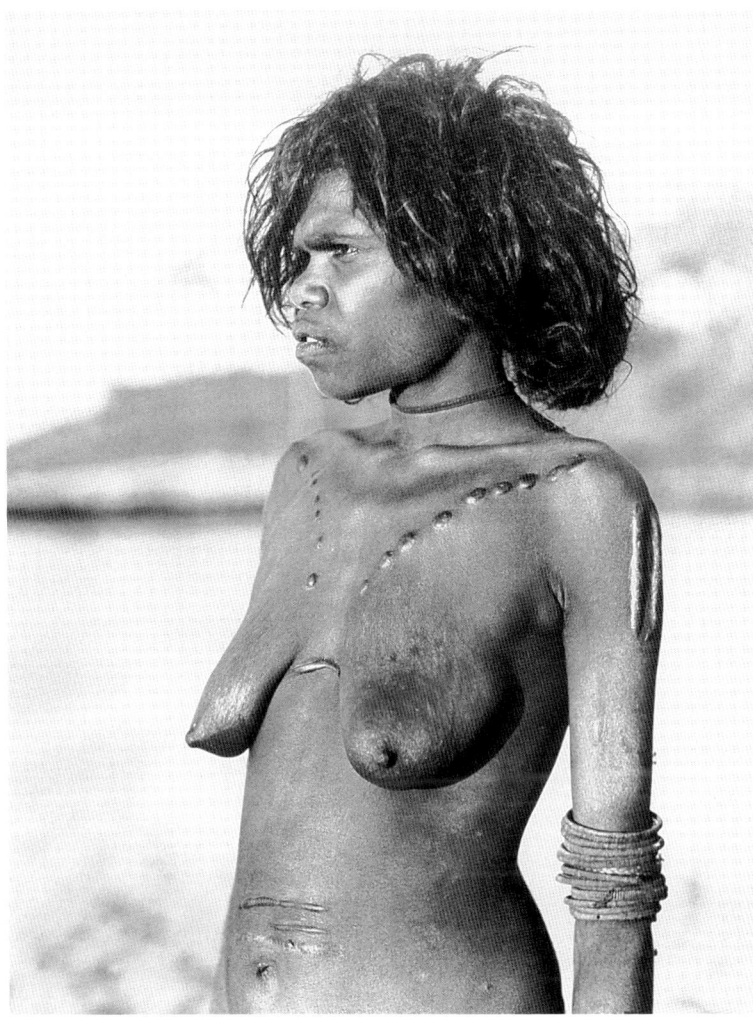

Gapita, a daughter
of Wonggu's.

As we left, old Wonggu broke into loud, broken wailing for his sons – 'My
children have all again left me'. It was not just ritual weeping. There was very
real grief and fear in the lamentation. I began to get anxious for I knew it would
not take much to put the party off the journey.

To the south of Arnhem Bay we picked up the tracks which subsequently
proved to be those of Bindjarrpuma and his group. When their camp site was
located, however, we found they had recently cut out a large canoe which they
had used to move westward, across towards Buckingham Bay. As following
them on foot would have involved swimming several large rivers, which was
dangerous, even with a large party of carriers, I returned to Yirrkala via Port

Bradshaw to wait for the *St Nicholas*, which was away on a store trip to Darwin.

Wonggu was still there so I called on him during August 27th and found him with four of his wives; when they saw us weary travellers they started wailing, beating their bodies with their hands and crying out.

They saw the sweat on our chests, our foreheads, our legs and our arms – they knew it had been a long, hard journey and they struck their bodies to hurt themselves so as to share our hardships through their pain. The expression was ritual but the feeling was real.

While waiting for the return of the *St Nicholas* I continued with injections for yaws to a number of babies and children, chiefly Wonggu's children and grandchildren. The old man was induced to muster those with sores and with much screaming and kicking we got the job done. As I have said, the treatment of yaws is one of the most satisfactory things one can do for the children, as the results are so quick and sure. In the following days I worked mainly on kinship and behaviour, including taking Wonggu's genealogy, established a colony of five mosaic-tailed rats (*Melomys*) and was taming a pair of possums in the hope I could take them south. People also brought me snakes for my collection.

The day after the return of the *St Nicholas* on September 10th we sailed to the western side of Arnhem Bay with Maaw as crew and with the help of Dhanyotjati as guide, located Bindjarrpuma and his group in the hills between Everett Island and Buckingham Bay.

An important mourning ceremony was about to take place and as I was known to this group through contact with neighbouring peoples, I had no difficulty in being present at this ceremony which lasted two or three days. After this, Bindjarrpuma told me his version of the killings.

During the last wet season he and his group had been camped in Arnhem Bay and were joined by a man named Gitjpapuy, who had come from the Upper Buckingham River, and a number of men, women and children of various groups who had recently travelled from Blue Mud Bay. These men brought a report that two men of Blue Mud Bay, Djimbaryun and Merara, had abused one of the sacred cult objects of Bindjarrpuma's group – an offence for which revenge would be expected and its justice recognised. Bindjarrpuma also said that he and his followers believed that Djimbaryun and Merara were anxious to get possession of two women who were married to a man named Nepaynga, who took part in the raid that followed.

Without waiting for any confirmation of the report about the sacred cult object or the rumour about the women, sixteen men set out on an avenging

above: Men painting a hollow log coffin in preparation for the final disposal of a person's bones.

Thomson witnessed this hollow log coffin ceremony in Arnhem Bay. It marks the culmination of the mortuary rites, when the bones of the deceased are crushed and placed inside the coffin, often many years after the death.

expedition – a *miringu* under the leadership of Mungitna. Three of the men who took part in this excursion broke away from the main party when they neared Blue Mud Bay and in a forced march, went ahead to reconnoitre. They located a camp of the Blue Mud Bay people, and returned to their fellow *miringu*, but when the avenging party went back to the camp of the Blue Mud Bay people they found the people had moved elsewhere. They followed the tracks. In the afternoon they painted themselves with mud as is the custom of men engaged on an avenging excursion, and that night they over took the people they were following. The night was very dark, with no moon. They sent spies out again, made a reconnaissance of the camp, and then slept. The camp was in a clear place. Before daylight they moved forward to attack it, dividing into three groups and 'shutting up' various roads (avenues of escape) from the camp. Then one of the *miringu*, an old man named Banggaliwuy, shouted aloud to wake the sleeping camp, saying they had the camp surrounded. Bindjarrpuma threw an iron-headed spear into the camp at random and struck Merara, who subsequently died from the wound. Gitjpapuy then threw his spear at a flying figure, wrapped in the paper-bark blanket, which is used as a protection from rain, cold and mosquitoes, not knowing who it was. He struck the figure; it was a woman named Guguk. Two days later she died. Another man, Garrarrambu, was also speared by one of the *miringu*, Gunbitjan, but he survived the wound.

No spears were thrown by the Blue Mud Bay group who were utterly surprised and fled in disorder. The attackers then withdrew to a distance to wait for daylight to break and to see whether they were pursued. Later that day the Blue Mud Bay people organised their own avenging party which overtook the attackers, who scattered, making no attempt to stand and fight. All escaped except Mungitna, who was killed with spears by a group including Wawit, to whom Garrarrambu stood in the relation of father. That evening the women of Blue Mud Bay cut up the body of Mungitna and placed the pieces on a burial platform. This is the customary way of dealing with members of a raiding party among certain groups of the Gulf coast.

The *miringu* eventually arrived back at their camping place near Everett Island, where a mourning ceremony was held to drive away the spirit of the dead Mungitna.

Subsequently a fight broke out over the possession of Yalwirduka, one of the two wives of Mungitna, who was wrongly (that is incestuously, according to their classificatory system of kinship) taken by Gitjpapuy. In the *mêlée* that resulted a woman named Wukunbuy, who was said to have taunted Gitpapuy, was struck by him with his spear-thrower and fell dead.

Both Bindjarrpuma and Gitjpapuy admitted without hesitation to the part they had played in the Blue Mud Bay raid and to their responsibility not only for the attack but, individually, for the several killings. However, Gitjpapuy declared he had not meant to kill Wukunbuy – it was an accident. Such accidents happen as it is the habit of the men to settle serious domestic quarrels with their spear-throwers.

I had not been asked by the Government to take any action in this matter, but I warned everybody of the gravity of their offence and cautioned them not to repeat it.

The search for Bindjarrpuma had taken me across some of the roughest country in Arnhem Land. It was a heavy undertaking but I had learned to live like an Aboriginal and no longer suffered the hardship and sickness which had handicapped me in the patrols of the previous year. Above all, I was now able to speak the language and to understand most of what was said and so no longer had to endure the months of intense loneliness which had been the greatest ordeal in 1935.

On these patrols we lived on what we could obtain as we travelled. We made a practice of breaking camp very early in the morning and we travelled hard until the sun was well up, spreading out to cover a wide area. By this time the native bees were active and could be followed to their nests, for the highly valued wild honey. We sought and ate lace lizards, snakes and their eggs and, on the estuarine reaches of the rivers, the shipworm (*Teredo*) cut from the water-sodden logs. These shipworms provided a sure food supply; they tasted rather like oysters but often their bodies were filled with mud which had to be squeezed out before they could be eaten.

During the heat of the day we halted, to shelter from the sun which beat down pitilessly on the dry, rocky hills and to cook what game we had collected. Often we made the halt at a lagoon, where we would comb the water for tortoises and for the short, thick, faintly striped fresh-water snake, *Hypsirhina*.

Late in September I returned to my base at Milingimbi to prepare for an inland journey among the people westwards of the Glyde River of whom little was known, although I knew some important ceremonies were about to be held.

On 3rd October, I sailed up the Derby River, and leaving the *St Nicholas* in the river as a supply vessel, I commenced work at Gaarttji among the groups whose territories extend from Cape Stewart to Central Arnhem Land and eastwards to the Glyde River.

top: It was from this base camp at Gaarttji between October 1936 and January 1937 that Thomson did some of his most detailed field work. This was a period of intense ceremonial activity, as Thomson's photographs indicate.

bottom: Gaarttji lagoon, which supplied much of the food to support people living at this camp, including wild taro, lily roots and seeds, fish and file snakes.

A large number of ceremonies connected with mourning and also with initiation took place in several of the big camps in this area during October and November and much new data was obtained.

On 24th October, I received a letter from Milingimbi Mission informing me that Fred Gray had reported trouble with the people at Arnhem Bay, and that he had written as follows:

> Have been working in Arnhem Bay again but this time 'Slippery' and about twenty men were there. Friend 'Slippery' tried to coax a few of his young bloods to clean us up while he cleaned the boat up, but instead they came and told me all about it. Of course, 'Slippery' denied it all when I talked to him about it but a couple of days after I heard fresh rumours so thought it would be wiser to get out, so got. Am afraid 'Slippery' is getting too strong – seems to have all the renegades with him. He is a terrible coward if he thinks other blacks are near.

A sequence of the Ngulmarrk ceremony held in the camp. The Ngulmarrk ceremony is one of four north-east Arnhem Land ceremonies of regional significance associated with the Waagilak creation story. The three others are the Djungguwan, the Gunabibi and the Marndayala. In this story two ancestral sisters sang through the complete song cycles of these four ceremonies in an unsuccessful attempt to stave off being swallowed by the great python from the waterhole at Mirramina.

above: Yilkari, the senior man associated with Mirramina in 1937, is seen here working on the first known painting of the story of the Waagilak sisters. The python can be seen coming out of the water hole and encircling the two sisters and their children in the centre panel on the left side of the painting. The large footprints are those left by the two women while singing and dancing around their hut to hold off the python.

The two wives of Yilkari, sisters Lurrparr and Dhirrumbuk, are sitting at Mirramina on the spot where the two ancestral sisters were swallowed by the great python on the Upper Woolen River.

above: Women dancing at the Ngulmarrk ceremony. Lloyd Warner records that this ceremony was introduced into the area from western Arnhem Land in the years immediately before his field work began in 1927. By 1970 it was no longer celebrated in this region.

Minyipiriwuy, in full ceremonial dress, which symbolically identifies him with his clan's totem, the shark. He holds a special spear called *warrnggurl*, which may be made only by men of his clan. It is not clear which ceremony he was participating in when the picture was taken.

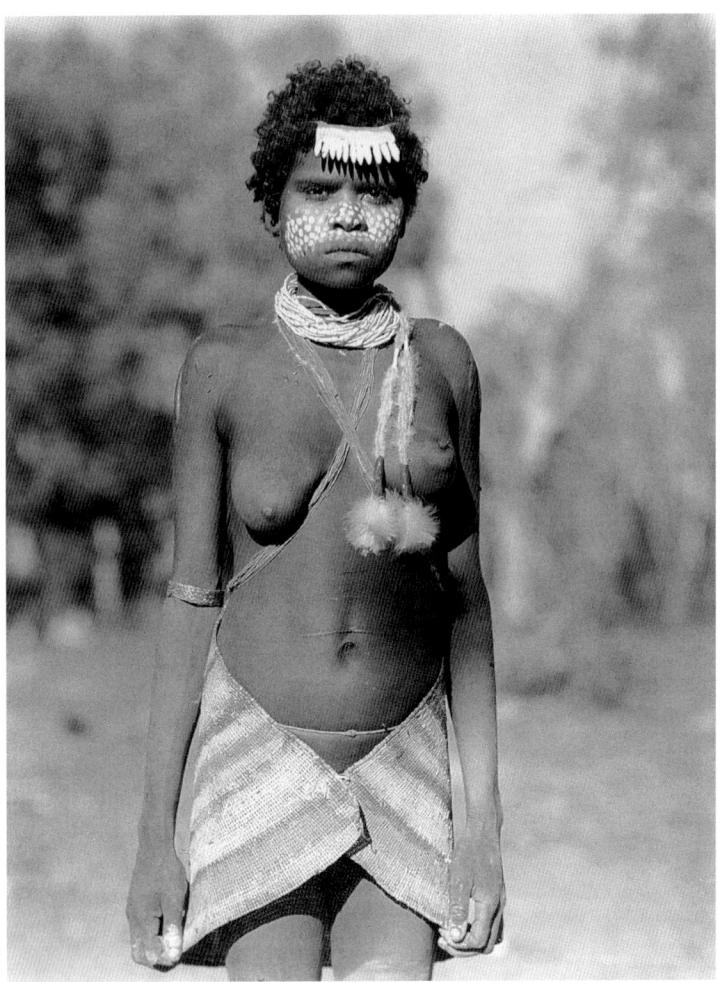

A young woman
decorated for the
Ngulmarrk ceremony,
wearing a headdresss
of crocodile teeth.

In view of the situation that I had already reported at Arnhem Bay I regarded it as necessary to inform the Minister of the matter and I dispatched the following telegram on 28th October, from Milingimbi:

Have arrived at Milingimbi after continuing work among natives of Northern Arnhem Land. Stop. Following my investigations of disturbances among natives of Arnhem Bay briefly reported September, Gray, trepanger accompanied by three half-castes subsequently worked this area and has reported to Milingimbi Mission trouble with natives. Stop. Gray states that natives planned attack his boat and kill his party and that he has found it necessary to retire. Stop. Have you any instructions. Stop. (Signature) Thomson.

Pending reply I returned to my field of work and subsequently received the following:

> Your telegram received if your programme will permit and it can be conveniently done would be glad if you could proceed Caledon Bay and ascertain reason for attempted attack on Gray. (Signature) Paterson.

Owing to the fact that there appeared to be some misapprehension as to the locality and particularly in view of the release of the three prisoners from Caledon Bay, I wired again on 1st November, as follows:

> Telegram received will proceed investigation as instructed. Stop. My telegram reads Arnhem Bay not Caledon as in your reply. Stop. Caledon Bay natives in no way involved. (Signature) Thomson.

My departure for Arnhem Bay was delayed for some little time owing to the fact that persistent rumours were brought to me that an Aboriginal was in the vicinity of the Blyth River armed with a shotgun, which he was reported to have stolen from the station country to the south of the Reserve. As this man had previously killed more than one Aboriginal I regarded it as a matter of urgency to investigate the reports. Accordingly, I again returned to the Derby River and travelling to the south-west with carriers, started for the Blyth River. A serious epidemic of influenza and a fever, apparently dengue, however, broke out at this time in the camps all over the mainland, and I and all my crew and carriers were for some time too ill to work or travel. I was obliged to make camp and to rest for several days on two or three occasions and a considerable time was thus lost. To make travel more difficult, the opening rains of the north-west season began to fall and bark shelters had to be made to safeguard equipment.

Eventually I reached the Blyth River, swam it with the carriers, and reached a camp of the Rembarrnga tribe, where I found that the man who was reported to have been in possession of the firearm had left some time, apparently several weeks, previously, for the south. The name of this man was Yanggarriny, a member of the Ganalbingu group whose territory lies in the vicinity of the Arafura Station on the Glyde River. He was reported by the people to have killed three men within the previous two or three years: one of these, an old man, he killed in 1935, and reportedly a third during 1936. In order to avoid the vengeance of the relatives of his victims he left late in 1935 for a 'walkabout' which took him to the railway line, where he is stated to have stolen the gun of which he was in possession on the Reserve. He was with a group to the west of the Blyth River for some time during 1936, but had left to go south towards the railway line, some time before my arrival.

Subsequently I made two long journeys to Arnhem Bay, and also to Buckingham Bay and spent several weeks searching for 'Slippery' and his group, but up to December I had not been able either to make contact with him or to find the tracks of his group. My own guides believed that, following the recent trouble with Gray, he had retreated farther inland, and as the first heavy rain of the 'wet' season had fallen before my search commenced, obliterating footprints, it was difficult to find a starting point. In view of the approach of several important ceremonies in the central area, and taking stock of the great area that I was endeavouring to cover, and the brief time at my disposal, I regarded it as inadvisable to devote further time to the quest at that stage.

The presence of Japanese-manned fishing craft, some of very large size and evidently equipped with powerful engines, was being reported to me at frequent intervals by the Aborigines at this time. On leaving Cadell Straits on Sunday, 29th November, I had met with five of these craft inshore at Elcho Island. I endeavoured to make an examination of the vessels but at each attempt they put out to sea, and owing to the lower power of the engine of the *St Nicholas*, which is auxiliary only, I was unable to approach them. I repeated the manoeuvre three times, but on each occasion they used the same tactics, so that there was no question that they were unwilling to give an account of their presence there.

On arrival at Milingimbi I therefore sent the following telegram to the Minister:

> Returning from patrol Arnhem Bay encountered five large fishing craft inshore at Point Bristow, Elcho Island Sunday morning last. Boats ran off repeatedly when approached, unable make close examination owing low power engine of *St Nicholas*.

I then returned to the base camp I had established at Gaarttji, south-south-west of Derby Creek in October, and enlarged and reroofed it with a heavy paper-bark thatch as I intended to use the camp as my base during the wet season. This area is on the fringe between the culture of the people of eastern Arnhem Land, the Rembarrnga and the Burarra (of Cape Stewart district) and the Gunwinggu peoples of the vicinity of Liverpool River. As an important ceremony, known as Gunabibi, was in progress near the Blyth River, I spent some time with these people, establishing a temporary camp inland, which I occupied until after

This picture, taken among Burarra speakers to the west, shows the finale of the Gunabibi ceremony when the initiates, hidden beneath the leaves, are returned to their mothers who can be seen sitting on the other side of the structure. Like the Ngulmarrk and the Marndayala, this ceremony was relatively recent in the area, having been introduced from the Roper Valley. While the mythology associated with the Burarra ceremony pictured here is different from that associated with the ceremony when held by the people in the Milingimbi area, the form and content of the ceremony are virtually identical. This ceremony celebrates fertility and has an age grading function.

Christmas Day. Living conditions were very severe at this period. Bush foods were scarce and quite inadequate at this season for the needs of the big group assembled for the Gunabibi and there was practically no animal food at all.

At the conclusion of the ceremony I returned to my base camp to witness the Mildjingi dog ceremony and to carry out further work. In the middle of January, news came of the loss of the Methodist Mission's supply boat the *Maree*, which left the missions without means of transporting stores. I returned to Milingimbi to arrange to make my boat, the *St Nicholas*, available to carry the necessary stores and supplies from Darwin for the missions and made my headquarters at Milingimbi for some time.

above: A boy being painted in preparation for his circumcision at a Djungguwan ceremony which is also used to commemorate the dead. Where this is the case one of the boys is likely to be a son of the deceased. This is the first time that a boy has a direct identification with the sacred patrimony of his own paternal country through the painting of the design associated with his country on his chest.

Being carried like a child for the last time.

top: Just before the circumcision.

bottom: The intensity of ritual life at Gaarttji is indicated by this photograph of a public sequence of the Mildjingi clan's dog Ngaarra ceremony taking place in the camp. The women are concealed beneath the conical mats in the foreground.

I lost Kapiu at this time as he had to return to Thursday Island because his wife was ill. Left only with raw Arnhem Landers as crew I was glad to use the mission boat crew while the *St Nicholas* was carrying mission stores.

For some weeks I carried out intensive work on social organisation, mythology and language in this area. It seemed to be of special importance to have a thorough knowledge of the people of this region and of their languages and customs, as they have appeared to a large extent in the Police Court proceedings in Darwin in recent years, both as prisoners and as witnesses.

I also made a close study of fishing methods, which are very specialised in this area, and paid a number of visits to see different kinds of traps being used. The most interesting was the ingenious *gurrka gurl* trap used on a small area of the north coast lying between the Glyde River and Buckingham Bay. Although this territory is inhabited by a number of small, closely allied clans, the right to use the *gurl* technique is restricted to the Nalladar, Djambarrpuyngu and Galbanuk group of the Liyagalawumirri, though in practice they are often assisted by their neighbours.

The *gurl* season comes towards the end of the 'wet', when the waters are receding and the estuarine fish, which have moved upstream in the heavy floods, are returning in large numbers to the mouths of the Glyde, the Woolen and the rivers running into Buckingham Bay. When the rivers have ceased to run like torrents and there is a nice balance between the retreating flood waters and the tide the people select a reach, among the mangroves, where the stream is moderately wide and is flowing steadily, and build a weir, far enough up-stream for the force of the tide not to overwhelm it. This weir, with one or more funnelled openings and an enclosed grating downstream, forms the trap.

For the weir, two strong forked saplings are driven upright into the ground on opposite sides of the stream and a long pole is placed across these. A palisade of strong saplings is now erected against the pole, on the upstream side, and driven deep into the mud. Against these is packed a mat of coarse grasses from the neighbouring plain, not only to act as a barrier to the passage of fish but to serve as a base and a reinforcement for the facing of clay which is plastered over all to make the dam effective. A very stiff blue clay, which withstands the water well, is found in many of the streams in this region. The weir is carried high enough to raise the level of the water about three feet, but care is always taken to relieve the pressure on the wall by permitting the water which is dammed up to over-flow the banks on either side and flow away in a shallow sheet – just enough to relieve the pressure on the wall without allowing the fish to escape.

above: The *gurrka-gurl* fish trap is used only on the Upper Glyde River. The first step in constructing the trap is the making of a weir.

Once the weir is constructed, funnels are inserted into it and a platform is constructed on the down-stream side, with a bark enclosure to catch the fish. The most commonly caught fish are various kinds of catfish and *Scleropages* (freshwater barramundi).

above: To show how the trap works Thomson has removed the section of the bark enclosure around the funnel nearest the camera.

opposite, top: One of several forms of complex fish traps used in north-east Arnhem Land. The fences direct fish, following the flow of the water, into the fish trap. This one was made by Burarra speakers on Cape Stewart. The two arms of the trap measured 32 metres and 30 metres in length.

opposite, bottom: The white baler shell allows people to see where the trap is as the grass grows higher and ensures its effectiveness by warding off ancestral ghosts who might interfere with its workings. The Burarra man in the centre is Milkudu.

The weir completed, the *gurrka gurl* is inserted. This is made from a single sheet of 'stringy bark'; the outer bark is stripped off and the sheet heated over a fire to make it pliable. It is then rolled to make a funnel or spout (the spout is the *gurrka*, the penis) and laced with strands of *Flagellaria* cane. This *gurrka gurl* is generally about three feet, six inches in length and tapers in such a way that when it is inserted the pressure of the water wedges it more securely into place. An opening is made in the wall of the weir, under the horizontal pole, and into this the *gurrka gurl* is thrust, held by a stake, hammered in obliquely, on either side. More of the blue clay is plastered round the opening, to prevent leakage which could open the way for erosion of the wall. Sometimes a second funnel is

used in the same wall but the volume of water through each trap must always be sufficient to carry the fish through.

A low platform of saplings, through which the water can strain, leaving the fish stranded, is now built immediately below the spout and surrounded by a wall of bark. Generally a layer of grass is spread over the 'grating' to prevent the loss of small fish.

As the trap operates chiefly at night, when the fish are making towards the sea, leafy boughs are laid over the tops of the bark enclosures to protect the catch from the early morning raids of sea eagles and other predatory or scavenging birds. Big hauls, mainly of cat-fish, and barramundi are often taken in this way and once the trap is built little effort is needed to maintain the supply.

In other areas different specialised methods of fishing have been developed by the people to meet local geographical and seasonal conditions.

Of the purely anthropological research carried out during the years 1936–37 the most interesting to me was the investigation of the specialised hunting methods of the clans whose territory borders the Arafura Swamp which I had crossed in October 1935. Then Raywala had told me that the open park-like country with its sward of fine green grass studded with tall paperbark trees became in the wet season a great swamp in which magpie geese (*Anseranas semipalmata*) in their thousands nested. He described how men from the surrounding area journeyed in a special type of canoe in search of the geese and their eggs, camping at night on tree platforms as there was no dry land.

During the 1935–36 wet season I had been in the South, but in 1937 I was determined to arrange my patrols so as to be able to join the goose-hunters in their strange life. So towards the end of March I took the *St Nicholas* up the Glyde River, to reach the Arafura Swamp. Conditions were difficult and dangerous. At high water the river was a wide, slow-running stream but a few hours later the tide fell rapidly and we found ourselves between two steeply sloping walls of sticky grey mud, so far down that we could see nothing of the surrounding country, in a river that had become a narrow raging torrent, dotted with logs, trees and debris being swept to the sea. We had to station a look-out man in the bow to watch for snags and floating debris and to clear the anchor chain, which was continually being fouled when the boat was anchored.

At low water, when I realised what was happening, the river was already running too swiftly and was much too narrow to turn a boat over forty feet in length and drawing six feet of water. So I put out as much anchor chain as I dared, got out a second anchor and put out bow and stern lines to the banks.

top: This fence trap is being placed on shallow mud flats in the Wessel Islands, with the bottom anchored and the fence lying flat on the mud so that the water flows over it as the tide comes in. At high tide the operators use bundles of sticks to hold the fence upright, leaving the fish to become stranded as the water goes out.

bottom: A detail of the construction of the fence.

But the current was running so swiftly that the vessel was in danger and I had to let go the stern lines, lest she go broadside to the current, and concentrate on keeping her in the centre of the narrow stream. Mosquitoes came in millions and I spent one of the longest and most wretched nights of my existence. Next morning I swung the boat on the full tide and took her downstream in search of a safe anchorage.

With the swollen flood waters and the strong tides, I was never happy about the safety of the *St Nicholas* during the weeks we were on and about the river. But there were some compensations amongst the discomfort and the anxiety. One afternoon, between expeditions with the goose-hunters, I was alone in the boat. It was low tide and at first I saw only the grey, discoloured water, the grey, muddy banks and, high above, a fringe of green mangroves. Nothing more. It occurred to me that the river's only claim to even passing notice was its resemblance to the great-grey-green-greasy Limpopo River, with the mangroves standing in for the fever-trees. But a moment later a fish, its body laterally flattened and marked by a series of black cross-bars, rose to the surface and protruded its curious, under-shot, disdainful snout. I recognised *Toxotes*, the archer or rifle fish.

Then I shifted my gaze a little higher and found the bank was teeming with life – hordes of fiddler crabs, each with one great over-developed, asymmetrical claw upraised as if in defence or threat, to protect his blue armoured body, emerged from unpromising looking holes in the ground, raised aloft a pair of eyes on long stalks – conveniently folded away when down below – and began to bow and scrape a kind of hatter's tea-party.

And dotted here and there over the great mud-flats were those curious and wonderful little jumping mangrove fish – 'mud – skippers' – which, because of their freakish breathing mechanism, are able to leave the water for long periods and leap about on dry land, using their pectoral fins rather like a seal its flippers.

But to return to the goose-hunters. When the geese began to tread down the grass in the swamp in preparation for nesting, the people of the neighbouring clans – the Djinba, the Ganalbingu, the Milyurpi, the Manhdhalpuy and the Nikki – converged on the swamp area and established their camps on the surrounding high ground. As a protection against the almost incredibly numerous and persistent mosquitoes they built a special type of dwelling. Generally these were large communal houses, beehive shaped, with the entrance low to the ground so that it could be readily blocked with grass to keep out the mosquitoes. The framework would be of pliant saplings, roofed with paper-bark.

above: As the dry season advances, people – in this case a group of men and women – may push grass barriers through shallow waters in the swampy plains, trapping a range of small fish against the surrounding reeds. The Djinang men here are Baku (far left), Bumbuwanga (centre) and Bilinyara.

At this same period, when the water level in the swamp is beginning to fall, a narrow channel may be scooped out by hand for ten or twenty metres so that the surrounding water drains into it, running to a small pool dug for the water to flow into. A basket is placed where the water drops into the pool and a range of quite small fish can be caught in this way. The pool has to be bailed out to keep the flow strong enough to wash the fish towards the basket.

Where this material was not available a different type of house would be erected – a platform, sometimes elaborately roofed, built high on stilts, so that a smoke fire could be kept going underneath at all times.

These camps are situated some way from the margin of the swamp, in forest where the 'stringy bark' (*Eucalyptus tetradonta*) necessary for the construction of the canoes is abundant. The canoes are of a special type, known to the Djinba as *nardan*, and as a rule each hunter makes his own. The most distinctive feature is the form of the bow, which is sharply pointed and shaped rather like a shoe; this allows it to drive through the heavy grass in the swamp and to ride easily over tangled water-weeds and logs. As in most bark canoes, the *nardan* is made from a single sheet of 'stringy bark'. The bark is stripped of some of the outer fibre and is subjected to a process of smoking to prevent it cracking. It is then folded along the centre, with the cambium side inwards, and wedged between two stakes driven into the ground, which hold the margins together while the seams are sewn with baste fibre or with split *Flagellaria* cane. It is the position of the seams which gives the *nardan* its characteristic form. The bow seam is started well forward at the keel and carried upwards and backwards at an angle of about twenty-five degrees. At the stern the edges are brought together and sewn at a point a foot or more from the end of the canoe, leaving a flat terminal stern about a foot in length, which is cut off quite straight. This not only allows a water-tight seam to be made but adds to the stream-lining of the craft and helps it in riding over obstacles. The bow-seam is caulked with clay and a plug of tea-tree bark is wedged tightly into the seam in the stern, from inside, to render it water-tight. Sticks are placed transversely to act as spreaders and to flatten the canoe and it is further strengthened by the addition of five or six strips of baste fibre stretched across above the spreaders.

Instead of a paddle, a pole ten or twelve feet long is used to propel the *nardan* through the water-ways. The poler stands in the stern and this serves further to raise the bow so that it slides more easily over snags. Driving the

opposite, top: Late wet season Ganalbingu camp with a sleeping platform. Sitting on the platform are Gunyirrnyirr on the left, Ngulmarmar in the front, and Guminydju and Mangan or Kikirri at the back. The woman sitting below is Dhapalany, a wife of Ngulmarmar. The group on the left includes Barmal, Gawala, Lanpupu and Milinditj. The two Liyagalawumirri women in the background are Maylilinybuy and Malpundhurr.

opposite, bottom: A group of men using bark canoes in open water in the swamp on their way to collect goose eggs. The shape of the prow helps them cut through the reeds; but even so, most canoes last only one or two trips.

The kind of house used at the height of the wet season. People sleep upstairs only when it is really wet on the ground. During the day they live in the space beneath the house where a bark canoe has been stored. Donald Thomson is seen here with Ngulmarmar or Kikirri.

canoe through the narrow openings among the trees which stand in the water, or through dense thickets of grass, is very hard work and calls for great skill and long practice. In stretches of open water he sits on the bottom of the canoe, on a sheet of paper bark folded to serve as a seat, and paddles with his hands. As the craft is light and offers little resistance to the water it can be propelled at considerable speed in this way. Apart from the pole, the only item of equipment is the bailer, generally made from one of the pieces of bark cut off when the bow is shaped; this is curled into the form of a scoop and tied with baste fibre.

Goose egg hunters poling themselves through the reedier parts of the Arafura Swamp, April 1937. From left to right: Djarri, Marrakaywarr, Gunyirrnyirr, Ngulang No. 2, Ngulmarmar, Mangari, Guminydju, Dhulumburrk, Kikirri, Dhunupirri.

I travelled always with a 'pole man' and with two men aboard the *nardan* was so deep in the water as to have very little free-board. Water continually slopped over the edge and with monotonous regularity the pilot would cry out, 'Wait! Wait! I bail'.

The life of a *nardan* is never long. The strongest may stand as many as three journeys but generally they serve only for one or two.

While the men are making the canoes, they send scouts into the swamp from time to time to watch the geese and to report on the progress of the nesting.

As soon as the geese begin to lay the hunting party – perhaps twenty men – moves closer to the fringe of the swamp and establishes a base. Here again the chief consideration is protection from mosquitoes and as they become worse as you get closer to the swamp so the houses were given a complete covering of grass, over the bark, as an additional barrier. People go into the houses before evening (when the attack strengthens), shut and plug the entrance with grass and light a fire in the centre, making a slight opening in the roof to allow the smoke to escape. If they should be overtaken at nightfall and obliged to camp in an area where no bark is available, they cut large heaps of grass, into which they crawl for protection.

As soon as the scouts report a reasonable number of eggs in the nests the hunting trips start. I joined them on two of these expeditions. The canoes – ten in the first expedition, twelve in the second – set out together but once we entered the swamp they scattered and each man hunted independently, so that the area was well covered. They kept in touch with one another with a long-drawn, carrying cry of '*hee–ee–ee*', quite distinct from the usual hunting cry of '*gai*' or '*ga-ai*'.

They were not comfortable days. It was hard physical work poling the *nardan* through the dense vegetation, which grew denser as the season progressed, and every forward plunge of the canoe brought down a shower of ants and spiders. Gorged leeches dropped from our bodies, leaving trickles of blood that ran into pools on the bottom of the canoe. Sharp 'cutting grass' lacerated our skin, which quickly became rough and dry and scaly from long immersion in water.

At dusk the long line of canoes would converge on a pre-arranged camping place. Since there was no dry land and the canoes were too small for sleeping, we camped in the trees, sleeping and cooking on crude platforms built on a foundation of more or less straight branches wedged into forks in a roughly rectangular form. Over this foundation they placed a layer of thinner branches, which in turn would be covered with large sheets of paper-bark. If the platform was to be used for cooking a bundle of swamp grass would be placed on the bark and plastered with a thick layer of sticky mud. This mud in turn would be covered with a sheet of paper-bark, on which the fire would be lighted.

On the sleeping platforms a mud base would also be made for a fire, whose smoke would provide some slight protection from the mosquitoes. So all night, on all sides, there would be the glimmer of camp-fires high up in the trees and an answering glimmer from the reflections in the dark water below.

When firewood was needed, one had to climb as far out along a branch as seemed expedient and break off the dead sticks within reach. Once this usually

A nest and eggs of a magpie goose (*Anseranas semi-palmata*). Djaari is behind and Kikirri is collecting the eggs.

inadequate supply was exhausted it was necessary to crawl backwards over the edge of the platform, climb down the tree to the canoe moored below, paddle across to a suitable tree, climb for the required wood – then repeat the whole performance in reverse. As no lashings or fastenings were used in making the platform one had to learn – quickly – where to place one's weight to avoid upsetting it.

As the hunters returned each went with his catch to the cooking platform, where the geese were plucked and cooked (any not required being partly cooked for carrying back to the camps at the end of the expedition) and perhaps a few of the eggs roasted in the ashes. The people eat the eggs in all stages and relish them when they are heavily incubated – they say they are sweet then. Then they would paddle off to the sleeping platforms which might each take seven or eight men. Even with the smoke the mosquitoes made sleep difficult and often the men sat huddled round the fires all night, beating themselves constantly with fans made from the wings of geese.

The platforms were rarely used more than once on any one journey, for in a day's travel the men might cover fifteen or twenty miles.

Because of the lack of sleep, the irritation of mosquitoes and leeches and the hard physical work involved, the expeditions seldom lasted more than a few days. Then, at the end of their endurance, laden with eggs and with half-cooked geese, they would rejoin the rest of the group in the mosquito houses on the perimeter of the swamp. Here they would make up some of the lost sleep and satisfy the craving for vegetable food which resulted from the diet of geese and eggs, while the women, tired of vegetable food, would feast on the geese.

This break would also give them an opportunity to dry out the canoes, re-caulk some and replace others. On the second expedition in which I took part one canoe was destroyed on a snag on a submerged tree and the man had to make his way home on foot. A second had an accident and had to have the stern re-sewn and a third, in which I was sitting in a pool of water, was staked but not seriously damaged.

During this time Raywala and a Djinba man named Djaari told me a good deal about the geese. They said that both birds build the nest – 'Two fella help one another along grass – one fella *miyalk* (female bird), one fella *dirramu* (male bird). This fella muster'im grass – muster'im grass – muster'im all way, all way – make'm soft fella ground'. They also said that the whole of the duty of incubation fell on the male and also the care of the young – 'That *miyalk* one, him bin make'm eggs, him go away altogether; no more come back'. They believed that the male might have two mates – that where five or six eggs only were found in a nest they were laid by the one bird but that where there were eight or more they were laid by two – 'Eight 'nuff for one – others, little fella sister'. They both also insisted that where a diminutive egg was found in a clutch – as it often was – this had been laid by the male.

On the 2nd May I saw the first young goose at Arafura and when I returned to the boat on the same day I found that one of the eggs I had in the hold had hatched. I waited to watch the rest of the clutch and found that they kept up an incessant 'cheep-cheep' – a querulous, chick-like 'cheep' – while they were hatching.

Raywala and Djaari (behind) sitting on a tree platform in the swamp with some of Thomson's gear while on a goose-hunting expedition, May 1937. Men remain in the swamp from one to seven days collecting eggs and spearing geese.

Early in the season, while the birds are still nesting, the hunter uses a special type of spear, with two or three prongs. With this he stalks the birds through the long grass, spearing them before they can take flight.

Later, when the swamps are drying and the *raakay* leaves show well above the water, the people dig deep holes in the swamp, in which they stand, up to their arm-pits in the water which seeps in, with a roof of pliant saplings, thatched with *raakay* leaves, over their heads. Under this camouflage the geese are taken by hand and pulled under the water at once, so as not to alarm others.

One man may take ten or twenty at a time and the hole may be used over and over again during the season for this type of capture.

Still later, when the water-ways are drying up and the geese are coming in to the permanent, heavily tree-fringed smaller but deeper water-holes, another technique again is used. They take a slender sapling, about six feet long, leaving small protuberances along its length and the bark is stripped at the thin end to act as a counterpoise. The hunter climbs out to the end of a thick, leafy branch over-hanging the water and waits until a flock of geese passes, flying low. Then he throws his stick; the protuberances prevent it glancing off the feathers, in which they tangle, breaking the wings of the bird and bringing it down. It sounds an improbable method, but it works.

When I returned to the *St Nicholas* after my second trip into the swamp with the goose-hunters the man whom I had left in charge reported that a big aeroplane 'with *minytji* like damper' had swooped low over the boat. I realised that the *minytji* were the circular colour discs of a Service aircraft – the aircraft which the RAAF had agreed to make available for aerial mapping had come looking for us.

We were still nearly a day's journey up the river but it was low water and we could do nothing. After a hurried supper of goose, goose eggs and catfish we lay down to get a short rest. As soon as the tide had turned and the moon was high enough to show the river as a shining pathway between dense black walls of mud and mangroves we swung the vessel and ran downstream, keeping a sharp look-out for the logs that were floating everywhere. It was a long, cold journey, running dead slow, with everyone weary from recent severe travelling. Next morning we reached the mouth of the river and ran for the Crocodile Islands. Here on the 4th May I found waiting for me the Seagull Amphibian which had been working in conjunction with HMAS *Moresby* near Darwin. During the next few weeks we were able to clear up some of the confusion of the rivers and to establish in broad outline the distribution and approximate areas of the various types of country.

It was during this aerial reconnaissance work that the full extent of the invasion of the Reserve was brought home to me. There were upwards of seventy Japanese pearling and fishing boats within sight at one time from the beach at Mooroonga Island in the Crocodile group. One of these vessels – the *Tenjin Maru*, which I had previously boarded in territorial waters – had a crew of fifteen men, so that at a conservative estimate there were perhaps seven hundred Japanese on the Arnhem Land coast at this time. Some idea of the extent of this invasion can be gathered from the photographs taken by me from the air.

above: Close to the swamp, mosquito-proof houses are essential. Known as *liya damala*, these houses are made from paperbark over a light frame, with grass to hold the bark in place. At night a smoky fire is lit inside and the door is shut. A small vent in the roof is the only connection to the outside. This picture shows Dhulumburk and his wives Milinditj and Lanpupu, and Djaari with Gawala.

A goose wing fan from the Gaarttji area.

These fleets represented boats from Darwin as well as from Thursday Island, supplemented by overseas vessels such as the craft cited above, with the crews of which they fraternised at the watering places. I considered that strong action in the initial stages of the invasion would have obviated much of the trouble that ensued, but during 1937 the crews of these vessels grew increasingly bold, and it became the practice of the fleets to resort to certain anchorages, particularly at the King and Liverpool Rivers, at Cape Stewart, Mooroonga Island in the Crocodile group, and Elcho Island, when the tides were unfavourable for diving. These visits were made ostensibly for shelter and water or for repairs. But the Aborigines began to congregate at these places and in order to conciliate and to ingratiate themselves with them the crews gave at first very large presents of contraband goods, such as tobacco and clothing, rice, fish-hooks, knives and other trade goods – presents out of all proportion to the initial value of the services rendered. News of these things spread throughout the Reserve. The normal activities of the Aboriginal population were entirely suspended in many areas, the people congregated at various rendezvous and at the King River particularly, the prostitution of women, including little girls, became the regular custom and a state of affairs inconceivable under Australian law was established and persisted almost unchecked. Authority was set at nought, the Reserve was violated, prostitution flourished and serious friction occurred between the people and the Japanese in which weapons were brandished and fighting only narrowly averted. An important aspect of this situation was the obvious danger of the introduction of diseases which, I understood, were actually epidemic in the East during this period. Many of the vessels came direct to the Australian coast from the Dutch East Indies, and even if they did not land crews immediately, they received Aborigines on board and the crews fraternised with men of vessels under Australian control. After the visits of the *Larrakia*, the northern coastal patrol service boat, the overseas vessels would remain for some time outside territorial limits, before they re-entered it to mingle with vessels from Darwin and Thursday Island, the crews of which enjoyed almost complete immunity within the waters of the Reserve. I was able to state from personal observation that the

opposite, top: Thomson and friends in front of an RAAF Seagull Amphibian used in aerial surveys. This photograph was taken by Harold Shepherdson, then a lay missionary at Milingimbi and the founder of Elcho Island/Galiwinku Mission.

opposite, bottom: One of the Japanese pearling luggers that Thomson boarded. Some of these boats had Japanese naval intelligence officers on board.

Women dancing at the beginning of the Marndayala ceremony which is a shorter ceremony for circumcising boys than the Djungguwan. This ceremony had been introduced into Arnhem Land relatively recently. The boys' mothers and mothers' mothers dance to protect the boys from harm coming to them during the ceremony. This dance marks a role reversal as women do not normally handle men's spears and spear throwers.

overseas vessels met during the night at watering places such as Elcho Island. The Aborigines knew that all this was in defiance of the white man's law, and the prestige of the white man fell greatly in their eyes. Unrest, instability and lawlessness increased among them, a state very near chaos resulted, it was a heavy task to keep the peace, and the chance of saving the remnant of these people suffered a blow which could have been irreparable. In the light of these facts, which I have only outlined, I urged again earnest consideration of my recommendations regarding the complete segregation and the maintenance of the inviolability of this Reserve which I advocated in my report.

I stayed at Milingimbi until the end of May and then moved to the Derby Creek area, where I was able to study the food gathering and preparation techniques of the women. The vegetable food, which it is their responsibility to provide, forms an important part of the diet. The supply is seasonal and each time

top: The boys to be circumcised are here lying under women's mats in the centre of the camp, each beside a young woman who is the sister of the man who will circumcise him. That is, the women are their future wives' mothers, women with whom they will have a strong avoidance relationship in future. The avoidance is a way of behaving respectfully.

bottom: The men approach the boys lying under the mat to take them to be circumcised.

A man representing
an ancestral dog
sniffs the boys' feet.

of the year has its own peculiar and characteristic products which, for varying periods, form the staple food of the family and to a large extent control its movements.

The main vegetable foods are the nuts of the Cycad palm (*Cycas media*), several species of yams, the rootstock and seed capsules of water-lilies (*Nymphaea* spp.) and the small globular corm of the mat-rush (*Heliocharis sphacelata*). About fifty other plants are also used in some form – fruit, tubers or roots.

Two men, standing on one of the many footpaths found along frequent lines of movement, look at a bushfire probably set for a hunting drive or to clear the undergrowth. Explorers' journals from across the continent frequently speak of coming across a native foot path or foot pad of this kind.

The most important single item is the cycad nut which is available for about nine months of the year. The nuts are gathered when they are just turning yellow, when they generally fall to the ground, and the small marble-like kernel is obtained by cracking the husk with a wooden mallet or a pounding stone. This kernel is then crushed and placed in a coarse mesh bag, generally made of Pandanus fibre. When the bag is full the mouth is laced with string and the bag is placed in a water-hole for several days to leach out the poison in the nuts.

These Marrangu women, Ngaani and Munuwa, are sisters, and are standing against a grove of wild taro (*Colocasia esculenta*) at Gaarttji lagoon.

below: Women prepare wild taro.

A Balmawuy woman, Lurrparr, preparing 'cakes' of water-lily seeds. The two species commonly used are *Nelumbo nucifera* and *Nymphaea macrosperma*. During the early part of the dry season water-lilies are an important part of the diet – the crunchy stalks being chewed like celery, the seeds in the pods eaten raw or ground into paste and cooked, and the roots roasted and eaten.

below: A Walamangu woman, Wanbuma, preparing the seeds of the cycad palm, *Cycas media*. These are highly carcenogenic when raw and require elaborate treatment including, shelling, crushing, leaching in running water for up to five days and cooking. They are finally made into cakes, which can keep for a number of weeks.

This round or cheeky yam *(Dioscorea bulbifera)* is slightly toxic and has to be grated and leached. The yam is grated either with a mollusc or snail shell or with the scapula of a wallaby. This is an important staple. The woman here, Burrmilikili, was the wife of Raywala.

As a result of this practice the water in these holes becomes exceedingly foul in hot weather. After this soaking the soaked mush is ground to a fine, floury paste, which is again washed and then wrapped neatly in paper-bark and buried in the hot ashes of the fire. The firm, coarse-textured cake that results is highly nutritious and keeps well. When ceremonies are in progress and food has to be sent long distances very large cakes are made in this way – up to twelve or fifteen pounds in weight.

At Derby Creek in June the staple food consisted of the seed capsules and roots of the water-lily, which grew in great quantities in the lagoons. The roots were roasted in the ashes of the camp-fire, from which they emerged looking most unappetising – like charred, mis-shapen pencils – but were unexpectedly good to eat. The seed capsules were either eaten raw or ground and made into cakes. For the cakes the capsules were broken up and sieved through the mesh of a finely woven bag to separate the seed, which was then ground to a paste between two stones – a large, flat 'mother' stone laid on the ground and a small 'child' stone gripped in both hands. This paste was then formed into flat cakes, which were wrapped in paper-bark and roasted in the ashes.

Later in the year, towards the end of the dry season, the corms of the mat-rush, *raakay*, became the staple vegetable food of the people near the coast, where it grows in the brackish water on the edges of the salt pans. The corms, which are generally eaten raw, are about the size of a hazel-nut and have something of the same flavour.

I first saw the women gathering *raakay* near Wonggu's camp at Matarawatj, near Blue Mud Bay, in 1935, but did not realise then what a valuable part of the diet this formed.

Yams were used all through Arnhem Land and always after roasting in the ashes, the outer skin was rubbed or washed off and the tuber finely sliced or grated. For the slicing, a knife made from the scapular of the red kangaroo was used by the Rembarrnga but the neighbouring groups, including the Wurlaki, Djinba, Djinang, Mildjingi and Gupapuyngu, used a fresh water mollusc shell, which was gathered in the dry swamp beds; these were strung on a length of bast and carried in the dilly bag until they were needed. After the yam had been reduced to coarse flakes it was placed in a bag and soaked for about twelve hours. Then the water was squeezed or drained out and the pulpy mass eaten. It was regarded as very good food – 'Sweet, that one!'

The people divide the annual seasonal cycle into six well-defined periods, each characterised by the climatic conditions which prevail and by appropriate house types and related food supplies. They also classify the country into types or formations as accurately as any ecologist. The following table shows the six principal seasons and their characteristics.

SEASONAL CYCLE

SEASON	CHARACTERISTICS OF SEASON	HOUSE TYPES
Late March and April *Mirdawarr*	End of wet season with scattered showers. Wind in south-east quarter but air still hot and humid. Grass long and rank. Vegetable foods becoming plentiful. Fish very numerous. 'Rain finish; him flower everything; grass long, him fall down'.	Houses chiefly for protection against mosquitoes, in frequent use.
Late April to August *Dhaarratharramirri*	South-east or dry season. Wind in east and south-east blowing almost incessantly. 'Cold weather time' (May to July), mini-mum average temperature 25.2°C. Grass drying off. Leaves of yams and other plants starting to dry and fall. Beginning of grass-burning season. Harvest of vegetable foods abundant and mature. The stringy bark is in flower.	
September and October *Rarranhdharr*	Hot dry season. Hot periods towards close of dry (south-east) season. Wind chiefly north-east, lightning frequent and first thunder heard. Stringy bark in flower.	Camps chiefly in open, for shade only; bark houses (when used) of open type with two openings in semi-permanent camps.
Late October, November and December *Worlmamirri*	The 'nose of the wet season', with or bringing thunder – late October. Period of maximum heat and humidity immediately before the rain season, characterized by violent thunder-storms of increasing frequency. Average temperature 29.9°C; wet bulb average over 21.2°C. Followed by two brief transition periods, each characterised by distinctive winds. These periods may overlap and may vary in relative length with the seasons. The transition period is named for the north-east wind and precedes the onset of the north-west or baarra.	See above. A few wet season types of house begin to make their appearance with the onset of first rains.
Late December and January *Baarramirri*	Short season with wind in north-west that marks the breaking of the wet. Called also munydjutjmirri from the fruit of munydjutj. Two kinds of north-west wind are recognised: (i) Baarra yindi, the big or gurrkamirri (male) baarra; (ii) Baarra nyumukurniny, the small or dhuykun (female) baarra. The first term applies to the more boisterous north-west gales, the second to the gentler breezes from the north-west.	Wet season houses of several types; often of stringy bark *(E.tetradonta)* sheets and tea tree *(Melaleuca)*; especially large communal houses called liya damala (the head of the eagle).
January, February and March *Gurnmul* or *Waltjarnmirri*	Gurnmul is the wet season proper. Divided into two phases: the first, gurritjarra, is again subdivided into three, each believed to be characterised by a subtle distinction in winds. Second phase of the wet – the period of torrential rains, yindi waltjan (the big rain).	See above.

SEASONAL ACTIVITIES	FOOD SUPPLIES
People generally sedentary and living in big camps. Nomadic movements restricted by flood waters, long rank grass and mosquitoes. Formerly, departure of Macassar fleets with strong south-east winds. Goose-hunting expeditions of Djinba and other groups into swamps. Fishing, especially large-scale communal fishing operations and drives, carried out where flood waters are receding; including basket traps set in weirs, nets, and the gurl in use only in valley of Glyde river.	Fish and shell fish abundant. Vegetable foods including yams *(Dioscorea sp)* which are fully mature in the late April to August period, becoming abundant. Magpie geese and their eggs abundant.
People nomadic; big wet-season camps breaking up. Systematic burning of all extensive grassed areas begins at this season in conjunction with communal drives for kangaroo, bandicoots, 'goanna'. Burning also carried out to ease travel and for protection from mosquitoes and snakes. Fishing continues to be important, with nets, 'grass barriers', in shallow waters on plains and salt pans, and other specialized methods. Hunting kangaroo and other game continues in conjunction with burning of grass. August to November (inclusive) is the most important period for ceremonial activities.	Vegetable food harvest abundant and varied and now fully mature. Water lilies important and collected in great quantities. Turtle eggs collected on coast. Fish still abundant. From August until March ngathu (fruit of *Cycas media*) becomes the most important single item of vegetable diet and also the staple food throughout the greater part of Arnhem Land.
Nomadic activities lessen after burning of grass, with intense heat and increasing scarcity of surface water. Poisoning of fish in waters now concentrated by evaporation. Spearing of fish continues in estuarine and coastal waters. Important period in ceremonial life.	Ngathu staple article of diet in most areas. Fish, tortoise and water snakes such as Macleay's Water Snake *(Hypsirhina)* and the Javan File Snake. Mundukul *(Liasis olivaceus)* taken in large quantities in inland (fresh) water. Corms of the Mat-Rush important in many coastal districts, and may form the staple food until wet season begins.
Nomadic movements much restricted. People generally concentrating in camps on permanent water.	Ngathu still abundant and forms chief staple article of diet until March. Numerous species of fruits such as wurnrdan *(Vitex glabrata)* and wild berries, particularly the sweet white fruits of *Flueggea microcarpa*, obtained at this season in very large quantities.
In former times Macassar fleets arriving with the onset of the north-west winds (baarra) and dispersing to sites occupied regularly for trepang fishing. People concentred in wet season camps leading almost sedentary life. Inland travel restricted by flood waters and by dense growth of rank grass.	Ngathu harvest finished. Important vegetable foods of baarramirri are the fruit narrani *(Syzygium suborbiculare)* dangi , dangapa *(Persoonia falcata)*, munydjutj *(Buchanania obovata)* or wurnrdan. Many native fruits, most of which occur only for brief seasons, eaten in large quantities. But during the height of the wet, from January to early March, vegetable foods are almost entirely lacking, being kauk'kauk (soggy or watery) and unpalatable.
See above.	See above.

On the 19th July I was present at a ceremony at Yathalamarra on the mainland in which the body of a Djinang man who had died the previous December was disinterred. The body had been buried right in the camp, which had been abandoned the same night. This is customary, but where the camp is a big permanent one, such as the camp at Gaarttji, the grave is made some distance away, so as not to disturb the camp. In that situation the man's own camp would be pulled down, piled in a heap and later burnt.

The body had been buried at full length, face downwards, with the head facing towards the east – towards the home of the dead. The grave had been covered with boughs to keep away dogs and goannas. If the body was to be left buried – which would usually mean that there was no one to take custody of the bones – logs and stones would be piled on the grave.

The body of the Djinang man was dug up by two close relatives, known literally as 'hand tabu' to the accompaniment of a 'sing' by two other men from the same clan. As each bone was taken out and washed it was placed on a sheet of melaleuca bark and then all were tied into a parcel, with the exception of the head, which was wrapped separately. On this occasion some of the long bones were broken to make them easier to parcel but generally they are not broken – and the skull never is – until the final disposal in a hollow log coffin called *dhupurn*. Even then, if the skeleton is that of an important man it will be left whole.

Shortly after this ceremony I returned to Milingimbi and witnessed a canoe arriving from Elcho Island bearing a stick at the stern with two calico pennants attached – a sign that they brought bad news. A canoe had been overturned in a storm in the Cadell Straits and although two people had escaped and reached the shore four others had drowned – a blind man and a second man with his son and daughter. The father of the two children had tried to right the canoe but he was hindered by the weight of an axe and a knife in his belt and a turtle rope attached to his body and he sank and did not come up again. That night a *Manytjarr* mortuary ceremony was held to drive away the spirits of the dead. A week later two further ceremonies were held, on elaborate ceremonial grounds laid out in the camp, which I later learnt related to the clan territory owned by the deceased.

In September 1937, I left Arnhem Land in HMAS *Moresby*, which called at Mooroonga Island to pick up me and my collection. The expedition had been successful. I had carried out everything I had been commissioned to do and achieved far more than I could have hoped when I set out alone more than two years before. And yet as I drew alongside the ship I experienced misgivings.

top: Many meats and large quantities of vegetable food are cooked in ovens. Stones or pieces of ant bed are placed on top of a pile of wood and heated. When the wood has burned to ash and the stones/ant bed pieces are very hot, aromatic green leaves are laid on top of them and the gutted animal or vegetable food is placed on top of the leaves. The whole is covered over with paperbark so that it is tightly sealed and earth is often spread on top to hold the paperbark in place. The oven is usually opened within one to two hours.

bottom: The two roundish roots are round yams (*Dioscorea bulbifera*) and the long root is the long yam (*Dioscorea transversa* or *alata* both of which are present in Arnhem Land). The latter are highly valued foods that require only light cooking. *D. bulbifera* and *D. alata* are grown in gardens by Papua New Guineans. Aboriginal people conserve *D. transversa*, and probably *D. alata*, by breaking off a small portion of the top of the root where it is attached to the vine that grows above ground and replanting it in the back-filled hole so that the root grows again within two to three months.

top: Women setting off to gather vegetable food with digging sticks, baskets and their mats, which this and other pictures indicate can serve a variety of purposes.

bottom: Part of the sequence of mortuary rites. The men sing to guide the spirit of the deceased back to the subterranean ancestral world while the women dance. Here the men are sitting around a circular sand sculpture *(wundjur)* which represents the waterhole that is the gateway to the ancestral world for members of the clan of the deceased person. Each clan has sand sculptures of a variety of forms, some of which can be very elaborate.

top: Several months after the death of a person their bones are recovered for final disposal. This man is going though a purification ceremony after having exhumed the bones.

bottom: The bones are then placed in a bark case, here being held by Raywala and a relative, where they will be stored until the final disposal in a hollow log coffin ceremony, which may not be for many years.

top: The bark container is wrapped and presented to a female relative of the deceased. This photograph of the presentation of the bone container is not related to the preceding sequence of photographs but is from a different occasion. However, it involves the same group of relatives, including Raywala , Wilinydjangu and Rerrnganydjun. The woman receiving the bones is Matay, the wife of Birriwun in the photograph on page 99.

bottom: Each clan has a variety of sand sculptures *(wandjur)*, the most complex of which relate both to the clan's focal sacred site and the ancestor that created it. This sand sculpture belongs to the Marrungu clan and represents the long-nosed beehive, with the sacred waterhole indicated by the circle at the point of the sculpture. Such grounds are mainly used to purify people who have had contact with others who have died recently. They are used at various stages in the mortuary rites.

top: Each clan has a message string of a distinctive design which is used to gather people for ceremonies. The messenger dons the string in this way on arrival just before presenting it to the people being invited. The man here is Gupapuyngu leader, Dhimila.

bottom: A mother with her newborn baby. The umbilical cord is wrapped in paperbark and falls off within a week or so. The cord is kept and usually ends up with the father. He may choose to send this to a well-known maker of *marradjiri* strings from a distant location – often 100 kilometres or more away. This man will spin the fibre into a long string of 10 to 20 metres and decorate it with either red parrot feathers, white feathers, possum fur or small strips of cloth. A year or two later the completed string will be returned to the father in a ceremony for which the father gives a substantial payment to the maker. The string is then cut up and used to make ceremonial arm bands, messenger strings and sacred objects.

Another way in which strings for the construction of ceremonial objects can be obtained is by sending a bone from a deceased child, such as a finger bone, to a distant string maker. If a person was sent the finger bone of an adult this obliged the recipient to avenge the death. Here the completed string is being handed over to the woman to give to her husband. The man is Magani of the Mildjingi clan, and he is presenting the parcel to the Djinba woman, Matay.

A close-up of the string to which the finger bone is attached.

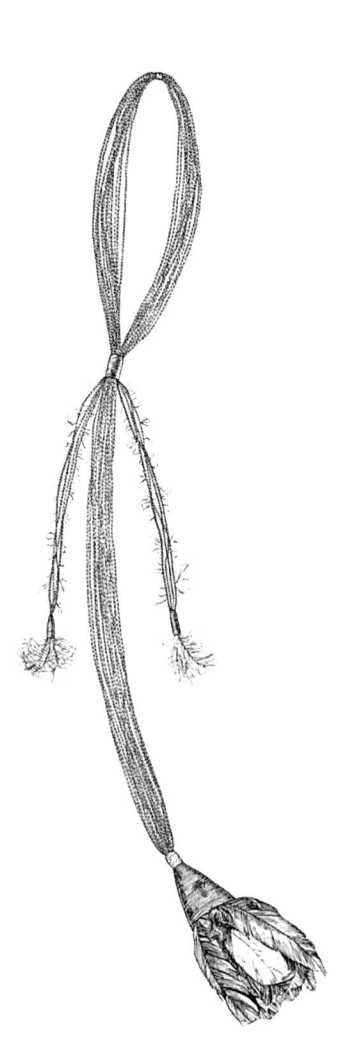

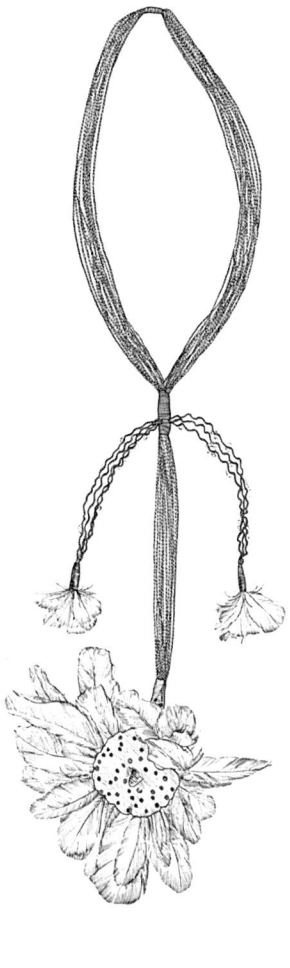

Ganalbingu *marradjiri* strings: each clan has their own form of these strings which are made as part of the preparations for a range of ceremonies and taken around to indicate to participants that it is time to gather for the ceremony. These two strings represent water lilies, their flowers, stem and roots.

Moresby was painted in readiness for her voyage south after a sojourn in tropical waters and she was immaculately clean. Suddenly I felt very old, very tired and very dirty. I looked around at the faces of my companions and realised that I did not want to go back to civilisation, that I knew and loved the Arnhem Land people and that I had more in common with them than with my own kind. I knew I would be lonely for them always.

On my return to the South I was invited to Canberra, called into the Cabinet Room and formally thanked by the Prime Minister.

I submitted my final report in December setting out my recommendations concerning policy in Aboriginal affairs in the Northern Territory. I emphasised

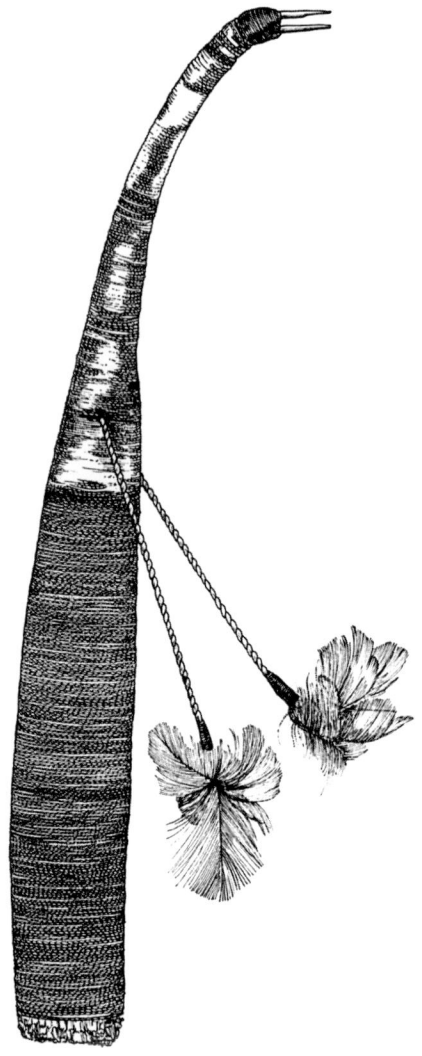

A White Reef heron *(Egretta
sacra) marradjiri* emblem
presented as part of the Wurlaki
marradjiri exchange ceremony
(see caption page 179).

that I had very little to add to the constructive proposals I had made in my
'Interim General Report' the previous year. I saw no reason to modify these recommendations after further research, particularly those concerned with arresting
the decline of population in which the Government was particularly interested.

I pointed out that the Government had ignored advice I had given it because
at almost every discussion of Aboriginal problems the objection had been raised
that 'experts differ', that is that many conflicting opinions are voiced. This was
exactly the position in 1933 from which arose my own investigations in the

field. In 1933, following the *mêlée* between Japanese trepang fishermen and people of Caledon Bay, and the killing, subsequently, of the two white men Traynor and Fagan, and later again, of Constable McColl, at Woodah Island in Blue Mud Bay, the Government was embarrassed by the lack of any reliable information about the country or its inhabitants and it was placed in the uncomfortable position of having to depend for its information at a critical period, on casual, unscientific, and often conflicting, accounts and hearsay. Greatly exaggerated reports were circulated throughout the world, and no information was then available even as to the numbers of the Aborigines inhabiting the region.

It was to meet this difficulty by making a survey of the people and obtaining critical data on their culture and social organisation, and in order to place the Government in possession of the necessary scientifically accurate data upon which to formulate a policy, that I undertook the long and arduous task that had just been completed.

The necessity for an understanding of the peoples and their cultures and social organisation as a preliminary step to administration was already recognised by the British Government, and was stressed in its Important Memorandum on Native Policy in East Africa, 1930, where the following principle is laid down:

> these considerations involve not only early investigation, but also continuous study of all the institutions of the native communities, in order that the action taken from time to time by the local Governments should be based upon adequate knowledge of the native habits and customs. It must be recognized that some acquaintance with, and some training in, anthropology, particularly with reference to African conditions has come to form a necessary part of the intellectual equipment of officers in nearly all grades of the East African Colonial Service.

A preliminary training in anthropology was also given to patrol officers in the Mandated Territories.

It was disconcerting, therefore, to be confronted with the same objection that the experts differ after a period of two years of intensive research on the problem. In this connection I cannot but feel that what was really implied was 'this is an uncomfortable doctrine, it will embarrass us, let us go to someone else and see if he will give us a different opinion'. I wish to stress the need, in discussions of Aboriginal policy, for an examination of the actual training and experience of the individual, for I do not think it is too much to state that most of the discussions that have taken place in Australia on 'the problem of the

Aboriginal' have been conducted by people who have a point of view, but very little real knowledge or training upon which to base it.

The object of my own recent undertaking in the field was, I emphasised, to make a survey of the present position and to present a plain, unbiased scientific statement of the facts. As an anthropologist, I may point out that the continuation of the present system will lead to such and such an end or that the result of such and such a policy will be so and so, but the decision and the ultimate responsibility for the action or the failure to act rests, of course, with the Government.

Although it is admitted that the problem of dealing with the Aborigines in the future is a complex and difficult one. I believed that the immediate problem that faced the Government, and the first moves, could be stated in simple terms. The real issue at that time was a decision as to whether the system in the past, of permitting the almost unregulated disorganisation and disintegration of native culture was to be permitted either in the same, or in some modified form, or whether the Government was prepared to face the alternative and make a real attempt to save the remaining Arnhem Landers. This admittedly required definite and even drastic measures.

It is not difficult to prove by a review of the facts that the result of the system of the past can only be decay and ultimate extinction. I admitted that my suggested policy required strong measures, and that neither it nor any one policy will meet with universal approval. I considered, however, that the criticism of Aboriginal affairs is in general diffuse, and often ill-founded, and that except where it is the outcome of real knowledge and experience, it should be discounted. It should be realised that the understanding of a native people is a specialist's business, and comes only from specialised training and experience.

At the outset I emphasised that I did not profess to have a proposal that would be popular in all quarters, that would silence all critics or that would bring political or economic credit. But I believed that as it was based on a survey of the experience of the past and a real desire to recognise the right of a primitive race to survival in a world with which it appeared at present to be incompatible, it would commend itself ultimately as a sound element of national policy. Moreover, it could be justified by reference to an overwhelming accumulation of scientific fact, and on humanitarian grounds, and I considered that it was the only means by which the stigma attaching to the administration of Aboriginal affairs in Australia could, in the eyes of posterity, be removed.

I was alive to the practical difficulties of what I proposed but I felt that in later years, long after the political and economic factors that were necessarily of paramount importance then, have changed, the data now available in Australia and the accumulated experience of the past that is now available, will be evident, and will give to any further neglect a very sinister aspect.

An unbiased review of the history of white contact with, and influence upon, the Aborigines over the past 150 years leaves no room for doubt that it is unfavourable to them. The conclusion is inevitable that they have suffered everywhere at first disorganisation of their social order, degradation and ultimate decay. Government institutions, missionary, educational and other endeavours to help and to uplift these people have not been able to arrest the decline. The claim is sometimes made in citing figures, often not very carefully collected, checked or authenticated, and selected from only two or three favourable years, that the population is actually increasing. Whenever these figures have been subjected to close scrutiny, an underlying fallacy has been revealed. On one station in Queensland, for example, the figures quoted were those used in obtaining an issue of Government blankets, and they included the numbers of Aborigines who came in from the bush, who did not really belong to the station, and whose numbers so augmented the strength of the establishment as to place the annual 'increase' far in excess of the death rate! Unfortunately accurate figures are rarely forthcoming, but where they are obtainable they reveal a rate of decline that is even more appalling than is generally realised. I had quoted exact figures for a station in North Queensland which show that under favourable conditions, and under full protection of a sympathetic Presbyterian Mission at Mapoon, and of the Queensland Government, a community declined, in only thirty years, from more than four hundred to less than twenty. A general review of the conditions all over Australia, and the comparative data available, show that the decline has almost everywhere proceeded at the same appalling rate. The decline in numbers of the people of the Roper River Valley, the Alligator River and Goulburn Island, are further examples of this. It is evident to any scientific observer who examines the evidence, that wherever the white or Asiatic races come into contact with the Aborigines the latter first become degenerate and ultimately die. The history of each of the States shows this so clearly that it seems needless to enter into details here

There is still another aspect of this problem. I do not think that even among those whose avowed policy is deliberately to stamp out the native culture – and I can cite examples of this policy which I have seen in operation – for example,

Wilinydjangu making a fish net. Wilinydjangu was an important man with six wives and a respected healer whose daughter was married to Harry Makarrwala. Lloyd Warner, in his book *A Black Civilization*, gives an account of him healing Makarrwala. He was a brother of Raywala.

in the 'dormitory system' practised on certain mission stations – the effect is ever followed to its logical conclusion. I think that it should always be remembered that in making black white men of these people we do them the greatest of all wrongs, since with our rigid adherence to the 'white Australia' policy, we are not prepared to admit them to real social equality, which would obviously be the only possible justification for such action.

I re-emphasised that a central policy objective should be finally to bring the whole of the administration of Aboriginal affairs in Australia under one control, since it was obviously desirable that there should be a uniform policy of administration, particularly as the Commonwealth has ultimately, to bear

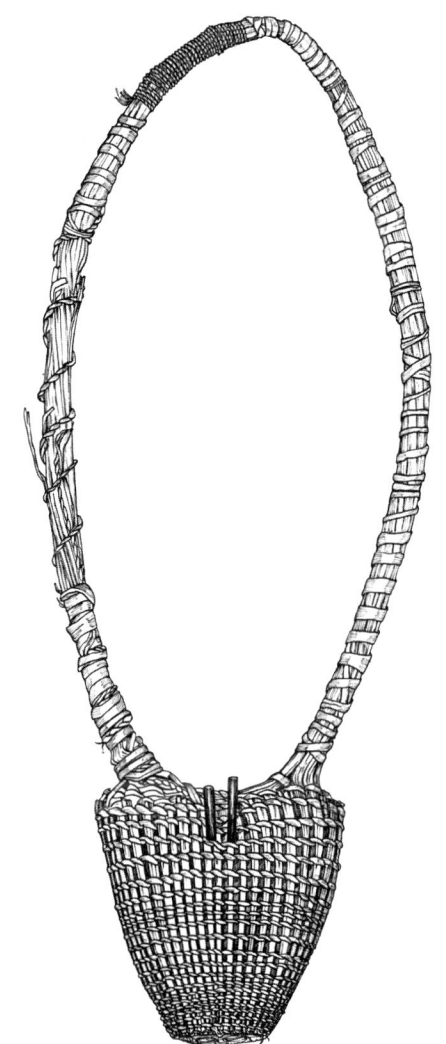

This is a power bag that belonged to Wilinydjangu, a healer. Such bags contained resin believed to be the blood of a victim of sorcery, or actual dried blood or small pieces of fat from such a person. Rubbed on the eyes, warmed and held on the stomach, or ingested by the nibbling of a small portion of the contents, a hunter was said to enhance his hunting success or the likelihood of seeing and catching a turtle.

the responsibility for the effects of the policies carried out by the individual States. I felt that the Commonwealth should itself first initiate the action by putting into operation its policy, when it would be in a position to ask the States to come into line. While the planned Conference between Premiers to discuss the policy to be adopted was an admirable step, I suggested that the most important first move would be the lead that might be given with a new policy by the Commonwealth which, then, had little to offer the States.

On 4th October 1937, I had proposed in a letter to the Secretary of the Department of the Interior that it might be of advantage to publish as an official

Malbudharr making a netted bag, in a typical position involving the use of the foot to maintain decorum.

paper or bulletin, an Anthropological Report covering a simple scientific outline account of the life and culture, material and social, of the people of Eastern Arnhem Land. The issue of such a publication by the Government in the near future might be regarded as a forward step and as a means of demonstrating the sympathetic attitude which I felt, at my recent visit to Canberra, the Government is adopting towards Aboriginal affairs.

One of the worst aspects of the problem was the unfavourable light in which the Commonwealth is placed by the contrast that was frequently being drawn between the state of native affairs in the territories held by Australia

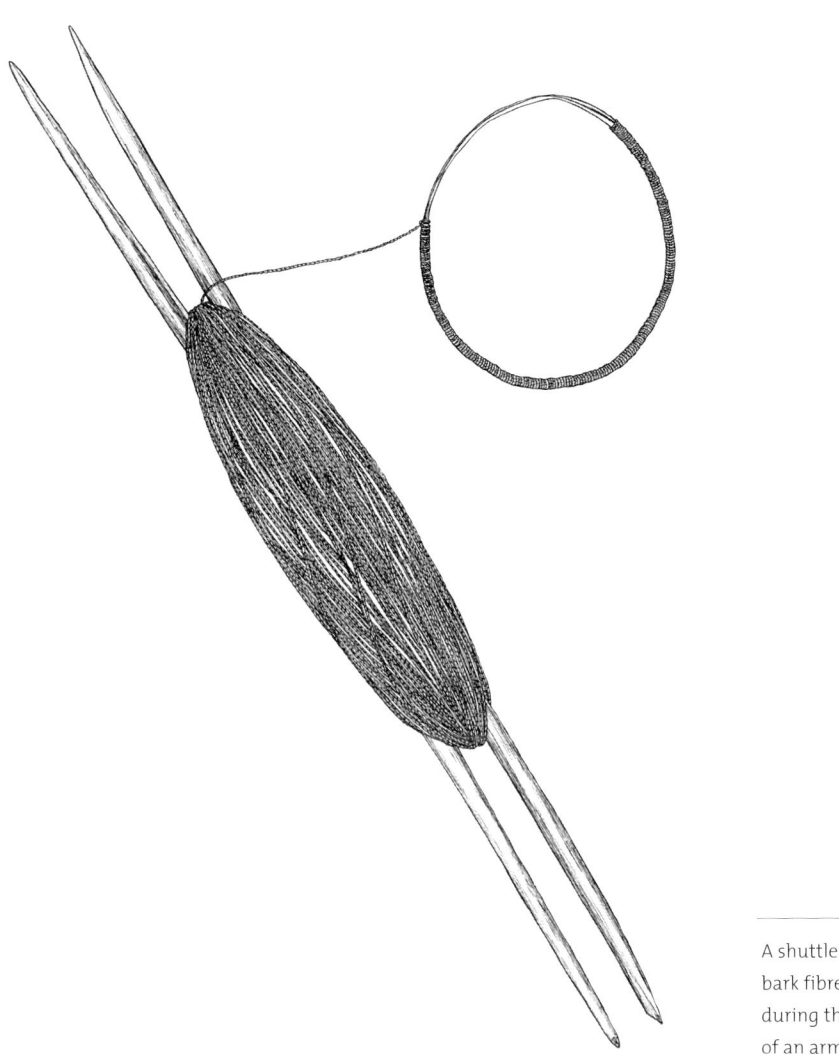

A shuttle holding
bark fibre string
during the making
of an armband.

under mandate from the League of Nations, and the condition of the Aboriginal in Australia.

I quoted, for example, from a newspaper leading article taken at random from among a number of cuttings at hand. It is from the Melbourne *Argus*, 24th April, 1937 (leader column):

> Much must be done before the Commonwealth Ministry can remove the bewilderment which exists abroad at the contrast between the policies of native control within the Commonwealth and in the Mandated Territories. On the one hand there

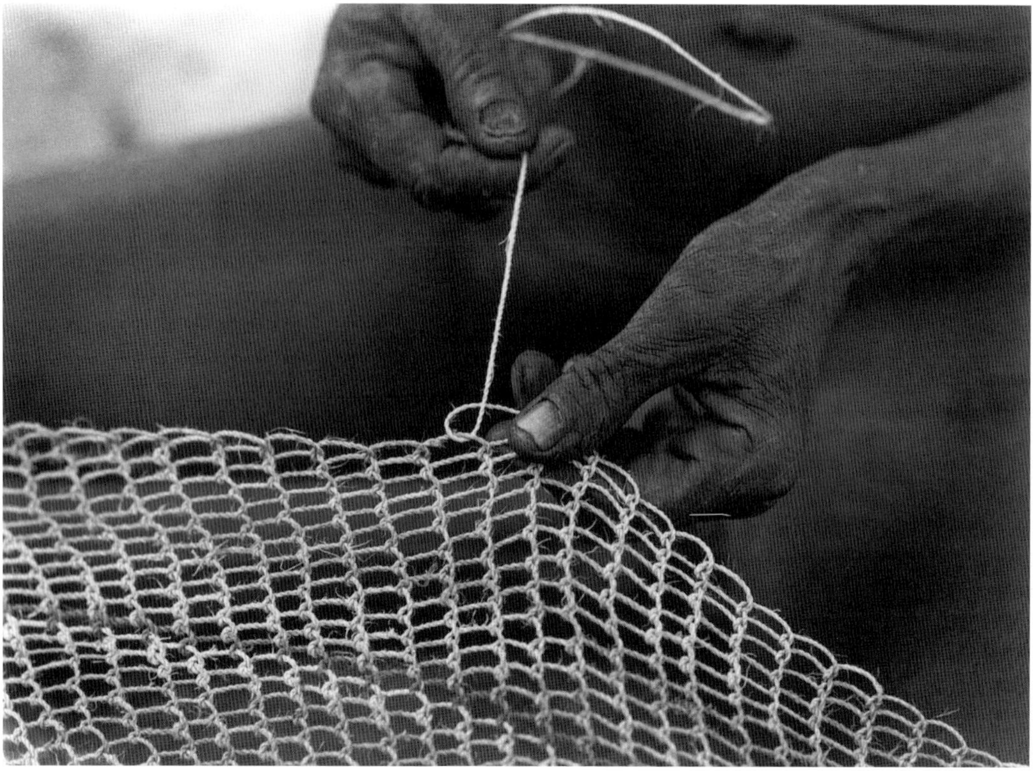

is displayed a recognition – and an application – of the scientific principles of Administration of native races which has earned the praise of authorities throughout the world. On the other hand, there is chaos, neglect, and lack of understanding which is hastening the prophesised extinction of the most ancient race among living humanity.

I reaffirmed my view that the Government should pursue a policy of absolute segregation. This did not necessarily imply a permanent segregation for all time, but it should be the policy to maintain these inviolable reserves for the Aborigines who are still in possession of their culture until a sound working policy and one in the best interests of the Aborigines is established, tested and proved, by experience, over a long period. I did not see that any really sound objection could be raised against this in any quarter, for ample opportunity would still be given to those whose work and interest is concerned with the welfare of these people, to demonstrate that the factors that have contributed to the decline and decay have been overcome, and that it would be in their best interests.

The objection that might be expected, for example, from certain missionary interests against any change of policy could be anticipated by approaching, at the outset, the bodies interested, and enlisting their aid in the establishment and maintenance of outposts or stations, on the outskirts of the Reserve, to act as 'buffers' and to prevent the entry of outside influence into the Reserves. The scope that is offered here for really valuable work should win the sympathetic co-operation of these workers and much good would result. Moreover, it would place these bodies in the best possible position to carry out welfare work among that section of the Aboriginal population – the detribalised and the semi-detribalised peoples – whose need, then seemed to be greatest, and who should therefore have the greatest appeal to Christian missionaries.

Much ill-informed criticism had been directed at this proposal but it has to be borne in mind that biologically the Aborigines have no racial immunity to even the most common European diseases, and that they have had no chance to acquire active immunity. The effect of this fact is necessarily that epidemics such as measles are very lethal among Aborigines. Culturally the highly specialised and

opposite, top: Close-up of netting stitch.

opposite, bottom: Men would spin both human hair and possum fur for ceremonial use. This man, Wathiya, has a so-called power bag around his neck, which will contain kapok and one or two small powerful objects used in healing.

The twining technique is used to make baskets and mats.

below: Wonggu making a mat. This particular form of mat is one that has been influenced by the Pacific Island missionaries sent to Yirrkala to assist with the work of the mission.

complex organisation of the Aborigines is unstable when it comes into contact with civilisation. It begins to crumble, and chaos follows in every case. The Aboriginal is unable to grasp the philosophy of our life; he sees, and is attracted only by the 'flashy' and superficial, the less important, the material things – tobacco, clothes, alcohol, and objects of material wealth. He will sacrifice everything to gain possession of these, and when he gets them he loses his own interest in his own culture, he loses his grip, he can get neither backward nor forward, and he dies, ultimately, in a dreadful state of spiritual and cultural agnosticism, adrift in a no man's land between the world of the white man and the black. It was not my intention to obtrude into this discussion any personal feelings or prejudices, but I would stress the fact here, that I was speaking not from hearsay, nor from any personal motive, but from the hard experience of between five and six years of living actually with these people – not just among them, but as few white men have ever lived before, and as no white man is ever known to have lived in Arnhem Land – in their camps, for weeks at a time, travelling with them, hunting with them, eating their food, attending their ceremonies, talking their language. I said this only to give force to my plea – to impress upon the Government the fact that I was speaking not so much as a white man, but rather as a friend and advocate of these people for whom I have a great regard, and an infinite pity.

But I knew no action would be taken. The crisis in native affairs had long passed. Because my undertaking to bring peace to Arnhem Land had been achieved the Government was no longer embarrassed and the problem of the Aborigines was no longer important. I felt I had failed utterly.

The Special Reconnaissance Unit

After my return from Arnhem Land I took up a Rockefeller Foundation Fellow-ship at Christ College, Cambridge, for eighteen months to July 1939. I was still much preoccupied with my experiences in Arnhem Land, both from the point of view of scientific study and of practical policy. I planned the outline of my anthropological account of Aboriginal life in Arnhem Land, wrote several papers, met Mr Menzies, the newly-elected Prime Minister to outline my views on policy in native affairs and joined the Standing Committee of the Royal Anthropological Institute on Applied Anthropology. Much to my great pleasure I was awarded, in 1939, the Wellcome Gold Medal by the Institute for my 'application of modern scientific methods to problems of native administra-tion'. This meant greater recognition of my work in Britain than at home in Australia.

At the beginning of July I set out for the United States, at the invitation of the Rockefeller Foundation. My time there investigating Indian life was cut short, however, by the outbreak of war. I returned immediately to Australia and in December was commissioned as Flight Lieutenant in the RAAF. The following March I was posted to the Solomon Islands where I organised and commanded the advanced operational base at Tulagi. One of my main duties in the fourteen months I spent there was to organise and extend the coast-watching system on behalf of the naval staff and RAAF, using Solomon Islanders. I returned to Victoria in April 1941, initially to a position of Staff Officer, Intelligence, Southern Area, but within a month was appointed Air Liaison Officer to No. 7 Infantry Training Centre on Wilson's Promontory, then known simply as Foster, to disguise the location.

This centre was set up to train men in guerilla warfare, and to organise them into what were then known as Independent Companies. I was sent along to consider relations between such Independent Companies and the air operations of the RAAF. With the threat of a possible Japanese invasion in the north I was immediately struck by the possibility of organising the people I had known in Arnhem Land into a special reconnaissance force with both a coast-watching role, like that of the Solomon Islanders and a harassing role like that of the Independent Companies, should the Japanese invade. I mentioned these ideas to my superiors who were most interested in them and who invited me on 11th June 1941 to give a talk, illustrated by my film, on the role of Aborigines in the defence of Arnhem Land. It was a small but select group of officers at Army Headquarters including among them the Director of Military Operations and the Deputy Chief of the General Staff. The idea was taken up almost immediately and by the end of the month I had been made available to the General Staff at Army Headquarters and set to work to produce two documents detailing my proposals.

The first was a five page paper entitled, 'The place of the natives of Arnhem Land in the defence of the coast of northern Australia with a proposal for the organisation of a force for scouting and reconnaissance'. In it I drew attention to the fact that the Arnhem Landers were a warlike people with their own well developed fighting tactics. The tactics of the *miringu* raid, such as the one Bindjarrpuma had led against the people of Blue Mud Bay in 1936, could, I felt, be used as the basis for guerilla warfare against small advance parties of Japanese. From the events at Caledon Bay in 1933 it was also clear that raids and surprise tactics against boats anchored offshore were well developed and could be used to advantage against the Japanese by a force under the command of a suitable white officer. I also mentioned that because Aboriginal contact with the Japanese had been very intense in some areas during the 1936–1937 pearling season, there was a need to assess unobtrusively the Aboriginal attitude to the Japanese and if necessary to destroy any false impressions about them.

My suggestion was not received favourably in all quarters. While the objectives of providing a coast-watching and reporting organisation were recognised as desirable there was objection on two main counts. First that I had proposed a boat be used instead of aircraft and secondly that I had suggested relying on the Aborigines rather than white stockmen. I pointed out in a formal reply that the roles of boats and aircraft are quite distinct, although of course complementary, and that detailed knowledge of ground conditions, essential for effective operation of guerilla troops, could not be acquired by aerial reconnaissance. It seemed to me however that the more fundamental objection was to relying on the

Aborigines. I stressed that it was easy to underestimate the value of Aborigines in the roles suggested and pointed up the inconsistency in the critic's proposal to use white stockmen who in turn would be dependent on their Aboriginal stockmen as guides. Further, I pointed out black or white stockmen were absent in Arnhem Land and few and far between in the Kimberley area. I stated my view that Arnhem Land Aborigines were quite reliable, straightforward and truthful in day-to-day dealing, if one had their confidence, and that if some white men had found them unreliable it was frequently that their approach was such as to encourage neither respect nor confidence. It was absurd to suggest that white stockmen were better equipped to live off the country or fight guerilla style in this area than the Aborigines were. From boyhood Aborigines lived by the use of ambush: they killed game from ambush and they killed their enemies in the same way.

Lieutenant Colonel Scott, head of the Special Operations Section accepted my arguments and on the 20th June 1941 drafted a paper for the Director of Military Operations entitled, 'Outline Plan for using local inhabitants in Arnhem Land and the Kimberley District in conjunction with detachments of Independent Companies on a guerilla basis'.

The plan was for two parties to work in the area: a land based party in charge of Captain H. G. Morgan working in the area west of Darwin to the Kimberleys and a sea based party under myself to the east in Arnhem Land. It was proposed that I should give training to members of Independent Companies in bushcraft so that in the event of invasion they could support themselves off the land.

Initially it was planned to set up a base fifteen miles up the Liverpool River, as this was one area where there had been much fraternisation between the Japanese and Aborigines, and a second near Melville Bay, but an appreciation of the strategic situation in the Darwin region by the Commandant of the 7th Military District had decided that an attack on the Darwin line of communication could only be carried out by using air borne troops operating from places such as Wyndham, Groote Eylandt and Bathurst Island. It was therefore suggested that my unit should focus on the shoreline opposite Groote Eylandt, making a base from which to monitor any invading force on Groote Eylandt and preventing the Roper River being used to gain access to the Stuart Highway. We were also to prepare for guerilla activity on the enemy's rear in the event of a landing and occupation of Darwin.

The second paper I produced was called, 'The proposed role of Arnhem Land natives in coast watching and reconnaissance and in guerilla warfare' and dealt in more detail with how the Aborigines might be used in the defence of the flanks of Darwin. One of the main points I stressed was the need to base the deployment of the Aboriginal force on the traditional territorial organisation. Specifically this meant arranging that the most influential men in each area should assume the responsibility of passing on any information to the nearest wireless station. One of the advantages of such Aboriginal units was that provided they were organised by sympathetic leaders there would be none of the problems of maintaining the morale of white troops chafing for action when isolated in what to them would be remote and hostile country. There was conversely no point in bringing the Aboriginal force into regular camp lines or barracks, nor should they be quartered near any large town if it were necessary to move them for training. Finally, I suggested the possibility should be considered of using a small body of Arnhem Landers for infiltration and reconnaissance in the islands of the Malay Peninsula. Arnhem Landers were peculiarly well fitted for this having had long contact with such people and some of them speaking Malay. I did not suggest that large numbers such as would depopulate their own country should be enlisted but only a small body who could be landed in emergency in conjunction with the Independent Companies and quickly establish themselves on a friendly footing among the Malay population. In contrast to Europeans, their presence would not be easily detected by the Japanese.

None of these plans, I stressed, should be implemented in a way that would disrupt or disturb the organisation of the people, unless this was made unavoidable by the threat of active invasion. At this stage all that was required was to organise a small number of Aborigines as the nucleus for any larger organisation which would only have to be set in motion in extreme emergency.

These plans were rapidly developed under the looming threat of Japanese invasion. In August I was in Darwin discussing plans for the disposition of the force; subsequently I travelled to Townsville, Brisbane and Sydney to locate a suitable vessel for the undertaking. I found the *Aroetta*, which I had known for several years before the war, and which was finally purchased for £2500 and completely refitted under my direction at a cost of £2200, including the purchase and installation of a new engine.

On 1st January 1942, the *Aroetta*, fully equipped, sailed for Darwin via Groote Eylandt and the coast of Arnhem Land. At this stage the force consisted of four hand-picked Europeans and five Pacific Islanders. Besides myself, there was Lieutenant A. E. Palmer and Sergeant T. H. Elkington whom I had met

Rerrnganydjun of the Balmawuy clan and his wife, Ngunguwana. There was commonly an age difference of around 20 years or more between a woman and her first husband. Men did not usually get married until around thirty while girls were married by puberty. It was this age difference at marriage, rather than an unbalanced sex ratio, that made polygyny possible. A mature-age man could expect to have at least two to four wives, while women could expect to have three or four husbands, in a lifetime.

recently while serving in the Solomons and who had owned and operated small ships in tropical waters for years. Both were used to dealing with non-Europeans as they had been earning their living as labour recruiters. The other Europeans were Sergeant K. R. Harvey who had served with me in the first RAAF detachment at Tulagi and Sergeant Ritchie, an armourer-airgunner.

In view of the nature of the work and the difficulty of obtaining personnel at short notice with the qualifications as well as the ability to stand up to the rough conditions, I had made a strong recommendation that the remainder of the party should be Aborigines or Islanders. I had in mind, of course, my faithful bosun from the *St Nicholas*, Kapiu. who not only knew the waters from our previous expeditions but who also spoke an Arnhem Land language. Kapiu enlisted in the Army and became the bosun for the whole period of his service, finally being made a full sergeant at a wage of £6 per month based on the rates laid down by the Queensland Government. Another person I particularly had in mind was Raywala, whose friendship, loyalty and faithfulness had contributed so much to the successfulness of my earlier work. The other five members of the crew were Islanders: there were two Melanesians, Gege, who had been my personal batman and cook at Gavutu and Edwin Serebo, engine driver, and three Polynesians, all of whom were enlisted in the Army and paid between thirty shillings and £2 per month with clothing, rations and medical attention supplied free.

After arrival in Darwin the gravity of the situation became more fully evident. There were reports of pro-Japanese activities along the Arnhem Land coast and anxiety was felt about the position of Roper River and the easy access it would give to the Darwin–Alice Springs line of communication. One thousand miles of coastline east of Darwin was without any organised military or naval patrol. Indeed on our trip to Darwin we had not sighted a ship nor once been challenged by an aircraft during the whole 600 miles from Groote Eylandt. We therefore set sail straight away on 12th February 1942, even though it was the height of the wet season, and, as it turned out, seven days before the first Japanese raid on Darwin, to carry out the following work:

- to make an intensive reconnaissance of the area from Darwin to the Roper.
- to re-establish contact with the Arnhem Landers, especially where Japanese influence was known to have been strong.
- to form the nucleus of the scouting and fighting unit.

We made the survey from Darwin to Croker Island quickly, learning that the entire area from Van Diemen Gulf to Goulburn Island was depopulated, with the Aborigines gathered in the mission. At Croker we found eighty part-Aborigines, three male and four female European staff and a beach camp of local Aborigines. Sergeant Harvey was able to perform an important task by repairing the wireless set used for coast-watching, as well as private traffic, restoring communication with Darwin. We reached Goulburn Island on 20th February and found Mr and Mrs Kentish, the Methodist missionaries, still in residence with their three children. A consultation was held with Mr Kentish regarding his role after the evacuation of his family, which was being arranged. He was carrying out normal coast-watching work so I suggested he move his set out into the bush under cover of a bark hut. I also impressed on him the importance of denying the Aborigines to the enemy as guides and the consequent necessity of keeping in the closest possible contact with the people. This was particularly important here because of the long association the Aborigines in the neighbourhood of Goulburn Island, King River, the Liverpool River and Cape Stewart had had with Japanese from Darwin, Thursday Island and overseas.

I also spoke to the Aborigines and made clear to them what had not been made clear to them before, that they were not at liberty to lend their services as guides, or bestow their allegiance at will. If they did, I emphasised, they would be treated as enemies. Mr Kentish expressed his willingness to carry on this 'propaganda' work, which I had commenced, although as a missionary he expressed doubt when it was suggested that he might also encourage the Aborigines to harry Japanese landing parties and kill them from ambush.

The next day we left for Milingimbi, calling at the Liverpool River on the way. Like Goulburn Island this too had been a region of intensive Japanese activity in the 1936–37 period. After a visit to a large camp there we sailed on.

The *Aroetta* reached Derby Creek on 25th February where we dropped off Raywala to make contact with his own close relatives and others in the region, who he was to muster at the Glyde mouth. I travelled by motor launch to Cape Stewart to contact a large group of people we had learnt were gathered for a ceremony there. We enlisted a number of people from this region in the guerilla unit.

Throughout this voyage eastwards, every effort was made to impress the Aborigines with the armament and striking force of the ship, so that a greatly exaggerated idea of its size and armament would be spread among the people. They were shown the racks containing tiers of rifles in the main cabin, and whenever possible machine gun practice was carried out to impress them, particularly at night when the most effective use could be made of tracer ammunition.

The object of these demonstrations was to stress the fact that the vessel was very much better equipped and more powerfully armed than the Japanese craft of a somewhat similar type as the *Aroetta*, which had been on this coast in large numbers. During this time valuable service was rendered by Raywala, whose loyalty never flagged and who carried on anti-Japanese propaganda in his language.

A reconnaissance was made of Elcho Island and the Napier Peninsula region west of Buckingham Bay. On March 4th we sailed to an anchorage behind Hardy Island on the western side of Arnhem Bay, I was anxious to re-establish contact with my old acquaintance Bindjarrpuma who still had his reputation

above: Men using swimming logs to cross a wide river, the man nearest the camera holding a bag aloft which appears to have fire sticks and, presumably, tinder in it.

The vertical firestick is twirled vigorously until there is glowing wood dust. This is then placed in the tinder, which can be seen beside the man's leg, and blown on to produce a flame. The firesticks are made from a variety of plants – often from vine thickets, commonly *Clerodend-rum* sp. or *Premna serratifolia*.

for being a powerful and aggressive man. While searching for him and his group, I planned to employ the interval in unloading the heavy cargo from the ship and in careening her in a sheltered sandy corner under Hardy Island to clean the copper. This work was carried out on March 5th and 6th, and the vessel refloated and loaded.

Meanwhile patrols into the neighbouring country had located Bindjarrpuma and his group. A meeting was held with him and his fighting band, and he and most of the able bodied young fighting men enlisted. By the evening of 7th March, thirty-six picked men, all good travellers and hunters, some of them renowned in single combat, had been collected. Only a nucleus was required to travel on the ship, and as I had decided to limit the enlistment in the meantime, as I wished to select a number from my old friends at Caledon Bay, I recruited nobody else from the north coast.

As I knew from my previous expedition Bindjarrpuma had been long engaged in raids upon his neighbours, and he was therefore very bad friends with the people of Caledon Bay. As these people represented the best fighting men, and I intended to work them in one unit, it was essential that they should first be brought together. In order to effect this, and to avoid the possibility of a clash between them when I was not there to prevent this, I set off overland on March 8th for Caledon Bay with this detachment.

At the outset I had promised the people that I would remain with them and lead them myself, for they knew me well and I knew their language, so that they had no fear that they might be led into a trap as might otherwise have been the case.

We arrived at Caledon Bay on the following day to find nobody there. Three days later we located them behind Trial Bay. I had not seen Wonggu since 1937 and the old man greeted me now like a son. I was struck by the irony of the situation. Last time I had seen him I had come to tell him the Government was not pleased by the attacks on the Japanese and that they had to stop. This time I had to tell him that I had come to enlist his support in preventing the Japanese from landing in his country, to tell him that the Government now wanted his sons to kill Japanese, and to recruit some of his men for service and training. He promised me at once the men I wanted, and offered me five of his six sons who were with him, to serve with me, including the three men – Natjiyalma, Maaw and Ngarkaya who had been gaoled for the killing of Japanese. But it took some time to convince these people that they could really kill Japanese who landed in this territory without incurring the ire of the

Natjiyalma fashioning
a spear head from
a piece of waterpipe
at Caledon Bay
in 1942 or 1943.

Government, and being visited with yet another punitive expedition, and Maaw for long remained sceptical. But that night the ring of iron on iron, the sound of forging of the 'shovel' spears was heard in camp, and the rasp of whet-stones on spear blades. From this time on, it would have been difficult indeed for even a large enemy landing party to have progressed far in the territory of these warrior people.

Negotiations were carried out between Bindjarrpuma's group, now working as a section with the ship, who were camped apart, for the formal 'squaring up'

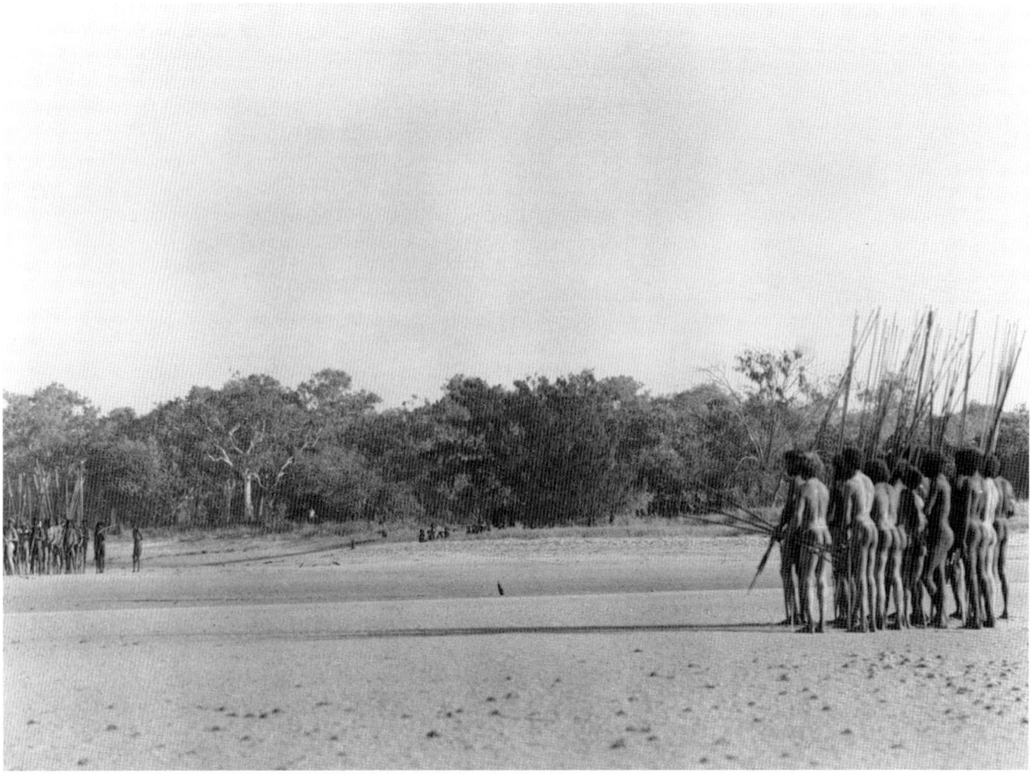

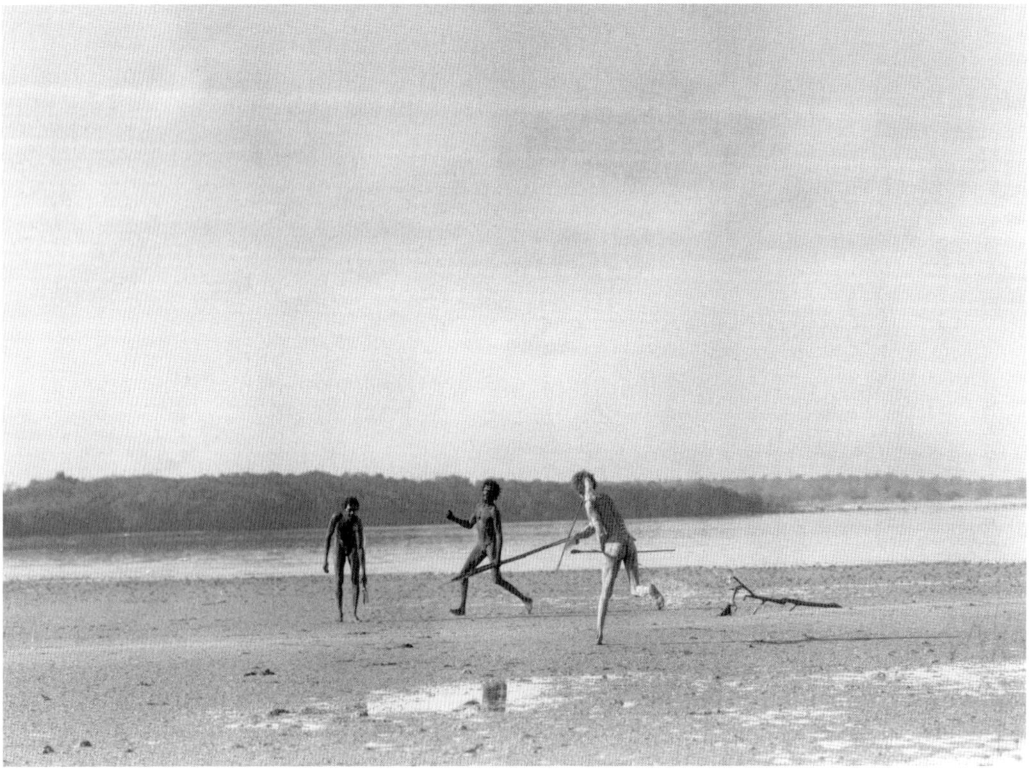

to settle their differences and to terminate the feud. In the meantime, to avoid a possible clash, I lived ashore in their camp.

This 'squaring up' means a formalised ordeal, called Makarrarta, in which the culprits or scapegoats in each group, who are held responsible for the killing of a member or members of the other group, become the champions and run the gauntlet of spears thrown at them before the assembled people.

If the culprit escapes and comes through the ordeal unmarked by a spear, he must still present his thigh to be speared, and a spear is thrust right through the leg muscles to let blood flow, after which the wrong which has been suffered is considered to have been expiated, and friendly relations are re-established between the parties. After this ordeal two of our men were crippled for a couple of weeks, but the bad blood had passed and the group had been brought together to work in unity.

It may appear that this has little enough to do with the raising of a native Unit, but as the relationship which exists between the members of the group and the success of team work depend on the appreciation of just these things, it is essential to understand the customs and behaviour. To have the full confidence of these people sufficiently to lead them, it is necessary to know their language and to be prepared literally to live and work with them. In return they will give loyalty and an unswerving devotion to duty which, if it rests on personal respect and attachment and has something of hero worship, is nevertheless very real. Properly led, under the severe conditions of their own territory, these people are capable of enduring hardships and suffering sustained privations, without flinching, that would be impossible to most white soldiers.

Discipline, which is essential in this, as in any other organisation, rests on very subtle factors, and is closely linked with that regard and respect which must be won, and which the Aboriginal himself must bestow.

Enlistment of the force required was now completed, and the fifty men of this small force were organised roughly into sections on a territorial basis, so that each section would be led by a man from its own group.

The names of the personnel of this force, and their territories are set out in the table overleaf.

opposite, top: Two groups, one led by Wonggu on the left the other led by Raywala, assembled for a dispute-settling ceremony, Makarrarta. The aggressors must run in front of the aggrieved, who then throw spears but rarely cause injury. However, at the end of the ceremony the aggressors, or one or two scapegoats, permit the aggrieved to thrust a spear into their thighs *(makarr)*, thus ending any right to continue the dispute. It was necessary to settle the disagreement in question here before members of these groups could work together in the Special Unit.

opposite, bottom: Raywala in the centre faces a spear thrown by Munyuku man, Wawit.

MEMBERS OF DETACHMENT FORMED IN ARNHEM LAND IN 1942 TO ORGANISE GUERILLA FIGHTING AND FOR RECONNAISSANCE AND SCOUTING

No.	Aboriginal Name	Group	Locality	Wife	Male child	Female child
1	Raywala (No. 1 Section leader)	Mildjingi	Glyde River	3	1	1
2	Buti	Liyagalawumırı	Upper Glyde River	3	-	3
3	Ngulmarmar	Djinang	Glyde River	2	3	2
4	Dainganngan	Daygurgur	Buckingham Bay	2	1	-
5	Ngunbaralli	Burarra	Cape Stewart	-	-	-
6	Wawuy	Gunwinggu	Upper Liverpool River	-	-	-
7	Billinyarra	Wurlaki	Derby River	-	-	-
8	Dingarilli	Djinang	Glyde River	1	1	1
9	Nupirni	Djinang	Glyde River	1	-	-
10	Mugabuy	Burarra	Cape Stewart	-	-	-
11	Millillilli	Djinang	Glyde River	-	-	-
12	Mulurk	Burarra	Cape Stewart	-	-	-
13	Ngulurr	Burarra	Cape Stewart	-	-	-
14	Gitjpapuy	Marrangu	East Arnhem Bay	1	-	-
15	Wuruwul	Ritharrngu	Upper Glyde River	1	-	1
16	Liadari	Gupapuyngu Daygurgur	Buckingham Bay	-	-	-
17	Djurrpum	Djambarrpuyngu	Buckingham Bay	-	-	-
18	Binyinnyiwuy	Djambarrpuyngu	Buckingham Bay	-	-	-
19	Wutjananwuy	Djambarrpuyngu	Buckingham Bay	1	-	1
20	Maawbanarra	Djinang	Lower Glyde river	-	-	-
21	Bindjarrpuma (No. 2 Section leader)	Wanguri	East Arnhem Bay	4	1	3
22	Nepaynga	Dharlwangu	East Arnhem Bay	3	3	-
23	Banggaliwuy	Djambarrpuyngu	Buckingham Bay	4	1	3
24	Djimbun	Djambarrpuyngu	South Arnhem Bay	-	-	-
25	Daipurriyun	Dartiwuy	SE Arnhem Bay	-	-	-
26	Kumbania	Dartiwuy	South Arnhem Bay	-	-	-
27	Yalparr	Dartiwuy	South Arnhem Bay	-	-	-
28	Bundamarrpa	Dartiwuy	South Arnhem Bay	-	-	-
29	Koigurro	Dartiwuy	South Arnhem Bay	1	-	-
30	Yirlungi	Dartiwuy	SE Arnhem Bay	2	1	-
31	Kandallsall	Dartiwuy	South Arnhem Bay	1	-	-
32	Natjiyalma (No. 3 Section leader)	Djapu	Inland, south of Caledon Bay	1	1	2
33	Maaw	Djapu	Inland, south of Caledon Bay	1	1	-

34	Ngarkaya	Djapu	Inland, south of Caledon Bay	1	-	-
35	Maawwunboi	Djapu	Inland, south of Caledon Bay	2	-	-
36	Djerliwuy	Djapu	Inland, south of Caledon Bay	-	-	-
37	Barndakka	Djapu	Inland, south of Caledon Bay	-	-	-
38	Wawit	Marrangu	Trial Bay	1	2	-
39	Mithili	Marrangu	Trial Bay	1	2	-
40	Nungunu	Marrangu	Trial Bay	-	-	-
41	Mullaiyal	Marrangu	Trial Bay	1	-	-
42	Butjiya	Marrangu	Trial Bay	1	-	-
43	Wakkureitpi	Marrangu	Trial Bay	-	-	-
44	Bullambi	Wanguri	South Arnhem Bay	2	-	4
45	Kumuk	(Dharlwangu?)	South Arnhem Bay	-	-	-
46	Mangirri	Gunibidji	South Arnhem Bay [*sic*]	2	-	3
47	Yirindilli	Gunibidji	Liverpool River	1	1	2
48	Kuninbal	Gunibidji	Liverpool River	-	-	-
49	Wulngana	Djapu	Inland, south of Caledon Bay	1	-	-
50	Marrilyauwuy	Waagilak	Walker River	1	-	-
51	Djungi	Djapu	Trial Bay	-	-	-

NOTES:

Section 1 consisted of seventeen men: numbers 1–13, plus 15, 16, 47 and 48 all from the area between the Liverpool River and Buckingham Bay. Section 2 consisted of sixteen men: numbers 21–31, plus 14, 17, 18, 19 and 20 all from Buckingham and Arnhem Bay. Section 3 consisted of 18 men: numbers 32–46, plus 49, 50 and 51 all from the Caledon/Blue Mud Bay Area.

Numbers 1–20 issued with wire for spears, knives and axes; numbers 21–31 issued with wire for spears and with knives; numbers 21, 22, 23, 27, 29 and 31 issued with axes; numbers 32–34 issued with wire for spears, knives and fishing lines and hooks; numbers 32, 34, 36, 38, 40, 44, 46, 48 issued with axes. Number 1 enlisted as a soldier at Darwin (D 178) 1942. Paybook No. 2976.

Numbers 22–31 men from Bindjarrpuma's group.

Numbers 32–37 all sons of Wonggu.

Numbers 38–43 all sons of Garrarrambu of Blue Mud Bay.

At Trial Bay on 13th March we received a signal from Headquarters with notification of a commission for Sergeant Palmer and on the 14th left for Groote Eylandt with the enlisted men to collect mail from the flying boat base there at Port Langdon. Two days later a pair of Japanese long range reconnaissance flying boats flew over the *Aroetta* at 3000 feet but did not drop bombs or make any demonstration. I assumed they were on a photographic mission, particularly as this incident almost immediately preceded the raid on Katherine.

From Groote Eylandt we took the men to Roper for a period of training. On the 17th March we arrived off the mouth of the Roper River, and the following day proceeded upstream. Two boats were lowered when the ship arrived off the estuary, and most of the detachment was then landed to avoid exposing all these men on deck in view of the presence of enemy aircraft. Just when the two boats, fully loaded, were leaving the ship, a heavy bomber approached, but it proved to be a United States machine.

Progress upstream was slow, on account of the depth of the *Aroetta*. Fully loaded, the vessel was now drawing eight to nine feet, and owing to the 'drag' over shallow areas, she had to wait for the tide at several places. Meanwhile the detachment ashore carried out a thorough reconnaissance along the banks of the country fringing the river in preparation for possible future operations against an enemy using the river to approach the Darwin–Katherine line of communication. On March 19th, the *Aroetta* arrived at Roper River Mission. The men, who had not tasted fresh meat for some time and who had been working hard on foot patrols, had been promised a bullock on arrival at the Roper River, and a steer was now obtained from the mission, slaughtered, and handed over intact to the detachment.

Advantage was taken of this period in the Roper River to drill the crew again regularly and to take in hand the newly recruited detachment.

It was not intended to attempt, in training these nomadic people, to turn them into orthodox soldiers or train them in parade ground tactics, although they were drilled with the crew, but merely to instil the elements of discipline, so that they would be capable of carrying out scouting work in conjunction with regular formations.

Nor was it intended at any stage to arm them with rifles. It was decided to encourage them to use their own weapons, the spear and the spear-thrower, which they understood, and with which they displayed great skill. Furthermore, in jungle warfare, where a small force was expected to harry a much larger and stronger force, this would have taken the form of harassing tactics chiefly from

Members of the unit being instructed in aircraft recognition aboard the *Aroetta*. From Thomson's reports it seems that only two enemy planes were ever spotted in his patrols in eastern Arnhem Land.

below: Wonggu and sons, Natjiyalma, Maama and Mawunbuy, painting a bark for Thomson at Caledon Bay.

ambush, picking off sentries and stragglers from the main body, killing men as they went to water, killing scouts and attacking detachments and outposts. And for these tactics, which would be carried out largely at night, the effect on enemy morale, of having men constantly picked off or wounded with spears, would be considerable, particularly as they would have no means of assessing the numbers of so elusive an enemy.

The men were encouraged, therefore, to carry as a full complement of weapons one spear-thrower, three fighting spears, either 'shovel-nosed' or stone-tipped, and one wire fish spear, so that they would be prepared at any time to hunt fish or game, as well as to fight.

Every member of the detachment was issued with the following items of personal equipment – two pieces of calico to serve as loin cloths or 'lava lavas', fishing lines, fish hooks, wire for fish spears, sheath knives and what tomahawks were available, the object of this issue being to assist them in hunting and fishing and so to render them more independent of stores supplied from the ship, since, with efficient equipment less time was required to secure game, fish, 'sugar bag' or wild honey and vegetable foods. In addition, it was intended by this to demonstrate to the Solomon Islanders, as well as to the white personnel, the methods of food capture and food preparation employed by the Aborigines.

Blankets were issued to the initial nucleus of the force, but these were used only when they were aboard the ship or in working or training camps close to the main party. At all other times the men travelled with their weapons and tomahawks only, for these people are expert in the arts of travelling light and living hard.

Each man received a weekly issue of at least three sticks of tobacco at all times. When they were carried with the ship, or were working in camp, so that they could not hunt, they were issued regularly with rice, flour and some tinned food. At other times they hunted for their food, for in this way alone they do not become dependent and so lose their skill in hunting and stalking, qualities which are essential to the successful operation of such a force.

Each day the crew of the vessel were sent ashore regularly for rifle and bayonet drill to maintain their alertness and efficiency, and to prepare them to handle a boarding party. At the same time as this work was in progress, the force was turned out on parade and drilled in elementary movements. They were taught to come to attention, to dress, and to know right and left turns. Regular inspections of kit and weapons were held to assure that these were well maintained. It was, however, considered highly undesirable to teach them to move in

The Special Force on parade, probably at Roper River Mission or near Katherine in 1942.

any orthodox formations which would at once reveal to an enemy the fact that they had been trained. Every man was issued with a brass disc, inscribed with his number, to hang around his neck, but they were instructed, in the event of a landing, to return these and to abandon the calico which might suggest a 'uniform' or at least indicate the presence of white men in the area.

The only man issued with a rifle was Raywala who was an enlisted soldier, and who was trained to use rifle and bayonet and carried out regularly the duties of sentry. But all members of the force were given frequent demonstrations on the avoidance of machine gun fire. They were also shown that a machine gun nest was as vulnerable to attack by stealth as another post.

Further, they were all instructed and given practice in the use of Molotov cocktails, in view of the plan to employ these to attack aircraft on the ground or fuel dumps if the enemy should attempt to occupy the aerodromes on the islands off the coast. They proved adept in the handling of Molotov cocktails and looked forward eagerly to an opportunity of demonstrating their skill.

The work of organising and leading the Aborigines was my own special responsibility as I was the only one who knew them and their language, and particularly because discipline among these people depends on personal relationships and loyalties. This is probably to a large extent the reason why so many stations owners and cattle men speak with disparagement of the loyalty and constancy of the Aborigine; they often work them, but rarely understand them and there appears no good reason why the Aborigines should give the loyalty and devotion of which they are capable to men who openly show their contempt for them.

While we were at the mission, the MV *Larrpan*, normally stationed at Milingimbi in the Crocodile Islands, and employed in the transport of stores to the Methodist missions on the north coast, arrived in the Roper River with evacuees from the Methodist mission stations. These people, the white women, half-castes and Fijian women from the missions of Croker, Goulburn and Milingimbi Islands, as well as from Yirrkala, were conveyed from Roper River to the railway line by military transport which had come down to meet them.

From March 19th to March 23rd the *Aroetta* remained at the Roper River Mission. In addition to the drilling of the crew and Unit, a considerable amount of general reconnaissance was carried out on both banks of the river. An appreciation of the situation in the Roper River at this time revealed the fact that it was wide open to any enemy party which might come upstream. No watching organisation of any kind existed and there was not even an Aboriginal camp for the first sixty or seventy miles from the mouth to give warning of an enemy landing or approach.

Arrangements were made with the missionary in charge (Mr Port) in the meantime, pending the setting up of a more permanent outpost, to send a party down to watch the mouth of the river and to build a pyre on a high hill as a warning. Some weeks later, a permanent outpost equipped with wireless, was established at Gulnare Bluff commanding a view of the mouth of the river and its approaches, in order to cover this very vulnerable area. On 29th March we set out in two three-ton trucks for headquarters in Katherine, arriving on the 31st March. In order to avoid the possibility of disorganising the men and to maintain discipline, which had been very good to date, it was considered advisable to establish a separate camp some distance from the regular camp area. A site was selected some two miles downstream on the banks of the Katherine

Lieutenant Palmer and Sergeants Elkington and Harvey taking a break at Adelaide River in 1942.

River, which, by arrangement with the Camp Commandant, was placed out of bounds to all the white troops in the area. No difficulty was experienced in keeping the members of the Unit within their own zone, but as their arrival had created some interest among the troops it was very difficult to enforce the prohibition. Yet once the edict had been issued it had to be enforced or discipline would have broken down. An undesirable feature was the fact that whereas the men had been encouraged to carry, and always maintain a certain number of spears, for both hunting and fighting, and which were to be their chief weapons in the event of guerilla operations against an enemy landing force, the white troops persistently endeavoured to induce them to trade these. This would have left the men without proper arms.

I now considered it advisable to proceed to Darwin Headquarters for a general discussion and for new orders, leaving Raywala in charge of the camp and detachment at Katherine. After discussions with Major Nunn and Major General Herring I was issued with a new Operation Order. I returned from Darwin with a renewed understanding of our task and a new name for the detachment – the Special Reconnaissance Unit. This meant that it was definitely established as an independent command to operate on the distant flanks of the area with a scouting and fighting role. We had the entire coastline from Cape Don to the McArthur River, as well as Groote Eylandt and the other islands off the coast, to watch, and to prepare against possible enemy landings – a coastline of more than a thousand miles. I knew also, for I had been told clearly, that no help could be expected. I can still recall now the feeling of pride that we all drew from this order, which told us to remain on the flanks and 'to harass enemy landings and progress in the event of landings on the east coast', and the determination that we felt that whatever befell us we would remain at our station. We did not overlook the fact that we were only four white men with a forty-three ton ship. But we knew that we had been entrusted with a responsibility and, should the enemy land on this coast, with an opportunity to serve, so great that it might never again be given to so small a body of men. It gave me fresh encouragement in the task of raising the Unit and training the people. Hitherto I had heard nothing but disparagement of this native force. I knew now that my faith in the force that I had been sent out to raise was shared by the GOC and his staff, and I returned with fresh heart to a task that proved always exacting and difficult, and often disappointing.

Darwin and Katherine had just been heavily bombed and it was widely expected that the Japanese would make a landing somewhere between Milingimbi and Roper River. The Unit's tasks were therefore:

- to establish a permanent and effective outpost, equipped with wireless, commanding a view of the approaches to the Roper River, which at this time was wide open.
- to establish an outpost sufficiently close to Milingimbi, Groote Eylandt and Roper River to enable night raids to be made to destroy enemy aircraft on the ground and sabotage fuel dumps. For this I chose Gray's camp at Caledon Bay not least because I knew Wonggu and his relatives to be implacably hostile to the Japanese.
- to disperse ammunition and equipment so that if the *Aroetta* were lost there would still be the means to carry on fighting.

Before leaving Darwin, arrangements were made to replenish all stores on the *Aroetta* to enable the vessel to remain for six months without further supplies, except for fuel.

In view of the plan to attack enemy aircraft on the ground, certain special stores had to be obtained. The vessel was already well equipped with demolition materials, but materials for the making of Molotov cocktails were inadequate. For this purpose a drum of bitumen was obtained in Darwin and a raid then conducted on all the hotels which remained after the first air raid to secure as many clear glass bottles as possible since these are the most suitable for this work. From these forays, conducted independently, the crew returned each with a sack of empty bottles on his back. Every man put his heart into the acquisition of equipment for the task ahead with a zeal that would not be denied.

We left Katherine on the 16th April to look for an outpost site at the mouth of the Roper. Raywala led the men on a foot reconnaissance. The best site found was Gulnare Bluff (Mt Moore) six miles from the river mouth, with commanding views over the estuary. Its main drawback was the lack of water, but it was decided it had to be established there and a search for water was conducted while this work was in progress. The camp was partially dug into the ground and camouflaged. Some difficulty was experienced at first in inducing the men to approach the post in such a way that tracks would not be worn, leading directly from the river to the site. By 28th April the work was complete and Sergeant Elkington was placed in charge with a detachment of twelve men headed by Bindjarrpuma, or Slippery as we now called him. The water problem was solved by two 400 gallon galvanised tanks secured from Roper Bar.

A few weeks earlier I had had an accident with the boat, hitting what I think must have been a waterlogged piece of timber. This damaged two of the blades, throwing the propeller out of balance. To avoid excessive vibration the engine now had to be run at low revolutions, greatly reducing her speed. We experienced much difficulty in securing a replacement so permission was granted for Lieutenant Palmer to fly to Brisbane to obtain one. We sailed the *Aroetta* to Groote Eylandt to put Palmer on the plane. There I decided that since I was assured of obtaining another propeller I could risk beating out the damaged blades in the hope that, pending replacement, this would increase its efficiency. Working in four feet of water we were able to bend the blades out with heavy hammers and to remove the rough edges with files.

With the *Aroetta* in much better shape we set out on a coastal reconnaissance on the 27th May.

During the ensuing week the *Aroetta* worked along the shoreline of Blue Mud Bay, calling also at Woodah and Round Hill Islands, and at various points of the mainland.

This is a dangerous shoreline for vessels drawing much water, it is shallow and uncharted with many banks and reefs, the more dangerous because the water is always dirty and discoloured. In the south-east season the sea rolls straight into the wide, open, shallow bay. Throughout almost the whole of the period in which the *Aroetta* was cruising in this area the engine had to be run at greatly reduced speed and the lead line used constantly to feel the way.

At each anchorage, detachments of Aborigines were sent ashore to reconnoitre and to examine the area for signs of recent occupation by strangers, or by Aboriginal hunting parties with whom it was desired to establish contact. A report had been received from Headquarters that an RAAF Gannet Aircraft was missing over Arnhem Land. Sergeant Elkington was instructed by wireless to send out patrols in his territory, and an extended search was carried out by us from the *Aroetta* at each anchorage without result. On June 2nd a detachment in charge of Raywala was put ashore west of Woodah Island, and instructed to carry out a patrol north of Blue Mud Bay to Trial Bay, and to meet with the ship there. On June 4th I took the *Aroetta* out of Blue Mud Bay and sailed north along the coast, anchoring in Trial Bay, where Raywala arrived with his detachment on the following night, after a severe journey in very rough country.

Between one hundred and one hundred-and-fifty people were living here, and it was at this time the chief camp of the people whose territories extended over a long stretch of coastline. Contact was made with Wonggu again. Except for aircraft sightings they had little to report, and no signs of strange ships or of Japanese activities had occurred in our absence.

While we were there a number of men from the area who had tired of routine work while at Katherine and gone away without leave, arrived back in their home camp. This was the only real case of poor discipline.

It was due in part to the dislike of discipline and restraint natural to a nomadic people whose territory has never been brought under administrative control, and in part to interference by white men on the Roper River. While the Unit was camped at the Four Mile Landing, the owner of Urapunga Station reported to the police at Roper Bar his premises had been entered, and alleged that clothing and food had been stolen. Without any evidence other than the supposition of his own station hands he accused the Caledon Bay members of the force of having entered his property. Subsequent enquiry proved that the

Establishing a coastal fuel depot, watched by Mardarrpa leader, Mundukul.

Caledon Bay Aborigines had nothing whatever to do with the matter. Investigation showed that none of the tracks resembled those of the Caledon Bay detachment, that the building had not been locked and that the station Aborigines were left in charge. It appeared probable that the sophisticated Aborigines of the settled station country of the Roper area, who were well aware of the sinister reputation of the Caledon Bay people against whom several excursions of a punitive character had already been organised by Roper police, took advantage of the presence of these people in the area, knowing that suspicion would inevitably fall on them. The Police Constable then at the Roper River made a call at the *Aroetta* during my absence inland at Katherine with Lieutenant Palmer, when an NCO only was in charge of the ship. The Caledon Bay and other Aborigines were camped at this time beside the ship. But when the police took the unwarranted action of visiting the ship in my absence, the men whose previous experience of the police was when they came to their territory and shot up the area, became uneasy, and a few days later slipped away and set off overland for Caledon Bay.

After their arrival I summoned Wonggu and held a meeting at which all the men, including those who had been AWL were present, and the seriousness of this action in returning without permission was instilled into them. Tact and compromise have to be used to temper discipline among these proud and warlike people.

This incident actually was a landmark in the development of the Unit for the old men of the group upheld me staunchly and as a result, all the men who had returned home volunteered to serve again, and returned with the vessel for a further period of work on the Roper and McArthur Rivers. A few days before the ship sailed, the people made a ceremonial presentation to me of a sacred object of great value, which is one of their methods of expiating a serious offence, generally a killing, when it is desired to make peace and avoid the starting of a blood feud.

In this way, therefore, by gaining the support of Wonggu of Caledon Bay and the other influential old men, and by establishing among the people themselves a sense of pride in service, and of shame in the idea of breaking faith in the undertaking that they agreed to complete, this incident was turned to good account. It should be added that these people served for the remainder of the reconnaissance with credit. None deserted again, and all were eventually returned to their home territories in the *Aroetta*.

I remained in Trial Bay for more than a week, in preference to extending the patrol north and west over a greater length of coastline, working hard with these people, from amongst whom we had already recruited many men. The need of an outpost in close proximity to Groote Eylandt and the approach to Roper River has already been stressed, and I planned to establish this base a little later, among the Caledon Bay people, either at Trial Bay or in Caledon Bay itself. For this reason close contact with them was now essential.

On the 13th June I took aboard the whole Unit and sailed to Groote Eylandt to pick up Lieutenant Palmer with the new propeller and shaft. We then sailed across to anchor off the outpost at Gulnare Bluff. Sergeant Elkington had nothing of importance to report. Both he, and all the members of the detachment, were in good health and spirits, but they were suffering severely with mosquitoes which were present in great numbers, and came out in hordes at night, and during the day they were much troubled with flies. Conditions at the outpost were severe and extremely monotonous. The surrounding country was flat and uninteresting, consisting of merely miles of salt pans and plains, intersected with man-groves. Nevertheless Sergeant Elkington and the detachment had carried on their work at this outpost: maintaining a constant lookout, keeping regular schedule with the ship each day, and carrying out patrols in the surrounding country. This NCO and his detachment had carried on their difficult and lonely undertaking excellently throughout.

In the meantime arrangements had been made to hand over this outpost on July 5 to No. 4 Independent Company, which was now in a position to supply the necessary personnel to take over the whole of the Roper River area, and so to free the *Aroetta* for patrol work farther out on the flanks.

Most of July was spent in a reconnaissance of the McArthur River, Maria Island and Pellow Island group. The *Aroetta* was to carry this out by sea while I travelled overland to meet her at Borroloola, after a visit to headquarters in Darwin to discuss the future of the Unit. Accompanied by five Aboriginal members of the force and one of the Solomon Islanders, I travelled to Darwin. An application was made for a separate colour patch and a definite establishment. I felt that such establishment and definite identity would assist in holding together this force and that it would further serve to foster pride in the Unit. Approval for this was granted. Approval was also given for the *Aroetta* to proceed to Townsville for a refit immediately after the McArthur River survey.

On the 9th July we were back in Katherine and set out a few days later for Borroloola. We rejoined the *Aroetta* on 27th July having observed the vulnerability of the low-lying areas just traversed. In the *Aroetta* we sailed to Groote arriving on the 1st August. This completed the first phase of the undertaking with which the force had been entrusted.

The men had now been thoroughly and systematically trained and understood what was required of them in the event of an enemy landing. Most of them had been away from their own territories and their women folk for several months, and it was considered that no useful purpose would be served by keeping them longer with the vessel, but that they should be repatriated and rewarded with gifts in return for the faithful service that they had given. It was intended that these men, generally representative and influential members of their groups, would form the nucleus of an efficient coast-watching system, and that by making regular contacts with them on each subsequent patrol they would be available when called upon, to muster their own clansmen in the event of enemy action in the area.

It was considered, therefore, that the most important undertaking that remained to be carried out was the establishment of a permanent outpost with the objects which were outlined earlier in this report, to serve as a base from which to conduct patrols or sorties, and particularly to serve as a permanent rendezvous where contacts would be maintained with members of the Unit. It was further planned, that once the nucleus had been trained, instead of attempting to maintain a large force which must grow 'stale' with inactivity, a few representative members only of each group should be held at the outpost. Those men could be ready to collect their groups together if required. Meanwhile, the others would be encouraged to continue to lead their normal existence as nomadic hunters. In this way it was considered that the most effective use could be made of these people, and their morale maintained at a high level.

For the reasons that have already been mentioned, Caledon Bay was finally selected as the site for the outpost and on August 4th the *Aroetta* arrived again in the area known as Gray's Camp, at the head of the arm or bay to the east of Middle Point in Caledon Bay. The whole of the Aboriginal force was landed here and a site selected for a house and garden – the house to be built of stringy bark. Good water was found in shallow wells close to the beach. Work was commenced at once on the construction of a house of two rooms, one of which was to serve as a store, and the other as living quarters. An area of about an acre was cleared, fenced with bush timber and sown with vegetables. The detachment, still fifty strong, was employed on the clearing of the ground for the garden, and on stripping stringy bark for the walls and roof of the house, the construction of which was carried out under Lieutenant Palmer's supervision.

The soil in this area is not fertile, being relatively poor and sandy, but to compensate for this we called at Low Rock on return from the Roper River and collected many bags and barrels of guano there which, though an unpleasant and laborious business, was well repaid, for the garden responded to an extraordinary degree, and within eight weeks of clearing the area it was yielding beans and salads for the crew. During my visit to head-quarters I had obtained some vegetable seeds from Lieutenant Campbell at Adelaide River, and also secured additional plants such as bananas and pawpaws at Groote Eylandt, Yirrkala and Milingimbi when on patrol.

opposite, top: The Caledon Bay outpost headquarters and gardens at Garrthalala.

opposite, bottom: Sergeant Ritchie instructing the men on how to avoid machine-gun fire, in front of the Caledon Bay headquarters in 1943. The group includes Mundukul, Wonggu, Djimbaryun, Mithili and Butjiya.

On account of the reputation of the Caledon Bay people for aggressiveness, I undertook the work of establishing the garden and outpost personally, and remained there for two or three weeks to set up the organisation. As arrangements had been completed at Norforce (the Army Headquarters in Darwin) for the refit of the ship in Townsville before the end of the dry season, it was necessary that the departure of the ship from this area should not be delayed for long if the vessel was to return to her station before the onset of the north-west monsoon – about the end of December or early in January. Before the ship left the area the men who had been recruited for the special Unit had to be returned to their own territory, and I planned, in conjunction with this, to carry out a final extended patrol along the coast of the Arafura Sea as far west as the Liverpool River, and to visit Cape Stewart, the Crocodile Islands and the Wessels before leaving the area.

By August 18th work on the outpost was completed and it was fully equipped, and Kapiu was placed in full charge of the outpost. Kapiu knew these people well, was on a friendly footing with them and was therefore deemed the most suitable man to place in charge at this time.

On August 19th the *Aroetta* sailed on a further extensive patrol to the north and Bindjarrpuma's detachment sent on patrol overland to Arnhem Bay. A visit was made to Port Bradshaw where a rough survey of the small boat or flying boat anchorages was made by Lieutenant Palmer and myself.

Medical work was carried out on this patrol as it had been in the past wherever we met groups of Aborigines. We carried a good supply of drugs and other medical stores including a small dental kit. Treating people created goodwill and won friends as well as relieving much suffering. As on my previous expeditions I found many people, especially the children, suffered severely from yaws and from many other tropical diseases. At almost every anchorage throughout the whole of the sixteen months covered by our patrols, the people would bring their sick, especially the children who were suffering from yaws, for treatment. The lesions of yaws disfigure and deform, but fortunately are readily cleared up by a few injections of certain arsenical preparations, particularly NAB which is administered intravenously. Large supplies of NAB had been provided by the Army for this work, and a full medical kit was kept always in readiness.

As an instance of the faith of these people may be cited a case that occurred just before the ship sailed finally from Caledon Bay in April. A woman was brought to me who had had her arm badly broken in two places by the falling limb of a tree. No apparatus was available, and at first I was at a loss as to what

I could do. At length, however, a sheet of stringy bark was obtained and by cutting this so that it could be bent to form an elbow joint, a good and comfortable splint was improvised; and after the rather painful task of setting the broken bones had been completed and a sling made from a strip of calico, the woman went off happy.

Although this work was exacting and laborious and occupied a considerable amount of time, it was one of the most important influences in maintaining the friendship and goodwill of the people throughout the area, and therefore, apart altogether from the human aspect, well repaid the labour and expense involved.

By September 13th this patrol of the northern coastline and the Wessel Islands had been completed, the Aborigines on board were all paid off and returned home, and the vessel returned to Caledon Bay. Everything had progressed smoothly there, and Pte Kapiu had nothing of importance to report during the absence of the *Aroetta*.

It was now necessary to prepare the outpost to carry on during the absence of the vessel in Queensland, and to establish two-way wireless communication. The set which had been impressed for the outpost at Gulnare Bluff was not giving satisfactory service, and accordingly I sent the *Aroetta* to Groote Eylandt to the Civil Aviation Flying Boat Base and to the RAM to endeavour to have the set repaired and tested, and to secure other W. T. [wireless transmission] material. Meanwhile, I remained at the outpost to complete work on the station.

On account of the limited personnel available on the ship, Sergeant Elkington was selected to take charge of the outpost, and to remain there during the absence of the ship in Queensland. It was estimated that the refit would occupy about six weeks, although as no priority was given to the work when the vessel first arrived in Townsville, a long delay occurred and this period was much extended. Sergeant Elkington, who had been in charge of the outpost at Gulnare Bluff and who had done excellent work there, volunteered to remain. It was not possible to leave the wireless transmission. operator as he was essential on the ship, and in addition the period of his secondment from the RAAF had long expired.

By September 19th all arrangements had been completed, and Sergeant Elkington was placed in charge of the outpost, with Operation Order 9 setting out the work with which he was entrusted, in particular, the maintenance of good relations with the people of the area.

On September 20th the *Aroetta* sailed for Groote Eylandt en route for Townsville. In December while the vessel was still at Townsville I received the following telegram from Norforce in Darwin, dated December 3:

Elkington reported through RAAF Groote natives entered house stole tobacco 22 Nov. Ringleader turned nasty took to bush with gang. Communications with Elkington difficult at time owing faulty W/T transmitter. RAAF Groote dispatched parry Gray's camp patched W/T and left airman. Now recommend Elkington have additional white man assist post maintenance. Post reported normal 28 Nov. but RAAF post Groote being withdrawn shortly and services airman only temporarily available. North Australia Observation Unit vessel from Roper been dispatched. Investigate but do not wish place untried NAOU pets Thomson area. Consider one Thomson's pets at Townsville should return Groote by flying boat. Would also appreciate ETA Aroetta's arrival these waters.

It was decided that I should return by air to clear up the trouble, and leave Lieutenant Palmer to bring the ship around later. I returned to Groote Eylandt by flying boat on the 27th December, and proceeded to Caledon Bay on the following day by the Civil Aviation Department's launch.

On arrival at Caledon Bay it was found that all but a few of the Aborigines had dispersed, and that the trouble which had occurred was primarily caused by the NCO who had been left in charge. It was ascertained that although sliding doors with secure fastenings and a padlock had been provided, and although he was provided with a strong box with a padlock to protect tobacco, he had been in the habit of leaving the post unlocked while he went on hunting trips in the bush. For some time, it appeared, the people had been helping themselves to small quantities of food and tobacco, and at first this had passed unnoticed. These depredations continued, growing progressively larger, until they were at length discovered by Sgt Elkington, who then threatened them with a Bren gun. Further troubles also occurred between this NCO and the people with whom he adopted an aggressive, overbearing attitude. If it had not been for the goodwill and faithfulness of Natjiyalma of Caledon Bay, whose sterling services have earned for him a special recommendation for recognition, and certain others of these people, serious consequences would probably have resulted. As it was, Natjiyalma and his father Wonggu kept the promise that they had made to me, and guarded Sgt Elkington and the post until my return, dispersing the others in the meantime. Despite the good work he had done at Gulnare Bluff, the attitude of Sgt Elkington and his unsuitability for work among Aborigines was indicated by entries in a log kept by him at the Caledon Bay post, from which the following are quoted:

October 14, 1942: Slippery and his gang turned up today, and this afternoon had a 'makarata' at the beginning of which there was nearly a row, so had to put my foot down and use the .303 as umpire.

October 18, 1942: Slippery very peeved because someone wants to pinch his wife. Bullets are the only things these people understand. They need a good, swift kick in the crutch.

It was particularly unfortunate that this NCO had been entrusted with the maintenance of this important post. Although the trouble which he experienced was largely brought about by his own actions, the signals which he originated at the time resulted in the visit of people to Caledon Bay who knew nothing of the territory or its people, and which greatly increased the difficulty of the task I had to face when I returned.

When on the 8th January the *Aroetta* arrived at Caledon Bay in the charge of Lieutenant Palmer, Sergeant Elkington was returned to the ship, and I remained ashore at the post to restore order and re-establish the good relations with the people. In spite of my own analysis of the cause of the small thefts of food and tobacco that had occurred, it was essential for purposes of discipline and control that, once the people knew that I was aware that they had stolen these things, some adequate form of punishment should be meted out. Under the conditions which prevailed, this was a matter of some difficulty. I collected the most reliable of the men whom I had worked with over a number of years and ordered them to muster all the men who had been concerned in the trouble at the outpost in my absence, setting a time limit on the date of their return.

Bindjarrpuma and his group were brought from Arnhem Bay on the Arafura Sea coast, but it speaks much for the sense of justice and the faithfulness of these people, when once they have been treated with consideration and fairness, that every one of those concerned returned to Caledon Bay and not only admitted, but told me in detail, what he had done. One of the groups was formed into a labour gang, and given some weeks of hard labour in the garden. They were also required to make a payment of a large number of fish. During this period they were ordered to remain at the outpost and were not permitted to leave the area on hunting expeditions. Every one, when the reason for this punishment was explained to him in his own language, admitted its justice and not one of them defaulted.

From the leader of another group a large sea-going canoe was demanded, this being the only wealth that he possessed. It was an object of great material value, involving probably days of search for a suitable tree, and then weeks of laborious work by a specialist in canoe building. But the most difficult problem was that of dealing with Bindjarrpuma and his followers, the most warlike group in the area. It was necessary to punish this man, to humiliate him, as well as to deprive him and his group of material possessions of value and to do this publicly. But it was equally necessary to convince him of the justice of the penalty. This would only have been possible to one he knew well or fighting would have ensued. On his arrival I greeted him as usual and then told him to fall in with his group of followers in full fighting array. This he did with a fine show of pride, for he was now on his mettle before his rivals, the people of Caledon Bay itself. Then I spoke to these people of the trust that they had betrayed, and finally ordered each man to lay down his spears on the ground. This was a tense moment. So far I had carried them with me, but to have lifted these spears at once would have been a fatal mistake. For a few minutes I talked to them, stressing the enormity of the betrayal of the trust I, as their leader, had placed in them, and the depth of my own humiliation. Then I told them that I was taking forty-two of their finest spears in expiation of their offence. After this I sent them back to their camp. For twenty-four hours they remained. If they had left instantly, this would have portended trouble. As it was, within twenty-four hours we were on our old footing except that my own prestige had been greatly increased throughout the whole area. But it had been touch and go. At such times it requires but one man to hook his spear in haste and the harm is done. Once finished, such a matter must never be held up before them. They must never be reminded of it or they have what they know as 'heart jump'; they go berserk. These are fighting people, killers, whom I would have liked to lead in action against the Japanese.

In a week or two after my return there were nearly two hundred Aborigines in camp at the outpost once more. For some time it was necessary for me to leave this post, and on this occasion Pte Kapiu, who had carried out the duties here so well on a previous occasion, was made Acting Sergeant and again placed in full charge. He carried out this undertaking with great credit.

Following upon the settlement of the trouble which had occurred at Caledon Bay during my absence with the ship in Queensland I proceeded, on January 21st for three days, to Advanced Headquarters, Norforce in response to instructions received by signal. Here a conference was held on the reorganisation of the Unit.

The spears taken from Bindjarrpuma's group as punishment.

As a result of this conference a memorandum was prepared by me setting out what I considered the minimum personnel required to man the ship on armed patrol. It was decided by the GOC at this time, in view of the difficulty of obtaining officers with the necessary experience and training to handle the natives, to close the outpost at Caledon Bay and to restrict the activities of the Unit henceforth to coastal patrol. On the 12th March 1943 we departed for Groote Eylandt for the last time.

The recommendations set out in this memorandum were adopted in the main, and later formed the basis of the war establishment laid down for the Unit, which was now reorganised under the name of 'Northern Territory Coastal Reconnaissance Unit, RAE'.

In my final report I made recommendations for six awards. For Lieutenant Palmer and Sergeant Ritchie who both showed a great loyalty and devotion to duty under very difficult conditions. For Sergeant Kapiu who even though advanced in years had left home and work from a sense of duty and loyalty to serve as bosun throughout the whole nineteen month period without a break. Not only was he a fine seaman but he also set a personal example to the other members of the crew and Force. So too did Private Makau who commanded the guard throughout the period and acquired considerable experience of armament.

Of the Aborigines two stood out. Although I have not said much about Raywala, he was my constant companion who set an example of loyalty and self-less devotion to duty of a standard few could follow. Prior to joining the Force his main experience of Europeans was punishment for a tribal offence in an area not under government control, yet he gave his liberty and placed service to country before love of family, which these people value more than life. Raywala was enlisted in Darwin in February 1942 and served until April 1943. He had established a reputation throughout Eastern Arnhem Land for his fighting prowess, and when enlisted he devoted the whole of his energies and influence to the work of undermining and destroying Japanese influence and prestige, and to assisting with the formation and training of the Unit. Raywala made many long, hard patrols over all sorts of country, often pressing on throughout the night without rest, in order to keep faith and to arrive at a rendezvous on time. This man's unfaltering loyalty and whole-hearted devotion, more than any other single factor, contributed to the building up of the Unit and the maintenance of order and discipline. Such was this man's sense of duty that when, in the beginning of 1943 after his return to Townsville in the *Aroetta*, he found that his wife and two young children had been stolen and carried off into the Interior and he was offered his release, he refused to desert his post, but insisted on remaining on duty until I relinquished command and he felt free from his obligation to remain with me.

This fine soldier, by his high standard of duty and honour set an example to the crew of the *Aroetta* and to all members of the Force, and won the regard, affection and respect of every member of the Unit.

Finally there was Natjiyalma, one of the five sons of Wonggu enlisted in the Force. Although Natjiyalma had been sentenced to life imprisonment for the killing of Japanese who had invaded his country some years ago, he served with the Force and was selected as leader of the Caledon Bay section. This man showed extraordinary faithfulness throughout, and rendered exceptionally meritorious service. Later when the outpost was established at Caledon Bay he gave most valuable assistance in organising the people and maintaining order and discipline.

Here Donald Thomson's reports end. The Special Reconnaissance Force was disbanded in 1942, as the war moved northward from the Australian coast. Thomson returned to the Air Force, was sent to Dutch New Guinea where he was severely wounded by pro-Japanese New Guineans and spent many months in hospital before being discharged from the Services and returning to the University of Melbourne. There he continued working until his death in 1970. His wife arranged for his ashes to be flown to the Northern Territory and scattered over the waters of Caledon Bay. Two of those in the plane over the Bay were Wonggu's sons, Djeriny and Maaw.

Notes

1 This sketch is based mainly on unpublished letters and other materials in three locations: the private papers held by Thomson's family, referred to as PP in the following references; Commonwealth Archives (here shortened to CA) files, A421:46/1999, A639:44/1/3089, A1:38/33269, A659:39/1/5250, A452/575; and records of the Australian National Research Council (ANRC) held by the National Library, and catalogued as MS. 482/846, 846A, 846B, 847A and 847B. Other important sources have been Thomson's published works, discussions with people who knew him, many hours spent working on his collections and several very pleasant visits to his house at Eltham where I talked at length with Mrs Thomson. PP: letter from Radcliffe-Brown to Thomson, 26 November 1926. Diary for 1923. Wilkins, in his account of the expedition, mentions that he met a holder of a Chair (biology clearly implied) at a leading Australian university who mentioned that he had 'dissuaded several promising young fellows from joining ... [the] expedition.' (Hubert Wilkins, Undiscovered Australia, Ernest Benn, London, 1928, pp. 14–15).

2 ANRC: MS. 482/846A. Notes of meeting 27 June 1929.

3 ANRC: MS. 482/846A. Letter from Lyle, director of ANRC, to all members of the Executive Committee on anthropological research, 1 April 1930. The eleven-page letter details the complaints of dishonesty by the ANRC treasurer against Thomson. Lyle strongly defends Thomson and in so doing outlines the details of his dealings with the Council.

4 ANRC: MS. 482/847A. Letter from Thomson to Radcliffe-Brown, 5 February 1929.

5 PP: Letter from Thomson to Mawson, 25 March 1929.

6 This paragraph is based entirely on the materials in the ANRC files which, in so far as they deal with Thomson, all relate to this matter.

7 See note 3.

8 ANRC: MS. 482/847B. Letter from Osbourn to Gibson, 5 June 1929.

9 ANRC: MS. 482/847A. An unsigned copy of a letter to Professor Wood Jones (a Thomson supporter), 24 September 1934.

10 ANRC: MS. 482/847B. Letter from Kellaway to Chapman, 5 February 1930.

11 See the partial chronological bibliography in Thomson, D., *Kinship and Behaviour in North Queensland* (ed. H. W. Scheffler), Australian Institute of Aboriginal Studies, Canberra, 1972.

12 See *American Anthropologist*, 1935, pp. 460–90 and 1936, pp. 374–93, respectively.

13 PP: A manuscript prepared to accompany plate. The plate was eventually published in the Melbourne *Herald*, 28 December 1947.

14 CA: A659:39/1/5250. Letter to the Minister for the Interior from Sir J. H. MacFarland, Chancellor, University of Melbourne, 18 December 1933, 4 pp; letter to Hon. J. A. Perkins, MP, Minister for the Interior, from J. G. Latham, Attorney General, 2 November 1933.

15 CA: A659:39/1/5250. Memo from J. A. C. [presumably the Secretary, Department of the Interior, Carrodus] to the Minister, 21 December 1933.

16 Melbourne *Herald*, 13 February 1934.

17 Melbourne *Herald*, 14 February 1934.

18 CA: A659:39/1/5250. Annotations on memo by J. A. [Warrenger?], dated by Minister, 25 April 1934.

19 CA: A659:39/1/5250. Memo from H. C. Brown, Secretary to the Minister, Department of the Interior, 22 June 1934, 2 pp.

20 CA: A659:39/1/5250. Letter from Thomson to Hon. J. A. Perkins, MP, Department of the Interior, 18 July 1934, 4 pp. and Perkins' annotations.

21 See note 19.

22 CA: A659:39/1/5250. Letter from Thomson to Hon. J. A. Perkins, Department of the Interior, 26 August 1934, 2 pp; draft letter, not sent, from Hon. J. A. Perkins to Thomson dated 29 August 1934; letter from Thomson to Hon. J. A. Perkins dated 27 September 1934, 3 pp.

23 CA: A659:39/1/5250. Letter from Thomson to Hon. J. A. Perkins, 27 September 1934, 3 pp. ; memo from J. A. Carrodus to the Secretary to the Minister, Mr Brown, 22 November 1934; letter from T. Paterson, Minister, to Thomson, 4 March 1935, with details of commission.

24 CA: A659:39/1/5250. Letter from Sir Arthur Robinson [Thomson's solicitor] to Dr Earle Page, 3 August 1935, 2 pp.; letter from Sir James Barnett, Chancellor, University of Melbourne, to Hon. T. Paterson, Department of the Interior, 28 October 1935, concerning film; an undated eleven-page report on financial expenditure in connection with investigations in Arnhem Land has the following figures:

Initial equipment	£ 199-5-7
Stores	£187-4-1
Transport	£117-9-10
Boat Expenses	£ 28-12-4
Wages [to employees]	£148 16-4
Camera supplies and film	£155-0-0
	£836-18-2

25   CA: A659:39/1/5250. Letter to Professor Wood Jones, Melbourne University, from T. Paterson, Department of the Interior, 21 May 1936, 2pp.; memo to Minister, Department of Interior, from J. A. Carrodus, 29 May 1936, 2 pp.; Melbourne Herald, 2 June 1936.

26   CA: A 1:38/33269. Letter from D. B. Copland, Acting Vice-Chancellor [University of Melbourne] to Hon. T. Paterson, Minister for the Interior, 4 June 1936, 4 pp.; Sydney Morning Herald, 4 June 1936; letter from the Minister to Professor Copland, 8 June 1936, 4 pp. For example, Melbourne *Herald* and *Argus*, *Sydney Morning Herald* and *Canberra Times* all of 16 June 1936.

27   CA: A1:38/33269. Letter from Mr J. W. Allen, Secretary, NT Pastoral Lessees' Association, Sydney, to the Minister of the Interior, 4 July 1936; letter from F. Gray of Caledon Bay, Port Darwin, NT, to the Secretary, Department of the Interior, 7 July 1936.

28   CA: A639:44/1/3089. Memo to Secretary, Department of the Interior, 28 March 1939, 2 pp.

29   Thomson was quite correct in believing that the Secretary of the Department of the Interior, Carrodus, was most hostile to him. See CA: A452/575. Memo from Carrodus to Minister, 2 January 1945, 1 p.

30   CA: A639:44/1/3089. Letter dated 28 April 1939.

31   PP: Letter from Thomson to Wood Jones, 29 March 1938, 2 pp.

32   CA: A639:44/1/3089. Letter from Thomson to Carrodus, 1 March 1938, 23 pp.

33   See R. Darrock, 'The Man behind Australia's Secret Army', the *Bulletin*, 20 May 1980.

34   The ignorance of the existence of this Aboriginal Special Reconnaissance Unit even in the Army is well indicated by an article in the *Australian Army Journal*, July 1965, where two officers, writing under the title 'The Aboriginal and Defence', suggest a very similar project without any reference to the fact that such a force had existed at one time. For more recent articles, also ignoring this earlier experience, see *Defence Force Journal*, 1979, numbers 14, 16, 18, and 1980, number 21. However, R. A. Hall, in two recent articles in this journal, has made some detailed reference to the Unit – see his 'Guarding White Australia: Aborigines' Contribution to Northern Surveillance during the Second World War'.

35   See Thomson's 'War-time Explorations in Dutch New Guinea', in *Geographical Journal*, March 1953.

36   CA: A452/575. Various letters on file all dated 1945.

37   See Thomson's eight-page pamphlet 'Justice for Aborigines', which consisted of reprints of articles from the Melbourne *Herald* of 28, 30 and 31 December 1946.

38   PP: Text of address by Dr C. Duguid for the Rocket Range Protest Meeting, Princess Theatre, Melbourne, Sunday 24 August 1947, 11 pp. The Rocket Range Committee also published a four-page pamphlet by Thomson, 'The Aborigines and the Rocket Range', May 1947.

39   See *Bindibu Country*, Nelson, Melbourne, 1975. This was a posthumously compiled account of the 1957 and 1963 expeditions. The documentation for the 1965 expedition was very limited.

Sources

The principal sources for Chapters 2, 3, 4 and 5 are:

Interim General Report of Preliminary Expedition to Arnhem Land, Northern Territory of Australia 1935–1936, 49 pp. This is a typescript that can be consulted in a number of libraries. A copy is held by Museum Victoria as part of the Donald Thomson Collection.

Parts of this report, slightly changed and supplemented with ethnographic material, have been published as:

Arnhem Land: Explorations Among an Unknown People, Parts 1, 2 and 3. *The Geographic Journal*, 1948, vol. 112, pp. 146–64; 1949, vol. 113, pp. 1–8; 1949, vol. 114, pp. 53–67.

Chapter 2 has had additional information introduced from Thomson's personal diaries and papers and from his own journalistic writings, mainly in the Melbourne *Herald*. The last paragraph has been added for continuity.

The Matthew Flinders reference is 1814/1966. *A Voyage to Terra Australis*. Libraries Board of South Australia, Adelaide (Facsimile edition no. 37).

Chapter 3 draws on pages from the published accounts, vol. 112, pp. 151–64 and vol. 113, pp. 1–6, supplemented from the unpublished Interim Report, pp. 9–12 and 16–22.

Chapter 4 is drawn from vol. 114, pp. 53–5 of the published account and pp. 22–6 and 28–30 of the unpublished account.

Chapter 5, apart from the opening paragraph, is drawn from pp. 42–8 of the unpublished report which I have altered to the first person in places.

Chapter 6 is based on *Report on Expedition to Arnhem Land 1936–37*, Government Printer, Canberra, 1939, 22 pp.

The three opening paragraphs have been introduced from Thomson's other writings and a few minor additions made from his personal papers here and there. The anthropological material is a composite of published and unpublished material. The basic accounts of the fish trap, bark canoes and goose hunters are to be found in *Man*, 1939, article 216; *Man*, 1939, article 109; and the *Illustrated London News*, 17 September 1938, respectively.

Chapter 7 opens with three added paragraphs but otherwise comes from: Report: the Organization of the Northern Territory Coastal Patrol and the Special Reconnaissance Unit 1941–1943. This may be consulted in the Australian War Memorial Archives, 741/5/9, Canberra. The text has been considerably re-arranged to create a chronological narrative.

Further sources: history

The most comprehensive account and analysis of the events surrounding the Caledon Bay affair so far has been written by Ted Egan (see below). The most easily available of the other published accounts that deal with it in some detail are listed here. Additional sources of information are the newspapers of the period, especially the *Northern Standard* (Darwin) and the *Herald* and *Argus* (Melbourne), which carried extensive accounts of the events and trials. Also important are the Commonwealth Archives and the Commonwealth Law Reports.

Berndt, R. M. and C. H. *Arnhem Land. Its History and Its People*, Cheshire, Melbourne, 1954. A general history of Arnhem Land that covers the events in considerable detail and indicates some of the archival sources.

Commonwealth Law Reports. 1934–35, vol. 52, pp. 335–55. Reports the case of 'Tuckiar and the King'.

Dewar, M. *The 'Black War' in Arnhem Land: Missionaries and the Yolngu 1908–1940*, North Australia Research Unit, Australian National University, Darwin, 1992.

Dyer, A. J. *Unarmed Combat: an Australian Missionary Adventure*, Bragg and Sons, Sydney, n.d. Written by a missionary from Roper River who was one of the three people appointed to the Church Missionary Society's 'peace expedition' sent to the Caledon Bay area in December 1933 to effect a reconciliation.

Egan, T. *Justice All Their Own: the Caledon Bay and Woodah Island Killings, 1932–1933*. Melbourne University Press, Melbourne, 1996. A master storyteller who spoke with all the survivors of the events, but especially the Aboriginal people involved, casting new light on a number of aspects of the events in eastern Arnhem Land. The author was formerly a Native Affairs patrol officer who worked in the area in the 1950s. He is now Administrator of the Northern Territory.

Hall, V. *Dreamtime Justice*, Rigby, Adelaide, 1962. An account by one of the four members of the Northern Territory Police Force who went to Caledon Bay to investigate the killing of the Japanese. It was during this expedition that Constable McColl was killed.

Haultain, C. T. G. *Watch off Arnhem Land*, Roebuck, Canberra, 1971. By the captain of the patrol boat *Larrakia* whose task it was to see that the Japanese pearlers observed the various regulations such as not landing on the mainland or interfering with Aboriginal people. He came across Japanese naval officers on the luggers collecting naval intelligence. He does not deal with the Caledon Bay affair but provides some of the background to the Special Reconnaissance Unit.

McMillan, A. *An Intruder's Guide to East Arnhem Land*, Duffy and Snellgrove, Sydney, 2001. A well-written and readable book but poorly referenced.

A biography of Narritjin Maymurru by Howard Morphy of the Australian National University is due to appear a couple of years after this current publication, with further fascinating new perspectives on what took place in 1932–33 as well as on the anthropology and history of the region more generally from the 1930s to 2000.

Further sources: anthropology

These three books reference the full range of anthropological literature on north-east Arnhem Land, including the important work of Ronald and Catherine Berndt.

Keen, I. *Knowledge and Secrecy in an Aboriginal Religion*, Oxford University Press, Oxford, 1994.
Morphy, H. *Ancestral Connections: Art and an Aboriginal System of Knowledge*, Chicago University Press, Chicago, 1991.
Williams, N. *The Yolngu and Their Land*, Stanford University Press, Stanford, 1986.

Illustrations

Sources

All but two photographs are by Thomson. The photograph on page 124 comes from the Herald and Weekly Times and that on page 162 (top) from Harold Shepherdson, who was a lay missionary at Milingimbi when Thomson was there. The drawings are all by Joan Clark who worked as Thomson's secretary from 1946 to 1952; they were originally intended to illustrate a planned volume, 'The Aborigines of Australia', that was never completed.

Notes on the photographs

Most of Thomson's photographs were taken on glass plate negatives – mainly half plates, although he did have a full-plate and a quarter-plate camera as well. Such glass plate negatives are not only heavy but also fragile. He could not have managed to take so many photographs had he not had the boat to carry and store his photographic and other gear. As Lindy Allen of Museum Victoria has pointed out, it took at least four minutes to put such a glass plate negative in the camera, take the photograph and remove the exposed plate, without allowing for setting up the shot. He used Thornton Pickard full- and half-plate cameras, and probably the quarter-plate camera too, although this has not been seen. He also used a Graflex Series B camera for hand-held shots. He developed the negatives in the field himself and sometimes made prints in which people showed a lively interest and about which, Thomson records, they made astute comments.

For a detailed account of Thomson's photography see:–

Allen, L. 'A photographer of brilliance', pp. 45–62, *Donald Thomson, the Man and Scholar*, B. Rigsby and N. Peterson (eds), Academy of the Social Sciences in Australia, Canberra, 2005.

Allen, L. 'Donald Thomson, photographer, and Donald Thomson photographs', *Bulletin of the Conference of Museum Anthropologists*, 30: 15–29, 1999.

Maps

Drawings

Photographs

Index